**Abel Ferrara** |

T0307735

## Contemporary Film Directors

Edited by James Naremore

The Contemporary Film Directors series provides concise, well-written introductions to directors from around the world and from every level of the film industry. Its chief aims are to broaden our awareness of important artists, to give serious critical attention to their work, and to illustrate the variety and vitality of contemporary cinema. Contributors to the series include an array of internationally respected critics and academics. Each volume contains an incisive critical commentary, an informative interview with the director, and a detailed filmography.

*A list of books in the series appears*
*at the end of this book.*

# Abel Ferrara |

Nicole Brenez

*Translated from the French by*
Adrian Martin

UNIVERSITY
OF
ILLINOIS
PRESS
URBANA
AND
CHICAGO

Library of Congress Cataloging-in-Publication Data
Brenez, Nicole.
[Abel Ferrara. English]
Abel Ferrara / Nicole Brenez ; translated from
the French by Adrian Martin.
  p.   cm. — (Contemporary film directors)
Filmography: p.
Includes bibliographical references and index.
ISBN-13: 978-0-252-03154-0 (cloth : alk. paper)
ISBN-10: 0-252-03154-7 (cloth : alk. paper)
ISBN-13: 978-0-252-07411-0 (pbk. : alk. paper)
ISBN-10: 0-252-07411-4 (pbk. : alk. paper)
  1. Ferrara, Abel, 1951—Criticism and interpretation.
I. Title. II. Series.
PN1998.3.F465B7413      2007
791.4302'33092—dc22 [B]      2006011276

Maybe it comes from being brought up in America and idolizing Patrick Henry and all these guys. It's about freedom of speech and will.

—Abel Ferrara (2002)

Give me liberty or give me death.

—Patrick Henry (1775)

# Contents |

*Acknowledgments* | xi

A CINEMA OF NEGATION | 1
Some Ethical Stakes in Ferrara's Cinema | 1
What Is Passion? Central Figures of Hypermorality | 22
"Going to the End of Being" | 68
Self-Consciousness: The Visionaries | 110
Cinema and Symbolic Reparation | 150

INTERVIEW: ABEL FERRARA | 165

*Filmography* | 173

*Bibliography* | 193

*Index* | 199

## Acknowledgments |

I warmly thank Bernard Benoliel, Emmanuel Bonin, Charles-Antoine Bosson, Stéphane Delorme, Philippe Delvosalle, Ivora Cusak, Fergus Daly, Agathe Dreyfus, Pierre Hecker, Alexander Horwath, Kent Jones, Bernd Kiefer, Maria Klonaris, Solange Marcin, Gabriela Trujillo, and Gaëlle Vidalie for their help with this book. Special thanks go to Thana's husband, Robert Lund.

Several parts of this book were encouraged and supported by commissions, some from eminent Ferrarans: Aimé Ancian (*Sofa*), Raymond Bellour (*Trafic*), Alain Bergala, Carole Desbarats, David Dessites (*Dreamlight Entertainment*), Catherine Gillet (Musée du Cinéma de Bruxelles), Danielle Hibon (Musée du Jeu de Paume), Luc Lagier (*Court-Circuit*), Jean-Pierre Moussaron (*Why Not?*), Olivier Pierre (l'Ecran de Saint-Denis), Muriel Thomé (*Court-Circuit*), Jean-Baptiste Thoret (*Simulacres*), Geneviève Troussier (Café des Images), Philippe Truffaut (*Court-Circuit*), and Jean-Pierre Vasseur (*Opening*).

This book originated in a course I taught at Université Paris I (Institut d'Art et d'Archéologie), directed by Professor Jean Gili. I fondly thank all my friends and students who attended this course so early on a Saturday morning; for their remarkable contributions, I would like to acknowledge Xavier Baert, Briana Berg de Marignac, Laure Bergala, Laurent Champoussin, Cassandra Cuman, Marc Dante, Séverin de Lajarte, Émeric de Lastens, Vincent Deville, Jean-Marc Elsholz, Yann Gonzalez, Florent Guézengar, Jérôme Momcilovicz, Pascal Sénequier, Seung-hee Seo, and Vivien Villani. In this context, Adrian Martin and Brad Stevens came—from Melbourne and London, respectively—to offer us magnificent seminars.

Thanks to Lionel Soukaz for his crucial remarks on *The Addiction*, which more than any other commentary prompted my reflections on this film.

Without the daily support of Michelle Brenez, Pierre-Jacques Brenez, and Titus Brenez-Michaud, I would not have been able to write a single line of this book. The manuscript benefited from indispensable rereadings by Ferraran experts, whom I can never thank enough: Aïcha Bahcelioglu, Sébastien Clerget, Stéphane du Mesnildot, Sylvain George, Pierre Gras, David Matarasso, Alberto Pezzotta, and Louis-George Schwartz. Special thanks to David Pellecuer for his inexhaustible kindness.

Adrian Martin—with the invaluable help of Helen Bandis and Grant McDonald, his comrades at *Rouge*—strengthened the content of the book by carefully verifying every shot and phenomenon described (as well as finding every citation) for the English translation. Raymond Bellour scrutinized the original manuscript with incomparabale care. I thank them all affectionately for the time they devoted to this project and for the rigor that is directly proportionate to their sensitivity and intellectual generosity.

At the origin of this book, as with so many others, there was an initiative by Jonathan Rosenbaum, without whom international cinephilic life would not be as living, fluent, and fertile as it currently is.

I warmly thank James Naremore, director of the *Contemporary Film Directors* series at the University of Illinois Press, for his trust and patience.

I dedicate this work to Brad Stevens, a true cinema historian, with affection, gratitude, and admiration.

# Abel Ferrara

# A Cinema of Negation |

## Some Ethical Stakes in Ferrara's Cinema

> To represent is already a murder.
> —Georges Bataille (1952)

### American Boy, European Friends

Abel Ferrara is to cinema what Joe Strummer is to music: a poet who justifies the existence of popular forms. Without them, the genre film or the pop song would be no more than objects of cultural consumption. In this material world run on injustice and terror, where "popular" is confused with "industrial," any cultural expression that does not hurl an angry cry or wail a song of mad love (often one and the same) merely collaborates in the regulation and preservation of this world. Is Ferrara, along with Jim Jarmusch, Tsui Hark, and Kinji Fukasaku, right to (even accidentally) redeem genre cinema? Would it not be preferable for them to desert the dirty terrain of what Theodor Adorno and Max Horkheimer named the "culture industry" and, like Jonas Mekas or Stan Brakhage, invent their own territories, forms, and artistic gestures? Ferrara's films offer an answer. How could anyone except a melancholic criminal speak to us in the name of the good (*King of New York;* 1990)? Who but a paranoid cop could make us believe for a second in the virtues of forgiveness (*Bad Lieutenant;* 1992)? Who today could bear to listen to a moral lesson if it was not acted out by a drug-addicted, leprous vampire (*The Addiction;* 1995)? Who could interest us, even for a moment, in the tired old questions of the family unit or the individual? Who could continue to arouse in us a desperate faith in sacrifice and love, unless they were almost autistic, completely crazed, haunted figures within films that cultivate advanced arguments concerning the need to destroy all filmic forms?

Ferrara was born on 19 July 1951 to an Italian American father (who turned from being a bookmaker to a stockbroker) and an Irish American mother. He is the youngest of six children, with five sisters. The Esposito family (renamed Ferrara by Abel's grandfather after he emigrated to the United States) originates in Salerno, south of Naples. Ferrara studied at the Sacred Heart Catholic School in the Bronx: "You were in, like, the front row and there was this giant crucifix, about eight feet tall, dripping blood."[1] In 1966, the family moved to the Peekskill district. At Lakeland High School, Ferrara met Nicodemo Oliverio (a.k.a. Nicholas St. John) and John Paul McIntyre. He and St. John formed a rock band, bought an eight-millimeter camera, and made their first ten-minute short, "The story of a kid who liked getting drunk with his friends."[2] Ferrara returned to New York to study cinema at the State University of New York at Purchase and made a series of very short films (one or two minutes each) on Super 8 and sixteen-millimeter, devised as protests against the Vietnam War. As part of his studies he spent a year in Britain, where he participated in his first professional thirty-five-millimeter shoot for the BBC. Then he returned to New York and reunited with St. John; together they started writing and making films and playing music.

Ferrara's œuvre can be read as a critical revitalization of the codes of genre cinema. He has tackled almost every popular genre: pornography (9 *Lives of a Wet Pussy;* 1976), gore (*The Driller Killer;* 1979), the rape-revenge movie (*Ms .45,* a.k.a. *Angel of Vengeance;* 1981), the thriller and film noir (*Fear City,* 1984; *China Girl,* 1987; *King of New*

York, and *Bad Lieutenant*), the television cop series (two episodes of *Miami Vice*, 1985; *The Gladiator*, 1986; and *Crime Story*, 1986), science fiction (*Body Snatchers*, 1993; *New Rose Hotel*, 1998), fantasy-horror (*The Addiction;* 1995), the film-within-a-film (*Dangerous Game*, a.k.a. *Snake Eyes*, 1993; *The Blackout*, 1997), and historical re-creation (*The Funeral*, 1996; *'R Xmas*, 2001.) Even music video has not escaped Ferrara's enterprise ("California"; 1996). Ferrara has now announced, among several projects that may be shot in Italy, that he will direct a comedy titled *Go-Go Tales*.

This critical interrogation of generic codes resembles neither a stylish reworking nor a simple exposure of cinematic clichés. It is a matter of formulating, thanks to an arsenal of basic, immediately comprehensible archetypes, certain primal, practical, and troubling questions. What are the limits of identity? What is an individual? What is a social subject? What are we conscious of? What are we responsible for? Adrian Martin has put it well: "Every problem in Ferrara's films is a social problem, a problem endemic to the formation and maintenance of a human community."[3]

It is telling that Ferrara made his most violently inventive film-tract when he was unwisely let loose at the heart of the Hollywood system. *Body Snatchers,* in this regard, forms a crucial diptych with Paul Verhoeven's *Starship Troopers* (1997). Ferrara's work introduces disorder into a cynical world; misunderstandings begin here, since some critics attribute this disorder to the films themselves. His films are increasingly accused of being badly made, murkily motivated, and confused—especially *The Blackout* and *New Rose Hotel.*

Crucially, there is no "angelism" in relation to evil and negation in Ferrara, no implicit belief in an ideal perfection or state of innocence. If scarcely a trace of utopia or any radical counterproposition can be detected, this is at least as much due to a fidelity to the negative as to the fact that everything in this world is already in a state of ecstasy, exaltation, and pure inebriation. As Ferrara said of Thana (Zoë Lund, née Tamerlis), the heroine of *Ms .45*: "Beyond the reasons that this girl has to kill—revenge, justice, all that—there is also pleasure of a sexual kind in violence."[4] So which is more cruel, the cynical world, or the man who merrily draws from it for his films, without pretending to change anything?

The aesthetic limitations of Ferrara's work are obvious. His cinema needs characters, narrative, mise en scène, and genre. More precisely and intensely, he needs the irreducible element at the heart of each of these modes: archetype, fable, staging, and standard imagery, respectively. As for Ferrara's public image, it is fascinating to the extent that it offers a smokescreen for the work itself. In the 2003 catalog for the cinephilic Locarno Film Festival, Ferrara is presented as "deranged." For the press, he will always be that big kid (now more than fifty years old) who strums his guitar instead of answering questions, lives in a perpetually dishevelled state, and leads journalists to the heights of poetically burlesque absurdity.[5]

In the range of figures allowed by the culture industry, Ferrara occupies the place of the "maverick"—half-Dionysus by virtue of his cultlike devotion to alcohol, half-Orpheus by virtue of the lyre that never leaves his side. Just as Madonna, Lili Taylor, and Béatrice Dalle have come to replace Marilyn Monroe, Frances Farmer, and Mae West in their public personae, Ferrara is reassuringly inscribed in the line of those grand eccentrics who maintain the fragile continuity between the industry and the avant-garde: Josef von Sternberg, Erich von Stroheim, King Vidor, Orson Welles (a photo of whom decorates Ferrara's bedroom), and Nicholas Ray.

Ferrara calls himself the "master of provocation."[6] His œuvre affirms the value of explosive outbursts. In the script for *Mary* (first written in 2000 and subsequently reworked)—the central subject of which is the shooting of a film about Jesus—the director, James, threatens the projectionist, forcing him to continue a screening; he ends up watching the film alone, gun in hand.[7] For Ferrara, images are a matter of life and death. Whether one creates or simply looks at a film, it must constitute an event in the existential sense of the word. He once stated, "You should be willing to die for a film."[8] But why accord such importance to images, to the realm of the symbolic? And how to deal with the requirements of such an exacting and lofty position?

This book is the fruit of an annual seminar devoted to Ferrara's work that I have been teaching at Université Paris I since 1996. I have been able to measure, over this time, the constant enthusiasm elicited in students and guests (some of them filmmakers) by Ferrara's films. Each two-monthly encounter is dedicated to a different dimension of the Ferraran corpus—for example, "The Dreamer Killer" in 1998–99, "Evil without Flowers: Ferrara and the History of Theories of Evil from the Ancient Greeks to Hannah Arendt" in 1999–2000, or "Right, Liberty, and Criminal Life" in 2003–4. This book does not terminate the analysis. We can see here one sign among many of the interest in and admiration for Ferrara shown over many years by French and other European cinephiles. His first major interview appeared, under the title "American Boy," in a 1988 issue of *La Revue du cinéma*, thanks to Alain Garel and François Guérif.[9] The Cinémathèque Française, under Jean-François Rauger's initiative, organized a comprehensive retrospective of Ferrara's career in 2003. In Italy, the first monographs on the director were produced in 1997, followed by several book-length studies.[10] The Venice Film Festival has often honored Ferrara's films: Chris Penn received an acting award for *The Funeral*, while *New Rose Hotel* received the International Critics' Award. Critical recognition of the same order has occurred in Ireland, Austria, and Germany. In Britain, Brad Stevens dedicated five years to writing and researching a magisterial reference book, *Abel Ferrara: The Moral Vision*.

Appreciative American commentaries are not entirely absent, starting with the essays and in-depth interviews by Gavin Smith and Kent Jones.[11] Yet it seems that Ferrara's work has encountered enormous resistance in the United States, where his four most recent films (*The Blackout, New Rose Hotel, 'R Xmas,* and *Mary* [2005]) have hardly been screened in cinemas. Asked what he would do if *'R Xmas* failed to achieve American distribution, Ferrara responded with his customary drollness: "'We burn the negative. We eat the negative with tomato sauce. On D. W. Griffith's grave.'"[12] Moreover, when a Ferrara film *is* produced and distributed by the American industry, it does not necessarily fare any better. As Jonathan Rosenbaum commented in 1994, "[C]ertain studios perversely want certain good films to fail, e.g., most recently and blatantly, Paramount and Peter Bogdanovich's *The Thing Called Love,* and Warner Brothers and Abel Ferrara's *Body Snatchers.*"[13] I want to show why the culture industry has good reason to repress Ferrara, just as it repressed Orson Welles, Monte Hellman, and Charles Chaplin.

There are three essential propositions underlying Ferrara's work:

1. *Modern cinema exists to come to grips with contemporary evil.* On this level, Ferrara's enterprise renews for the twenty-first century

what Roberto Rossellini accomplished for the twentieth. To respond to this challenge, Ferrara's work produces forms of synthesis at the levels of the individual films and the sum of his work as a whole. From a thematic viewpoint, his work explores the articulation of two of the century's emblematic criminal logics, the Mafia and capitalism.

2. *In contrast to other filmmakers who are drawn to the same conception of history—that the only story is the story of evil—Ferrara follows an optimistic conception, thus preserving a sense of tragedy.* This gives rise to the elaboration of characters who are in revolt, whether political (revolutionaries) or psychic (the great tormented). Such characters pose anew the question of the individual, but they all derive from the prototype of the visionary.

3. *The treatment of historic evil requires the invention of filmic forms that express what is inadmissible in terms of behavior, morality, narrative, image, sound, and especially in terms of architechtonic and compositional invention.* Provocative storylines (concerning murder, injury, apparent amorality, rape, and violence of every kind) are merely the currency of a structure of inadmissibility, the reign of injustice. Ferrara's work seeks to elucidate the basic elements of this structure in terms of an economy that is at once psychic and political.

### Ferrara's System: Synthetic Genius and Kinetic Forms

*Figurative Synthesis*  Two films manifest Ferrara's genius for figurative synthesis in a particularly clear way: *Body Snatchers* and *The Addiction*. (Plot synopses for all films analyzed can be found in the filmography.)

The "snatching" principle lends itself to an infinite play of metaphors. Discussing Jack Finney's 1955 novel *The Body Snatchers*, which has so far inspired three films (with a fourth reportedly on the way), Ferrara declared: "The book—it's beautiful. It's a metaphor like an image in a million mirrors—y'know what I mean? It's infinite."[14] His version of the *Body Snatchers* story covers at least three dimensions of human experience: it is a "family romance" (a teenaged girl symbolically kills off her family); a futuristic essay on industrial pollution and global militarization; and a retrospective meditation on "Hiroshima man," in which all is shadow, a "haunted outline," where every silhouette can only be envisaged from the viewpoint of its imminent disappearance. This is figurative work on the most violent act of aggression ever inflicted upon humanity. *Body Snatchers* asks the historical question, What can the destruction of Hiroshima or Nagasaki tell us about the liberal, democratic society responsible for it? Its collective political question is, What can the individual do when faced with the deathly logics at work in the industrial standardization of the entire world? And its intimate, biological question is, What is revealed to us by this dream of a teenaged girl, Marti (Gabrielle Anwar)—a lethal fable invented so that she can do away with her brother, mother, and father—about the life-drive, the reproductive function of which she supposedly embodies?

How does the film interrelate these three dimensions? This can be determined clearly in the sequence depicting the Malone family arriving and setting itself up at the military base. The father, Steve (Terry Kinney), is about to lead a scientific inquiry into the toxicity of certain chemical weapons. Two worlds are depicted in parallel montage: the private world of the family with its warm, childlike atmosphere, and the dark, menacing world of the military camp. The latter is presented via a successive piling-up of collective evils: general world pollution; an explicit reference to the history of armed conflict, namely the first Gulf War (General Platt [R. Lee Ermey] reproaches Steve, "You know absolutely nothing about biological and chemical warfare"); an allusion to Nazism, via the nocturnal spiriting away of an anonymous victim by a fearsome commando unit; a triple superimposition of military, industrial, and criminal orders; and a reference to Hiroshima in the striking, spatially mismatched shot of three soldiers' shadows in the dust behind the kneeling Steve. These shadows inscribed in the toxic dirt—recalling the outlines of bodies imprinted onto Hiroshima's walls—anchor the figurative treatment of the snatchers as sketches, obscure silhouettes and undecidable effigies within a specific historical abomination.

The question of the scene thus becomes, What is the relation between the two universes, intimate (the family) and collective (war)? Major Collins (Forest Whitaker) forges this link when he asks Steve, in the middle of the latter's examination for toxic chemicals, "Can they affect the brain patterns? Can they interfere with chemo-neurological processes? . . . Simply, can they alter a person's view of reality?" This is the practical question explored by every Ferrara film: How does evil attach itself to bodies and the psyche? In *Body Snatchers,* this question immediately receives a doubly affirmative response: evil attaches itself to bodies by spatial invasion, when a troop of soldiers instantly arrives to deposit suspicious boxes in the Malone home (the paternal bedroom thus becomes a toxic depot), and by mental invasion, when all the children in day care except Andy (Reilly Murphy) hold up their identical drawings of bloody viscera, evidence of the barbaric confiscation of their imaginaries.

From this example, the method of Ferrara's style can be deduced. It proceeds by a figurative and kinetic synthesis. The film ceaselessly establishes links between phenomena by way of circuits of propagation, contamination, and invasion. *Body Snatchers* begins this process by describing the destruction of intimacy by collective evil in order to deepen our understanding of the way in which intimacy is itself invaded by the germs of hatred and cruelty. As we will see, this is what is at stake in the film's depiction of the maternal.

*The Addiction* explores a historical synthesis. It offers, for cinema, a balance sheet of the twentieth century. The principle of vampirism—a

Terry Kinney, Forest Whitaker, and the soldiers in
*Body Snatchers*.

Terry Kinney and the shadows of three soldiers in
*Body Snatchers.*

particularly rich figurative schema—signifies the Vietnam War, Nazism, drugs, all contagious diseases such as AIDS, American imperialism, and poverty. Ferrara's work, in coming to grips with modern evil, can be envisaged as an ever more carefully argued-out description of *capitalism as catastrophe.* This polemical enterprise begins with *The Hold Up* (1972), a fifteen-minute short written by St. John (credited under his real name, Oliverio). In synopsis, the film's politics are crude: a group of workers, victims of economic retrenchment, hold up a service station. They are arrested. The boss's son-in-law is freed, while his two accomplices, ordinary workers, end up sentenced and imprisoned. Criminalized capitalism, complicit unions (the sackings are announced by the union delegate), generalized corruption, and institutionalized injustice: *The Hold Up* paints the backdrop upon which Ferrara's features (*King of New York, Body Snatchers, New Rose Hotel*) will develop much fuller and more violent elaborations. The final shots of *The Hold Up* radically depict the factory as a prison—like a visual reprise of the celebrated sequence in Rossellini's *Europa '51* (1952) where Ingrid Bergman, returning from her first day of factory work, declares to Giulietta Masina, "I thought I was seeing convicts." The assimilation of factory to penitentiary inaugurates Ferrara's succession of metaphors for economic alienation. The capitalist system is figured as a toxic military base in *Body Snatchers;* the underground drug economy greases the wheels of the above-ground economy in *King of New York;* and industrial, scientific, and state-run networks nestle within criminal organizations in *New Rose Hotel.*

So what becomes of the human? In *The Driller Killer* and later *The Addiction*—twin films in many respects—capitalism is shown from the viewpoint of its victims: the depressing poverty of urban dereliction, bums, junkies, and all the little people who are economic castoffs, slowly dying in the street, at anyone's mercy. In *Body Snatchers,* over the course of the fifty most terrifying, synthetic seconds in narrative cinema, the human is transformed into rubbish. In a slow-motion sequence-shot, the false, snatched mother, Carol (Meg Tilly), moves toward a truck, carrying a garbage bag that contains the remains of the real mother. Much is fused in this image of man-as-ashes: the Nazi ovens, the obliteration of bodies in Hiroshima, and the contemporary transformation of genetic patrimony into industrial property—three of the principle modern attempts at annulling humanity, whether by pure and simple disappearance (Nazi camps, Hiroshima) or by industrial reduction to the state of raw material (genetic industrialization). The dark, speckled brilliance of the asphalt upon which the menacing mother advances with her bag of remains evokes an archaic, mythological kind of figuration: the inaugural turbulence of atoms, as per Heraclitus and Lucretius. It is as if Ferrara aims to show the origin of life along with its symbolic disappearance. The narrative premise of *Body Snatchers* evokes a fatality without remission, clinched by the fact that it is the mother who performs this gesture of getting rid of humanity. She who gives life fulsomely propagates death, not only physically but also symbolically; the quotidian banality of her gesture renders it all the more ineluctable. But the lap-dissolve that begins the sequence-shot, superimposing the disturbed face of Andy upon the cosmic asphalt, suggests that it is all the nightmare of a young boy. In *New Rose Hotel,* however, there is no longer either dereliction or bodily waste—the human factor is contained on a computer disc, no longer anchored in warm, living bodies. It has been entirely coded and can thus be entirely erased.

*A Polemical Enterprise*    Ferrara has often expressed his admiration for the exacting artistry of John Cassavetes, Rainer Werner Fassbinder, and Pier Paolo Pasolini. Several principles unite the respective works of these four filmmakers. First, a practical principle: the constitution of a variable but faithful group of collaborators (Ferrara's team includes the writer Nicholas St. John, the composer Joe Delia, the cinematographer Ken Kelsch, the editor Anthony Redman, the producer Mary Kane, and the writer/actor Zoë Lund). Second, a stylistic principle: the exclusive privilege accorded by these filmmakers to the description of human behavior via gestural, actoral, and emotional invention. And a third, a fundamental theoretical principle: these filmmakers explicitly conceive of their work as a vast enterprise of political critique. This conception is most evident in the cases of Pasolini and Fassbinder.

For Fassbinder, each film constitutes a polemical treatise on Germany, past and present. His work never ceases to investigate five points: 1) the remnants of Nazism in contemporary Germany; 2) the moral nullity of liberal democracy; 3) the historical hypothesis that capitalism can accommodate itself to any political regime whatsoever, whether democratic or fascist; and, as a corollary to that, 4) Nazism as the ideal regime for capitalism, since it reduces workers to a "workforce" that does not need to be supported, only exhausted to the point of death and then instantly replaced (I. G. Farben paid Auschwitz prisoners); and 5) the servile ideological role of the culture industry.

Pasolini's work is organized on the basis of a central critical point: acculturation. This engenders a melancholic hypothesis concerning the disappearance of certain archaic forms of Italian civilization. While Fassbinder's work (like Ferrara's) declares itself to be entirely negative and purely polemical (in the great tradition of the Frankfurt School), Pasolini's work presents at once a negative side (the angry description of the forms of human nature's destruction) and an affirmative side (an affirmation of the survival or the force of the good and the beautiful, which is for him mythological barbarity, elaborated in *Medea,* 1970; *The Gospel According to Matthew,* 1964; and *Love Meetings,* 1965). Both filmmakers are bent on preserving particular forms of beauty: neoclassical beauty, like the angel in Pasolini's *Theorem* (1968) or the gay boys in Fassbinder; and subproletarian beauty, like the *ragazzi* in Pasolini or the way Fassbinder films his own body (in *Fox and His Friends* [1974], for instance). This is a dimension completely missing from Ferrara's work; the beautiful appears nowhere in his representations. The beautiful and the good are either resolutely absent (as in *Body Snatchers*), rendered as repulsive (the "healthy" character in *The Blackout,* Susan [Claudia Schiffer]), profaned (the nun [Frankie Thorn] in *Bad Lieutenant*), or treated as a catastrophic, unliveable eruption leading to death (the crisis of L. T. [Harvey Keitel] at the moment of his redemption) or to self-annihilation (the ambiguous resurrection of Kathy [Lili Taylor] at the end of *The Addiction*). In Ferrara, the journey of goodness is rendered as endless suffering. At the antipodes to the sporadic Hellenism that appears in Fassbinder or Pasolini, the only "beauties" in Ferrara are criminal, Baudelairean, infernal bodies.

*Modern Forms of Allegory* Ferrara, Cassavetes, Pasolini, and Fassbinder plumb, within the order of figuration, a common resource: the elaboration of modern cinematic allegory, in forms determined by these filmmakers' polemical enterprises. Cinematic characters often represent exemplars or values such as law, revolt, or normality, but that is a matter of emblems or archetypes, not allegories. Allegories presuppose a strong conceptual construction. The conceptual elaboration of an allegory, sometimes complex and unfamiliar, opposes itself to the principle of recognition, the already seen and already known, which is the realm where archetypes work. It is in this sense, perhaps, that Walter Benjamin claims that "[a]llegory is the armature of modernity."[15]

Consider, for example, the character of Willie (Hannah Schygulla) in Fassbinder's *Lili Marleen* (1981). A singing star, Willie is a purely logical figure representing the point of confusion between antagonists: she maintains the link between Nazism and the Resistance (as a symbol of the Nazi regime, she has a lover inside the Resistance); between the German and Russian armies, which halt fire in their trenches to listen to her songs; and between the Jewish music that she replaces on the radio and the censorship that she herself suffers. In short, she is a modern allegory—not an entity that cloaks a concept in a body by means of a panoply of emblems (Justice with her scales and sword, Cupid with his garland and arrows) but a logical movement of passage between conflictual entities. Fassbinder's intent is strongly critical, since Willie is ultimately a figure for the German people.

Ferrara's allegorical invention is especially kinetic: his characters allegorize not fixed notions but questions or problems. Marti in *Body Snatchers* represents what is archaic in the human psyche; Kathy in *The Addiction* represents the (highly ambiguous) principle of historical guilt; Matty (Matthew Modine) in *The Blackout* represents the workings of an abandonment complex. Note, however, that Pasolini, Fassbinder, and Ferrara classically maintain character as the figurative site for allegory, whereas Jean-Luc Godard works by constellation and dispersion across several figures, as the filmmaker Gaspard Bazin (Jean-Pierre Léaud), relating the technique to its pictorial origins in Titian, outlines clearly in *Grandeur and Decadence of a Small-Time Filmmaker* (1986).

*Dynamics of the System*   Pasolini, Fassbinder, and Ferrara proceed from the same cinematic origin: Rossellini. In all three cases, it is a matter of systematically coming to grips with contemporary evil. "Systematic" here means permanent, recurrent, and exclusive—for nothing is beyond the question of evil. But the formal translations of this systematicity for each filmmaker are rich and diverse. The elementary form of systematicity is the program, in the sense of a plan laid out in advance and progressively explored. This is the source of Rossellini's inventiveness, not only in his great educational television works but also his postwar cycle of films. Rossellini set out to make a series of films on the disasters of war. Four installments were shot: *Rome Open City* (1945) and *Paisà* (1946) on the Italian resistance to fascism, *Germany Year Zero* (1947) on the physical and moral catastrophe provoked by Nazism, and *Stromboli* (1949) on displaced people. Another installment, a film on Hiroshima, was conceived; and Ferrara, in a sense, realized this project with *Body Snatchers*.

But Ferrara's work invents other systematic forms at the heart of individual films as well as across all of his films: composition by anamorphosis (a key image is translated and metamorphosed in the course of a film, just as an anamorphic image can only be viewed correctly under certain conditions, such as through a lens or in a mirror that "unsqueezes" it); films conceived as counterparts of each other (*Ms .45* is the female version of the male fable of *The Driller Killer*); scenes conceived as gestures of repentance for (or even a repainting of) other scenes (the rape in *9 Lives of a Wet Pussy* is expiated in *Ms .45*); the progressive stretching from film to film of a figure that is initially simple in its symbolic operation, pushing it to its limits (the serial killer); the systematic declension of the same psychic motor—namely, passion—for all central figures; and narrative inversion, to posit a "reverse shot" to the entire system (in 'R Xmas, how to get free of evil when it is no longer experienced as criminal transgression but as an everyday norm). Generally, proof that a filmmaker's œuvre is coherent is not especially remarkable or impressive. But in Ferrara's case, this proliferation of systematic forms—on iconographic, narrative, stylistic, and logical levels, and from film to film—never ceases to amaze.

## Anamorphic Structures

*Preservation of Tragedy*  One concept unites Ferrara's work with that of some of his contemporaries: *the only story is the story of evil.* Two possible positions instantly follow from this. The first is fatalistic (in the manner of Marguerite Duras's famous phrase from *The Truck* [1977], "The world hurrying to its end, that's the only politics"), demanding a frontal description of "the disaster," whatever and wherever that disaster may be. The second position is tragic, maintaining a principle of resistance to evil while knowing all along that this resistance is doomed to failure. Ferrara is on the top rung of tragedians, even though, as a filmmaker, he is essentially boundlessly optimistic. Not because goodness (in the sense of an advent of social justice and thus of moral pacification) can ever become a reality, but because the annihilation of evil can be envisaged as the negation of negation. This is evident in the endings of *Bad Lieutenant, The Addiction,* and *The Funeral.*

In this respect, the frenetic treatment of goodness via the figure of the delirious ambulance driver (Nicolas Cage) in *Bringing Out the Dead* (1999) constitutes Martin Scorsese's response to Ferrara's use of *Mean Streets* (1973) in *Bad Lieutenant* and *The Addiction.* In all these films, fables of compassion and redemption have no efficacy unless they borrow the attributes (and the visionary stylistics) of crime stories: gestures of goodness are inverted into gestures of aggression; love of one's neighbor becomes an almost cannibalistic desire; and empathy with the suffering of others leads to a criminal vertigo. In contemporary cinema, goodness, love, and compassion can no longer be represented with the kind of simplicity for which Rossellini provided the definitive model in *Europa '51.* There must now be a true guardian of the law (not order but morality), whether psychopathic, incestuous, and mute (such as Takeshi Kitano in *Violent Cop* [1989]); drugged, libidinal, and mystical (Keitel in *Bad Lieutenant*); or hallucinating, irrational, and ineffectual (Cage in *Bringing Out the Dead*). Such a treatment of goodness, via the paradoxical adoption of traditional attributes of evil, culminates in the portrait in *'R Xmas* of the cop (Ice-T) as a tempting, corrupt, anguished figure—in short, the serpent who must save Eve (the wife-mother, played by Drea de Matteo) from amorality lived as normality.

*Fold and Pleat: Formal Logics of Metamorphosis* To imagine the annihilation of evil there must be an exploration—not a simple antagonism of two opposed entities (good versus evil) but an intensification or deepening of a single entity. Ferrara's films are structured like passages through the looking-glass; it is a matter of passing from the recto to the verso of a given situation or image. This gives rise to a typical narrative structure of Ferrara's work. Films are organized upon a single major fold, where the beginning finally meets or "touches" the ending to offer a striking comparison, or a more gradual pleat, where the major fold is progressively translated throughout in a series of small folds (akin to a pleated skirt) over the entire structure of a film. *Ms .45* is a representative example of a film with a major fold joining the start and end, while *The Addiction* and *The Blackout* offer models of the pleating structure.

Bad Lieutenant is exemplary in its demonstration of these dynamics. In terms of its major, overarching fold, it opens on a daily situation—a father taking his two sons to school in a pleasant suburb—in order to arrive, finally, at the catastrophic version of this same scene: L. T. driving the two young punks through a devastated New York. Whether folding or pleating, Ferrara's narratives generally take an ordinary daily scene all the way through to its transformation into a disaster. They are organized according to two principal procedures: either they depict the integral time of a single folding trajectory (*Ms .45, Bad Lieutenant*), or they ceaselessly repeat and renew the inaugural fold in an echoing, insistent, and hence pleated way (*The Driller Killer, The Addiction, The Blackout*). Ferrara's films are organized on the basis of a fully imaginary form: metamorphosis, a complete alteration or transformation in form, structure, or substance—a process that can seem magical or diabolical. Two major instances of metamorphosis offer possibilities for compositional invention: metamorphosis of the protagonist or of the film itself. The dynamic of Ferrara's œuvre arises from the way it endlessly renews the relationship between these two instances.

Let us observe some examples of this dynamic. *Ms .45* and *Bad Lieutenant*, the two films Ferrara made with Zoë Lund, operate upon a harmonious coincidence between the protagonist's trajectory and the film's own unfolding. *Ms .45* recounts the progressive metamorphosis of a young woman, Thana, into an implacable avenger. The film takes us from an ordinary scene (a fashion preview in a garment factory) to its nightmarish revision (the fancy-dress office party that ends in bloodshed). Its ending thus elucidates its seemingly casual opening: the fashion preview poses human costume as an ordinary disguise for a social mise en scène of bodies entirely founded on relations of power and submission (the regal and contemptuous buyer, the cunning dresser, mistreated models, and passive workers). The final fancy-dress party, which puts the studio staff back into the scene, develops the film's underlying postulate all the way to the end: relations between people, especially sexual relations, can only be criminal. The invited couples swap tidbits about vasectomies and how to buy virgins from Third World countries. The sexual horror institutionally acknowledged and left at the dialogue level as a factual referent is immediately translated into a fantastic plot event. The double rape of the virginal Thana is thus reinscribed in a general economy of body-exploitation perceived by the western imaginary as the natural order rather than an absolute injustice, signaled by the off-handedness with which the interlocutors discuss prices for young girls. Thana's violence responds to this institutionalized horror: to kill everyone, from the factory boss (this derisory representative of the industrial order) and his colleagues to all the available men, women, and transvestites. No massacre will ever be proportionate with the real abomination. The figure of Thana brings to light the phenomenon of ordinary sexual violence—first as a private phobia, but ultimately as an ultrapowerful force in the daily world economy, the possibility of exploiting any body of any age in any way. As Lund stated in 1993, "*Ms .45* is not about women's liberation, any more than it is about mutes' liberation, or garment workers' liberation (the character was a presser), or your liberation, or my own. Notice that her climactic victim is not a rapist in the clinical sense. He is her boss. The real rapist. *Our* real rapist."[16]

The anamorphic trajectory of *Ms .45* is thus clear: the final catastrophic version (the bloody ball) brings to light the intolerable character of the socially domesticated violence lurking in the inaugural ordinary scene (the fashion preview). As at the end of *The Deer Hunter* (1978), where the protagonists' journey into hell allows us to finally see the germinal violence surreptitiously at work in the gesture of a little boy playing sweetly in his room with a plastic revolver, here the rape-and-massacre fable develops the logic of aggression at work in the apparently anodyne gesture of a sleazy boss caressing his employee's hair and takes it all the way.

*Bad Lieutenant* recounts the path of a tormented character towards conversion; like *Ms .45*, the film takes us from an ordinary scene to its devastated version. But this major folding trajectory enriches itself through a gradual, pleated structure of echoes and metamorphic waves. A fold at the film's start takes us directly from the private (the family) to the public (the job), from L. T.'s two sons in the black car to two girls, shooting victims, in their white car, female corpses that L. T. regards (in a point-of-view shot) as sexual objects. The fold closes itself at the end of its trajectory on an exact reverse (the two young Latino rapists). But in between, it is also translated at least twice further: across the sexual couple (a woman and an androgyne) with whom L. T. dances, and the two young women in the stationary car whom L. T. orders to mime fellatio—as if to testify more clearly to the totally phantasmic nature of this echo. Ferrara's scenes are less plot events than visual echoes. Their logic is not especially Aristotelian, for they are not determined by linkages of cause and effect or before and after. They belong to a psychic process: the *reproduction of a trauma in multiple aftershocks.*

Two figural energies are put to work here. The first is figurative elasticity, which concerns the amplitude of the vibration between the matrix and each of its singular echoes. For example, the erotic couple with which L. T. drinks and dances (a voluptuous naked woman and an androgyne) does not really resemble what it relays (the initial pair of boys) unless it is inscribed within the entire chain of visual transfers. The second figural energy is iconographic fertility, which concerns the possible diversity of the echoes (L. T.'s sons become women, androgynes, rapists). These two processes and their attendant energies—the extent of visual approximation that the matrix can bear (all the way to apparent dissimilitude) in figurative elasticity and the constant renewal of the motifs (all the way to their apparent dispersion) in iconographic fertility—attest to the gravity of the complex that the film addresses.

*Liquidation of Western Philosophy* The Addiction offers the clearest anamorphic structure of any Ferrara film to this point in his career; it features a double metamorphosis. On the level of its protagonist, the film offers the metamorphosis of a philosophy student into a vampire, and thus of a moral problem (collective historical guilt) into corporeal destruction (somatization). From the viewpoint of the film itself, the metamorphosis is the permanent conversion of historical information (images of the Vietnam War, Nazi death camps, and so on) into physical events (vampiric attacks). The film is an essay on the psychic effects of images that are so powerful that, once shown, they take over the fictional bodies: Kathy experiences, as if for the first time, the slides of the My Lai massacre, and her intellectual torment (who is to blame? how to make amends?) metamorphoses in the very next sequence into a fantastic vampirism. Encountering an image, and encountering a Vampire named Casanova (Annabella Sciorra): it is the same scene, first as documentary and then as allegory, and this conversion will reproduce itself with each new discovery of a documentary image. Vampirism offers a simple, universal, popular iconography for the treatment of a complex and universal political question: how to live with the knowledge of historic evil—the unending chain of genocides, public and private massacres, the reign of injustice, oppression, and corruption? How not to die from all this pain, anguish, and guilt? Kathy incarnates and overexposes the torment that western civilization strives daily to repress.

The film's ending, with its sudden logical spin, responds to the simple conversion at its beginning (the slides incarnate themselves as vampires), offering a metamorphosis so rapidly dialectical that it defies our understanding. Kathy, drained of all blood, seems to pass away peacefully after having received her last rites. Her ghost returns to place a rose on her grave, which proves either that the peaceful laying-to-rest remains tentative, or that Kathy is the first in a line of angels who are a source of torment rather than protection. At the same time, on the strict evidence of what we see and hear, this problematic figure intellectually self-destructs, since she exits the film with these words spoken

Christopher Walken and Lili Taylor in
*The Addiction.*

in voiceover: "Self-revelation is annihilation of self." Nothing is liveable any longer: neither knowing the world (one can die from anguish), nor making amends (liquidation is never complete, torment always returns; the "unhappy consciousness," as Hegel called it, has no historical use-value), nor self-awareness (which marks the fulfillment of a disaster, not its solution). Kathy's character symbolically exhausts every option of western philosophy.

*Beginning from Fantasy*  Other Ferrara films dissociate the protagonist's trajectory from the work's own unfolding. *Dangerous Game,* like the films based on total metamorphosis, proceeds through incessant variations upon the same scene (a husband-wife quarrel). But these characters do not undergo any metamorphosis; on the contrary, they are locked up in their closed identities, caught in the stickiness of the self—starting with the confusion of actor and individual. Here it is not differentiation but its absence—an indistinctness—that creates the conditions for a pathology. *Body Snatchers* has metamorphosis as its very subject: the fiction of extraterrestrial replacement works well as a treatment of anthropological mutation in the age of the genome, that is, the menace to the living posed by industrialization in an advanced capitalist regime that now readies itself to confiscate our human, genetic patrimony. This film plainly obeys the anamorphic logic of Ferrara's work. At the start, in an eminently familiar domestic gesture, Marti, riding in the back of the family car, pushes away her stepbrother, Andy; at the end, she hurls him from a helicopter down into a world consumed by blood and fire. The fold is perfect. However, Marti's problem is precisely that she refuses the proper metamorphosis to adolescence. One can read the Snatchers story as a psychoanalytic fantasy (or *phantasm*) arising from a general repulsion towards the body. To fantasize a body that is empty and never subject to chance, without difference from the Other, with no future: the Snatchers, far more effectively than any overt menace, are not only the catalyst that allows this family romance to develop (erasing a young girl's father, mother, brother, and the whole world); they also offer a fantasy of the body delivered from its own weight, from conception, gestation, and child bearing. The Snatcher thus represents the Other as not the human but the female. To restore living reproduction to a vegetable (no longer animal) model allows the invention of a mode of gestation that no longer takes place within the body but anywhere in the exterior world (hence the imagery of pods in a swamp)—no longer an intimate, individual process but an anonymous, collective administration (the nocturnal military management of the pods); no longer an organic, affective fusion (the fœtus) but a reproduction that is always already separate from its source. That such a fantasy of engenderment of the living can be a part of a young girl's dreams, paradoxically, is what singularly expands our grasp of what is human. Here we catch a glimpse of one of the anthropological horizons of Ferrara's cinema: to reopen our conception of the human, starting from that aspect of humanity that is unresigned to the facts of being only itself—including the apparently most ineluctable and definitive biological determinations of human being.

*Depicting the World* A number of cases of figurative anamorphosis, structural or local, can be found in Ferrara's cinema: for example, between the scenes of dancing and urban confrontation in *China Girl,* or between the release from prison at the start and the exit from the train station at the end of *King of New York.* This is not merely a matter of rhymes aiming to establish a thematic coherence but of constructing a film through the form of a passage between altered images. The stake of this recurrent construction (certain films, such as *Cat Chaser* [1989] and *'R Xmas,* follow different logics) is not the closure or self-abolition of the film (as is the case in *Violent Cop,* where the reprise of the same shot of the cop crossing a bridge at the start and end signifies the desperate futility of the protagonist's sacrifice) but an intensification by reprises and variations. Ferrara films plunge into the deep, unspoken, scandalous significations of a scene, a gesture, or an ordinary situation. Such a structure declares itself to be at once classical (in the sense of perfectly totalized) and eminently contemporary: it is the structure of the antiworld. One of the origins of this antiworld structure can be found in Lewis Carroll's books, *Alice's Adventures in Wonderland, Through the Looking-Glass,* and *Sylvie and Bruno:* we must pass through a double of our world to understand the original. In cinema, the two most popular models of such "shadow world" fables are Victor Fleming's *The Wizard of Oz* (1939) and Alfred Hitchcock's *Vertigo* (1958), which dramatize, respectively, a crossing over into the doubled world and the construction of a double that is brought into our world.

Contrary to such traditional fictions of destiny or becoming, contemporary American cinema massively construes fable as nightmare, narrative as anamnesis (an obsessive remembering that is also an erasure of past trauma), and thus (retroactively) the world as Limbo. Brian De Palma's *Carlito's Way* (1993), Scorsese's *Casino* (1995), Jarmusch's *Dead Man* (1995), and David Lynch's *Lost Highway* (1997) all elaborate this kind of nightmare. Ferrara uses the same structure but transposes it into a realist context. In the process, he returns to an early, precocious occurrence of this form: Cassavetes's *The Killing of a Chinese Bookie* (1978). The opening and penultimate sequences of that film depict the same character, Cosmo (Ben Gazzara), abandoned by life on a sidewalk—in between, the fable unfolds within dreamlike Limbo-spaces (centered on the nightmarish insistence of Cosmo's debt). Another concept—à la John Carpenter's *Village of the Damned* (1995)—is to present the world as already its own double. *Body Snatchers* unites both major modes: anamorphic intensification of a family scene, plus the fantastic re-elaboration of the world as a terrestrial hell.

To put it another way, the great contemporary fabulations address the question of what can be depicted or represented. But they do this in a way completely opposite to the Freudian dreamwork, which dresses up a normal, standard situation in an oneiric image capable of opening an access-path to consciousness. Rather, it is a matter of exhuming the latent violence in a standard image (daily life), with the intention of reconstructing its most obscure and least acceptable determinations. Ferrara's work on this level belongs to a collective American aesthetic movement. Its specificity at the heart of this current can be measured by the way it places a crucial structure—the narrative possibilities of what can be represented—at the service of a radical, critical project.

## What Is Passion? Central Figures of Hypermorality

### Forms of the Person: The Exigency of Infinity

In coming to grips with the questions of evil and guilt, Rossellini found it necessary to renew fiction in order to restore our relation to belief and reason. Ferrara works on the same problem, but at the level of the body. His films invent powerful modes of somatization, or the translation of psychic, political, and economic phenomena into corporeal terms. This enterprise of translation never ceases reinventing the relation between mental image and concrete image, opening up an astonishing repertoire of altered bodies: suffering, wasted, angry, convulsive, collapsed, haunted, even absent. His characters throw the telephone out the window because the bill is too high (Reno, played by Ferrara himself, in *The Driller Killer*); shoot out the radio because it broadcasts bad news (L. T. in *Bad Lieutenant*); kill any man who insults a woman (Thana in *Ms.45*); compulsively machine-gun the facades of Chinatown real estate (Mercury [David Caruso] in *China Girl*); erase the world to transform it (Frank White [Christopher Walken] in *King of New York*); kill in order to grasp that the only story is the story of evil (Kathy in *The Addiction*). Ferrara's protagonists—Reno, Thana, L. T., Frank, Kathy, the Tempio brothers (Walken, Christopher Penn, and Vincent Gallo) in *The Funeral*, Matty and Mickey (Dennis Hopper) in *The Blackout*—represent figures of possession. Burdened with an undiminished fury, these characters are filled with an overflowing pain and a sublime ethical project that leads them to death.

*System of Ethical Life* What logic underpins Ferrara's system? First of all, two models should be set aside. This logic is not a doctrine that can be applied from one film to the next, over and above the content of the individual fictions. Even if the character of Johnny (Gallo) in *The Funeral*—violent, communist, hypersexed, and full of integrity—seems like the most seductive and idealized figure in his films so far, Ferrara nonetheless declares himself to be a perfect dandy who believes only in "antipolitics," brandishing the motto, "I'm a limousine liberal."[17] Nor does the Ferraran system rest upon the principle of taxonomy or cartography—the exhaustive filling-in of an already mapped territory. Rather, his aesthetic system proceeds from a logic of extension and a politics of reprise. It is because of these reprises that we see—as one rarely does in cinema, beyond the major example of Godard—an artist reflecting on the sense of his own work.

A first form of reprise is reparation: posing a film as an act of repentance for (and also "repairing" of) previous images. Two instances of this process can be cited. The first is purely axiological: the relation between the two episodes of the television series *Miami Vice* that Ferrara directed in 1985. "The Home Invaders" (episode 20) represents the televisual norm in its brute state: a band of young Latin American thugs burgle a rich Miami family; our friendly detectives (led by Sonny Crockett [Don Johnson]) identify, apprehend, and punish the culprits. Beating up a guy who is poor, young, immigrant, and clandestine in the name of respect for private property is considered honest work, a mission, a necessity—helpful, and also good fun. In an agonized stab at redemption for this (in its own way) criminal subjugation to television's rules, "The Dutch Oven" (episode 27) embodies the general transgression of such rules. This time, the fiction depicts the murder of a bad guy by a female cop, Gina (Saundra Santiago), and the guilt that this engenders. Ferrara employs a wayward approach to narrative that favors description over action and liberates the possibility of working with mental images—a prelude to the complex superimpositions in *The Blackout*. In the context of a popular television series, "The Dutch Oven" constitutes an astonishing disavowal of police activity, problematizing the law on political and affective levels.

The second instance of reparation evokes a figurative deontology (a science of duty or moral obligation, or a code of ethics). In one sequence in *The Blackout*, a video artist (Mickey) directs an extra ("Annie 2" [Sarah Lassez]) to seduce an actor (Matty) and obtain from him the image lacking from the film-in-progress titled *Nana Miami:* a murder. Immediately absorbed into this fiction, the extra is drawn into a criminal economy. She disappears twice over, assassinated as a character and repressed as a memory, confused with the model for whom she offers a shadow-double. *New Rose Hotel* begins from the same situation and extends it to the scale of an entire film, so as to finally arrive at its moral reversal. Two men (Fox [Christopher Walken] and X [Willem Dafoe]) direct a young woman (Sandii [Asia Argento])—utterly interchangeable with the other women on stage with whom we first glimpse her—to seduce a third man (the Japanese scientist Hiroshi [Yoshitaka Amano]). But this aspiring actress proves herself to be not only a simulator incarnate but also the supreme femme fatale—the mythic Pandora who annihilates her designated victim, her creators, and mankind in general.

However, what is morally unbearable in *The Blackout*—to summon up a body, render it secondary, and supplicate and sacrifice it, all in ten minutes of film—is ultimately pressed into the service of its crowning image. The superimposition of the murderer and his victim evokes an iconographical reference: the adoration of the Virgin, or hyperdulia.[18] The film includes this representation on two conditions: First, that the Virgin disappears, physically erased by the man who adores and symbolically kills her, since she is already dead and thus insignificant in the shadow cast by the gigantic, absent body, "Annie 1" (Béatrice Dalle)—the Mother, wife, star, and (in terms of Lacanian psychoanalysis) "block of the Real." Second, this Virgin must also be the Mother, but one whose son has been aborted. However, even this figural apogee will not suffice. *New Rose Hotel* reinvents this figurative guilt even more profoundly. Sandii, the woman who was initially only an extra, becomes a central character: the angel tattooed on her belly rises (in a lap dissolve) over the entire world, and the actress destroys everything in her path. The entire film is organized according to a logic of denial that transforms destructive power into passionate affirmation. In an era of integral industrialization of the living (from which the *zaibatsu* draws its resources), woman no longer constitutes the indispensable source of human life—she has become a mere accessory. Nevertheless, if we attribute a universal power to destruction (Pandora), woman remains an absolute origin. From *The Blackout* to *New Rose Hotel,* figurative repentance arranges itself around stakes of an anthropological order.

*Critical Intensification: The Case of the Individual* The exacerbated form of repentance leads us to the general dynamic of Ferrara's system. It is characterized by a second form of reprise (also found in Orson Welles and Fritz Lang): critical intensification. Observe the evolution of a crucial Ferraran problem, the notion of the individual. Ferrara's protagonists represent figures of the human insofar as the human is kept distinct from the individual, or insofar as intimate experience is kept distinct from individual experience. What is the individual today? (In tomorrow's world, the question will be easy to answer: an individual is anyone you can clone.) The individual is a subject identical to itself, anchored in identity, resolving itself (at least practically) in its relation to the Other, whether under types of self-alteration (for instance, the experience of illness) or collective experience (the relation to diverse kinds of human groups, such as family, clan, or tribe). According to our modern western conception, the individual is assured of his or her singularity, irreplaceable, a subject of rights and morality. To this extent, the individual becomes a bad object for the moderns. "[T]he isolated being is the individual, and the individual is only an abstraction, existence as it is represented by the weak-minded conception of everyday liberalism."[19]

The individual amounts, on the good side, to the sovereign subject and, on the bad side, to the autotelic subject (the subject as an "end in itself"). The entirety of modernity, from Nietzsche to the Frankfurt School, is in opposition to this concept of the autotelic subject who facilely becomes a simple object of identity. Ferrara's cinema permanently shoves this crucial idea in our faces: *the human is that which cannot find its limits*. Nothing could be closer to Ferrara's cinema, on this level, than the philosophical and literary work of Georges Bataille. Both share the postulate that an ethical life henceforth consists of finding forms of faith at the heart of human negativity—an enterprise that Bataille calls "hypermorality." "[T]he Evil—an acute form of Evil—which [literature] expresses, has a sovereign value for us. But this concept does not exclude morality: on the contrary, it demands a 'hypermorality.'"[20]

There are four kinds of hero in Ferrara's films. First, we have those that take themselves outside individuation and identity (the wasted or the nameless, like L. T. in *Bad Lieutenant* and almost all the characters in *'R Xmas,* or representative types, like the body snatchers). Second, there are those that directly problematize the question of identity, either through being actors (Sarah [Madonna] in *Dangerous Game,* Sandii in *New Rose Hotel*) or being mad (Chez [Chris Penn] in *The Funeral*); because they are addicts, as in all of his films; or because they are addicts, mad, and actors at once (Matty in *The Blackout*). Third, Ferrara's heroes find themselves beyond individuation (the King of New York, the saintly figure that L. T. becomes in *Bad Lieutenant,* the formless larva into which Kathy is transformed in *The Addiction*). Peina (Christopher Walken), king of vampires in *The Addiction,* is presented as both super- and subhuman: superhuman because he is immortal; subhuman because he is burdened with the arrogance of keeping himself in shape, citing Baudelaire, and managing to drink tea, describing himself as "almost human." And fourth, Ferrara's heroes die in the process of upholding a tragic defense of the individual, as Major Collins in *Body Snatchers* kills himself to affirm the privilege of singularity over uniform collectivity.

Contrary to the American ideology of narcissistic conquest, Collins's suicide places the individual in a purely defensive position, with no choice other than self-erasure. When he disappears, so too does the humanist hypothesis of a worthy and righteous sovereign subject. Beyond him reigns the military, industrial, and psychic order—the American democratic capitalism responsible for Hiroshima and Nagasaki. A good synopsis of *Body Snatchers* can be found in Adorno's *Minima Moralia:*

> It is the signature of our age that no-one, without exception, can now determine his own life. . . . Even the profession of general no longer offers adequate protection. . . . It follows directly from this that anyone who attempts to come out alive—and survival itself has something nonsensical about it, like dreams in which having experienced the end of the world, one afterwards crawls from a basement—ought also to be prepared at each moment to end his life. . . . Freedom has contracted to pure negativity, and what in the days of *art nouveau* was known as a beautiful death has shrunk to the wish to curtail the infinite abasement of the living and the infinite torment of dying, in a world where they are far worse things to fear than death. The objective end of humanism is only another expression for the same thing. It signifies that the individual as individual, in representing the species of man, has lost the autonomy through which he might realize the species.[21]

*"Realize the Species"* Is the individual in Ferrara's work thus reduced to a simple principle of resistance against all it encounters, or nothing more than the shocking scenography of its own liquidation? On the contrary, Ferrara's cinema is tragic because it insistently fixes upon the "realization of the species"—something that real history (which Ferrara's cinema tries to describe in the most rational way possible) is intent on whisking away. After the statement made by *Body Snatchers*—that the whole world and all minds are being poisoned by capitalist industrialization—after the disappearance of the human, and since "nothing is possible any longer" (the final line of Pasolini's *Medea*), then what is there to say or do? For starters, one can verify and deepen this description of the state of things in more specific ways.

*The Funeral* and *The Blackout*, despite their differences, represent two "family romances" that transpose the universal investigation undertaken by *Body Snatchers* into the context of domestic intimacy. The same conclusion is reached: the self must be erased to accomplish the "religion of humanity" that Emile Durkheim posed as the good version of individualism.[22] In *The Funeral,* Chez, the sick brother, must destroy destruction, the logic of pride and vengeance set up by his family. In a perfectly rational act of *amour fou,* he must kill his eldest brother, Ray (Christopher Walken), "kill" Johnny's corpse, and finally kill himself. Maybe then the wives and fiancées, capable of reflection and kindness, might be able to live. In *The Blackout,* a man (Matty) must die in order to fail before the woman who initially desired his presence. The allegory contained in the final image—the male ghost inclined towards the sweet, nude, female ghost arising in a superimposition out of the dark sea—constitutes the complete unfolding of the way in which one being can lack another. The final question of the victim-phantom to the executioner-phantom who has rejoined her in death—"Did you miss me?"—represents the sacred development of the ordinary, lighthearted dialogue of the wife-husband greeting at the film's start (Her: "I missed you" / Him: "Yeah? I missed you too, baby" / Her: "Impossible . . ."). The slightest lack in the other's desire is developed to the point of catastrophe, opening a fissure in the couple's fusion and triggering a deluge of scenarios of death and abandonment into which the characters dive. Whether on the plane of morality (*The Funeral*) or emotion (*The Blackout*), Ferrara's characters cannot live if not in a state of *amour fou.*

What kind of humanity is this? That of the "just man," in the realization of whose name the singular individual can abolish himself. This is the ethical grandeur of Ferrara's work, its fierce call to dignity. It wreaks violence upon the concrete individual in the name of an ideal of fusion and love, while fully knowing and describing the pathological, morbid nature of this ideal. This is the same logic expressed by Walter Benjamin when he refutes the sacred character of particular existence in the name of an ethical life: "The proposition that existence stands higher than a just existence is false and ignominious, if existence is to mean nothing other than mere life. . . . However sacred man is (or however sacred that life in him which is identically present in earthly life, death, and afterlife), there is no sacredness in his condition, in his bodily life vulnerable to injury by his fellow men."[23]

At the start of *The Blackout,* a man and woman (Matty and Annie) embrace; their kiss, instead of manifesting joy and mutual understand-

Matthew Modine in *The Blackout*.

ing, masks their disquiet and distance. In the unfolding by successive
anamorphoses of this affective gesture across the film, there is a long
figurative movement of successive correction and the tragic advent of
the just man, he who has recognized, traversed, and absorbed all that is
negative, plunged to the point of drowning himself in an abyss of lack
so that, beyond his disappearance, the glimmer of an instant of pure
adoration might finally appear. *Body Snatchers* establishes an analytic
synthesis of the human and social condition that is beyond any specific
time or place. This account, however, was further verified and specified
by Ferrara, by confronting it with historical reality. *The Addiction* and
*New Rose Hotel* each take up, in their own way, the figurative schema of
*Body Snatchers*—in a body-to-body encounter, the self is captured and
stolen. Both use the same archetype: Pandora, incarnated by Peina in

*The Addiction* and Sandii in *New Rose Hotel.* But *The Addiction* treats the historical dimension of the problem in a recapitulative way. Kathy absorbs the collective catastrophes of the twentieth century (Nazism, the Vietnam War, poverty, pandemic diseases, and so on). *New Rose Hotel* treats the matter in a prophetic way, asking, What is the destiny of the body in an industrial regime of genetic licensing? Both films develop the same idea of a general erasure of the human race, whether by physiological and genetic confiscation (*New Rose Hotel*) or by moral and metaphysical subtraction (*The Addiction*).

Both films end on a moral lesson of sorts. In *The Addiction,* this lesson is that the speculative faculty must be cultivated as an ultimate weapon—"self-revelation is annihilation of self," like a resistance fighter who hides on his person the cyanide capsule that will allow him to remain free in death. *New Rose Hotel* takes another path. By preserving—against all historical evidence—biological prerogatives within the female belly, the film introduces us to the critical virtues of denial.

The problem can also be posed the other way around, as in *'R Xmas.* In this film that ends with "to be continued," hypermorality is confused with ordinary morality. As in *The Funeral,* criminal life is the normal state of the family, but now this state is lived as a peaceful happiness, no longer as a paranoiac, twilight madness. The protagonists live inside the serenity of evil, and the trajectory of the story comprises their blind and difficult journey towards the recovery of their rights. The true transgression henceforth consists of acceding to justice—obviously not to false legality, the bad capitalist jurisdiction that all previous Ferrara films critique, but a state in which "right and grace are confused."[24] *'R Xmas* establishes the most terrible of claims concerning evil: no one can get away from it anymore; the individual henceforth bathes in it like a blissful reign whose negative nature is no longer perceived. No one can even imagine, as far as the human horizon extends, what a new understanding of sovereignty, or a possible form of justice, could be. Another, completely different option would be to pose the problem of evil without passing through the negative, as Scorsese envisaged in *Bringing Out the Dead,* an amicable, brilliant response to Ferrara's cinema. It reverses the frenetic, agonised treatment of madness, crime, and misery in *Mean Streets, Taxi Driver* (1976), and *After Hours* (1985)—not to mention

*Bad Lieutenant, King of New York,* and *The Addiction*—into the realm of compassion, charity, and the problematic of healing.

Film after film—whatever the conditions of production—the systematicity of Ferrara's work is elaborated with a calm certainty. How does this level of systematicity sometimes remain unperceived by critics as mastery? There are two possible reasons: Ferrara's cinema actively explores the forms of lack in a radical way—especially in *New Rose Hotel,* his masterpiece on this topic. More generally, because of the insistent motifs that constantly return, the psychic confusion of the characters is attributed to the work itself—which, in fact, treats this subject magisterially. So let us pose again the question of the individual, this time from the vantage point of its interiority.

*Rough Beast, Scrap Heap, Authentic Virtue*  Consider the sequence in *Bad Lieutenant* where, under the sound of "Let's Get High" by the Lords of Acid, L. T. goes to explain to his bookie, Lite (Anthony Ruggiero), that he intends not to settle his debt, instructing him instead to re-bet it. This scene offers an accumulation of forms of negativity on at least three levels. On the level of the narrative situation, L. T. is plunged into a spiral: he gets himself into ever deeper debt, puts himself in lethal peril, and continues to deny the risk. At this level, the scene could be taken to depict a simple "descent into hell": visual obscurity, a trajectory complicated by the need to visit a cavern (the bar) with a death's head, red chromatism, a religious thematic, and a backdrop of gothic debauchery (a dancer in a cage). But this picturesque iconography of hell stylishly declares its ornamental nature. It decorates a plastic and mental negativity that is more dangerous, one related to the elementary alternation between the visible and the invisible.

L. T. is a character who refuses to recognize anything, neither death nor the real. His path to the bar—staggering, eyes closed, totally lost in himself under the influence of crack—represents his blindness in physical terms. The stroboscopic light, in force from the moment of his descent, constitutes the plastic manifestation of this evident blindness. At this second, plastic level of the scene, the strobe effect can be understood in several ways. It allows us to reconstruct the psychic state of L. T.—hallucinating, confused, and prey to sensation. It transforms obscurity into a mode of self-perception—the passages of darkness, like so many small, insistent blackouts, de-realize phenomena, making them tremble and shudder. It leaves no room for any mode of apprehension beyond the alternation of blindness and dazzle, nothingness and excess. Perhaps most importantly, the stroboscope guarantees the indifference of the visible and invisible. Light and dark are no longer opposed; they work in concert to aggress and confuse figures. *Bad Lieutenant* contains one of the first truly symbolic uses of the stroboscope in cinema, after the tremendous plastic constructions of Ronald Nameth's films (Andy Warhol's *Exploding Plastic Inevitable,* contemporary with its technical invention in 1967) and the psychedelic installations of USCO in New York during the 1960s and 1970s. These works constitute the euphoric model to which Ferrara's scene offers a dysphoric avatar.

The third level of the scene creates a particularly acute form of negativity, thanks to its play on all-pervasive indistinctness. L. T. is not a character who alters or degrades himself, as does Kathy in *The Addiction* or Matty in *The Blackout* (characters who suit the "descent into hell" schema rather well). On the contrary, he is a compact, heavyset figure who is never really touched by anything. This is violently verified by the piling-on of factors that annul various sorts of differentiation at each of the three stages of the sequence (entry/bar/return). The first stage is spatial annulment: By mismatches of position from one shot to the next, L. T. and his mentor-dealer (Nicholas DeCegli) are alternately placed in the guide position as they make their way through the dancing crowd. The spatial orientation, in front or behind, hardly matters; nor does the before or after, who guides or who follows. It is no longer the case that light illuminates or that space situates. The second stage is metaphysical annulment: L. T.'s central declaration to Lite—"No one can kill me. I'm blessed"—testifies to his delirious presumption, an impunity that annuls all chance or becoming. The dialogue here refers back to Budd Boetticher's *The Rise and Fall of Legs Diamond* (1960), in which another hero swears that nothing can kill him, that he is blessed—with his companion's response providing the text for the mother's evil litany in *Body Snatchers* ("You're all alone. Who are you gonna turn to now? Where you gonna go? Who you gonna trust?" in the former, matching, "Where you gonna go? Where you gonna run? Where you gonna hide? Nowhere. Because there's no one—like you—left" in the latter). L. T.'s vital formula amounts to a radical denial; he is the very character of denial, the existential repression of death. The third stage, temporal annulment: In the return corridor, it is always—against all plausibility—the same Lords of Acid fragment, the same blue shadow, the same staggered walk; time has evaporated. The only changes are subtractive: the crowd has disappeared, the strobe has stopped, Lite is gone, and all traces of teeming activity have vanished. It is as if L. T.'s entry (stage one) constitutes the objective version of the scene for which his return (stage three), after the existential declaration (stage two), offers the subjective version, thus rendering it even more dreamlike, hallucinatory, and solipsistic. To put it another way, this nightclub sequence establishes a vast formal machine of annulment, modeled on L. T.'s denial: nothing matters, no accident can happen, everything can remain indistinct. L. T. is a figure of dark unconsciousness, closed in on himself, almost autistic, and totally impervious to suffering (he sees corpses as sexual objects and exploits a murder scene as an opportunity to grab a bag of drugs). He is the very figure of blindness avowed, named, and intensified.

In the terms of my argument, such a character represents not a drug addict or a corrupt cop but rather the contemporary incarnation of what Hegel calls "authentic truth," which "has only one figure: that of heroic immersion in ethical totality."[25] Hegel is opposed here to Kant's famous precept, "Act only in accordance with that maxim through which you can at the same time will that it should become a universal law."[26] Does a law need to be discussed? No, according to Alexis Philonenko: "[I]f the duty exists, there is no need to reflect, it is immediate, beyond discussion" (63). Philonenko describes the concept of authentic virtue as an absolute moral obligation, opposed to the "compatibility of understanding" for which Hegel reproached Kant: "Only immediate engagement in the ethical substance, without discussion or reasoning, in which the individual raises himself to the totality by sacrificing the particularity which defines him, testifies to the authenticity of existence" (64).

L. T. incarnates a raw engagement with immediacy "without discussion or reasoning." This is not only because of his action at the nadir of material life, immersed in the lower depths, in essential needs and a life of drives. It is also because he replaces understanding with crazy affirmation ("I'm blessed"), on the one hand, and a bet, on the other hand, which in his case does not proceed by deliberation and calculation but illumination ("I was at the game today, face to fucking face with Strawberry"). Thus, instead of understanding, he gives free reign to the powers of sensation, instinct, and chance. He does not lead the inquiry into the nun's rape; he stumbles onto its culprits by chance. Thus it is to this figure of authentic virtue, for whom nothing can be discussed, that truth will be revealed: the factual truth of the identity of the rapists and the spiritual truth of forgiveness. The work of negativity in the nightclub sequence here finds its true meaning: to represent the pure immediacy of engagement, which is not a positivity but a lack of distinctness between self and exteriority, a total passion totally experienced instant by instant. Ferrara translates this passion in terms of unconsciousness and inebriation.

The few trembling steps taken by Kathy as she leaves the vampire orgy in *The Addiction* correspond to the blind stagger of L. T. leaving the nightclub. The figurative elaboration of *The Addiction* is inverse and complementary to that of *Bad Lieutenant*. The theoretical consciousness of the student who rationally analyzes historical reality—the somatization of which corrupts her organically to the point of transforming her into the ultimate, unassimilable scrap heap, a scumbag retching from the misery of having imbibed every imaginable anguish right down to the dregs—corresponds to L. T.'s psychic repression, which cuts him off from reality so that he can stay immersed in the evil he has absorbed via huge doses of crack and heroin. The unchanging L. T. can only disappear through magical sleight of hand; he is all or nothing. His death solicits neither agony nor becoming. Death does not come for him dramatically; it simply happens, with no great show. Hence the immense urban billboard at the foot of which, we assume, L. T. gets rubbed out: "It All Happens Here." Complementarily, after being turned into a vampire by the Vietnam images, Kathy in *The Addiction* lives out her torment like an interminable anguish. She disintegrates from within, losing her teeth, her flesh, and even her gestures. On the sidewalk she metamorphoses into a deformed bag lady, bathing indistinctly in her own blood as well as the blood of her victims, a filthy scrap almost indistinguishable from the stretcher on which she is carried. But even this "thing" does not disappear; just this side of formless, Kathy returns again and always, like an insoluble problem. She returns as a sick person on a hospital bed, blessed when the rays of grace shine down on her; damned when the vampire suddenly halts the process, in repose after receiving the last rites; dead and gone when her name appears on a gravestone; and, finally, as a ghost at the cemetery. In contrast to L. T. in *Bad Lieutenant,* Kathy does not enjoy the relative luxury of a gradual disappearance. In a protracted, terrifying trajectory, she experiences every form of self-alteration and self-annihilation, abandoning along the way the remains of a false ego-integrity—the kind of integrity that western civilization thinks of as mental health but whose narcissistic, cruel, and morbid character the film has unmasked. Where L. T. wants to see nothing, Kathy wants to understand everything; where L. T. implodes, Kathy dissolves herself—two inverse and complementary somatic economies that render the same sacrificial logic.

*Hegel/Bataille/Ferrara* Why drag Hegel in? Not to appeal to some distant authority but because he is, on the same level as Ecclesiastes, Dante, Thomas Hobbes, and William Blake, a great inventor of negative forms. Negativity assures the dynamism of his dialectic, a system of relations in which every phenomenon, subjective or objective, contains a negative dimension, and its fulfillment will always be the negation of the negation. This functional importance of negativity fascinates all the moderns, particularly Bataille, who retains only the negative from Hegel. Ferrara's work resurrects, for cinema, this culture of negativity—not as a doctrine or even simply as a tool but as a speculative asset whose fundamental techniques are nourished by a Hegelian inventiveness. In this culture that (to put it bluntly) treasures thesis, cultivates antithesis, and destroys any possibility of synthesis, knowledge belongs to the reign of the negative. In *The Addiction,* for example, the get-together at Kathy's place after she has been awarded her doctorate degree transforms a traditional celebration of knowledge into an orgiastic outburst of destruction. Ferrara's work on death, crime, scandal, the sacred, sacrifice, disfiguration, the human, and the inhuman returns us to a systematic exploration of the powers of the negative. Take two simple examples, beginning with the indissoluble connection established by Hegel between reflection and evil: "In independent self-certainty, with its independence of knowledge and decision, both morality and evil have their common root." In fact, good "comes on the scene as the opposite extreme to immediate objectivity, the natural pure and simple, as soon as the will is reflected into itself and consciousness is a *knowing* consciousness. It is in this opposition that this inwardness of the will is evil. Man is therefore evil by a conjunction between his natural or undeveloped character and his reflection into himself."[27]

Thus, good and evil spring from the same source. Evil is not anterior to good; reflection is in itself negative. This is what Hegel calls the "necessity of evil."[28] Transposed into Bataille's existential terms (Bataille is to Hegel what Proust is to Schelling or De Palma is to Hitchcock, a fetishistic re-elaboration at the heights of analytic brilliance) the Hegelian proposition becomes: "Evil, therefore, if we examine it closely, is not only the dream of the wicked: it is to some extent the dream of Good."[29] We can here recognize Ferrara's hypermoral heroes: the so-called bad lieutenant, immersed in evil and by that path alone acceding to grace; Frank White in *King of New York,* who arranges or personally commits any crime whatsoever in his quest to bring a new era of goodness upon New York; and Kathy in *The Addiction,* propagating knowledge—which means terror—among everyone she meets. To have a benevolent mission (implicit in L. T.'s case, explicit in Frank's) is already to engage in dirty work. The time frame of *The Addiction,* corresponding to the conception and completion of Kathy's thesis, dramatizes this schema—the principle of an "accursed reflection"—in its pure state. On a minor level, Kathy uses her research to drag victims off to the library or the cafeteria; on a major level, she cannot finish her thesis once she has encountered evil face to face in the form of Peina, king of the vampires.

The second Hegelian example concerns the truth of being:

Nothing, pure nothing: it is simply equality with itself, complete emptiness, absence of all determination. . . . Nothing is, therefore, the same determination, or rather absence of determination, and thus altogether the same as, pure *being. Pure being* and *pure nothing* are, therefore, the same. What is the truth is neither being nor nothing, but that being—does not pass over but has passed over—into nothing, and nothing into being. . . . [E]ach immediately *vanishes in its opposite.* Their truth is, therefore, this movement of the immediate vanishing of one in the other: *becoming.*[30]

This is the point of departure for Hegel's entire theory of dialectics. Bataille conserves essentially the negative part of this: "by an exasperated inversion, [Sade] wanted the impossible and the *reverse* of life. He was as decisive as a housewife who skins a rabbit hurriedly and deftly (the housewife also reveals the reverse of the truth, and in this case, the reverse is also the heart of the truth)."[31]

This astonishing metaphor of the skinned rabbit as an emblem of authentic life is made literal in *The Driller Killer.* The landlord (Alan Wynroth)—obviously a viewer of Roman Polanski's *Repulsion* (1965)—offers Reno a skinned rabbit; in the next scene, he takes it, reaches into it and removes the bones and viscera, and proceeds to hack it apart with stabs of his knife. In this rabbit, Reno literally discovers the insides, the flesh, the meat, the inverse, that is, the nonlife in life without which life cannot exist. Once the rabbit has been turned inside out—once the protagonist has experienced innards and death—Reno converts his artistic torment into a concrete gesture, making crime and expressivity equivalent. *The Driller Killer* organizes a metaphoric montage: the inner ordeal, which cannot resolve itself in painting, converts itself into an external crime, the murder of homeless vagrants with a drill. In his studio, a mental night reigns; in the street, a physical night. In the studio it is a matter of making a gesture, painting a surface (to represent, among other things, motifs of laceration). In the street, he commits an act that consists of penetrating bodies until they die, through the front, the eye, the stomach. Artistic torment is transposed into criminal life. *The Driller Killer* composes a sublime eulogy to art as utterly a matter of life and death.

Having noted these happy coincidences between our three explorers of the negative, one major divergence must be remarked upon. As a good Hegelian, Bataille logically strives to deny the culture of negativity. This gives rise to hilarious formulations such as: "While yet alive, Hegel won salvation, killed supplication, *mutilated himself.* Of him, only the handle of a shovel remained, a modern man."[32] For Bataille, it is a matter of going beyond the founding Hegelian principle, which consists of sealing all phenomena in the dialectic of the accomplishment of absolute Spirit—thus making this system of thought a philosophy of effort and work. In Bataille's view, this profane logic of labor, of a necessary "project," must be abandoned. We must deviate from that course to reach a sacred philosophy of what he calls "non-discursive existence": laughter, ecstasy, destruction. It must come to pass that "man *ultimately* ruins himself in a *total* effacement—of what he is, of all human affirmation."[33]

In this respect, Ferrara's work occupies a position between Hegel and Bataille. His cinema revels in the Bataille-style forms of going beyond, which represent our typical ideals of transgression (and as such constitute the privileged marks of comic excess within the culture industry): laughter, ecstasy, meaninglessness, obscenity, and effacement. But he keeps the logical Hegelian framework: his protagonists (and, with them, the films) complete their mission and truly exhaust their concept. L. T. (willful blindness) transforms evil into grace and redemption in *Bad Lieutenant;* Kathy (accursed reflection) goes to the end of man's inhumanity in *The Addiction;* Chez (malady of death) destroys destruction in *The Funeral;* Matty (image laboratory) replays exactly the scene that has eluded him in *The Blackout;* Sandii (femme fatale) preserves the feminine as the source of all life in *New Rose Hotel;* and we can deduce from the provisional ending of *'R Xmas* that the wife (crime as normality) will find her way to the law. To put this another way, to date there is no trace of the senseless in Ferrara. The plastic forms of tearing, rupture, scandal, and perhaps mystery find their place within the framework of demonstrations that are always logical and complete. It is the same as in Rossellini, Pasolini, and Fassbinder—and the opposite of Godard, who leaves room for disorder, suspense, and enigma.

Such a way of thinking about being determines an ethic of forms, leading to major aesthetic consequences. The image only has meaning in ceaselessly measuring itself against what is unbearable and inadmissible: cruelty, inner opacity, and all that defies understanding. Thus, the image often presents itself as the coinage of the unrepresentable, as a ruin, a fallen image. Ferrara's cinema—whose stylistic origins can be found among the American "No Wave" punk films of the 1970s, especially the work of Vivienne Dick and Scott and Beth B.—naturally adopts every kind of image that supposedly belongs to low culture: trash and gore, but also cliché, advertising, and music video. The outsized treatment of motifs of the good life in *The Blackout* (palm trees, sunglasses, and sports cars) brings to its peak this *plastique* in which nothing is more sumptuous than a cliché or as flamboyant as a moral panic.

*Being Is Nothingness: Theory of the Vampire* One instance of the negative recurs throughout Hegel: the dead. How to define the dead? It is not a foreign negation coming from beyond but rather from within the living, which must consume itself to go on. The living is in itself inorganic nature: "[I]t consumes itself, suppresses its own inorganic reality, feeds on itself, organizes itself from within."[34] It is impossible not to see the "novelistic" version of this Hegelian proposition in the theory of the vampire expressed by Zoë Lund in *Bad Lieutenant*'s shooting-up scene. Cut off from its scientific and conceptual origins, already shorn of its dialectical becoming, this vampire theory returns the living being wholly to its self-destruction:

Vampires are lucky.
They feed on others.
We have to feed on ourselves.
We have to eat our legs,
To have the energy to walk.
We have to come, in order to go.
We have to suck ourselves off.
We have to eat away at ourselves
'Til there's nothing left
But appetite.[35]

This organic image, transposed to the level of psychic life, brings us to the exigency of infinity that characterizes the human. In contrast with the object, the subject ceaselessly seeks to transgress its limit, to go towards the infinite, the unconditioned. "The true nature of the finite is to be infinite, to suppress itself as being. The determinate has, qua determinate, no other essence than this absolute disquiet not to be what it is."[36]

Such is man, in a state of pure disquiet, the human being "that never is what it is and always is what it is not,"[37] without end. The subject must pose itself as an Other to become a self. Bataille transcribes the Hegelian dialectic while suppressing becoming, so as to retain only this absolute disquiet: "He who does not 'die' from being merely a man will never be other than a man."[38] Ferrara retains, according to the same negative dialectic that authorizes a number of its novelistic versions (especially Dostoyevsky's), only the distortion born of this relation to the infinite. In his films, the hypermoral heroes are burdened by a "disquiet of infinity," which determines the forms of personhood in Ferrara as *experience that always overflows the individual subject*.

Certain major procedures are employed throughout Ferrara's œuvre to constitute these figures that overflow finitude. They can be summarized as follows: the elaboration of an ontology of destruction; the figural treatment of the relation to death; the use of scenarios of the double; the laying bare of intimacy; and a devastating belief in truth. The prodigious logical energy of Ferrara's œuvre annuls its paradoxical character. These dynamics determine the work's nature as a critical passion.

## Ontology of Destruction: The Critical Function of the "Great Criminal" Figure

*The High-Water Mark of Subjectivity*  Refusing finitude, never finding their limits, Ferrara's protagonists exist in a permanent state of rage, like the bad lieutenant whose fury is exercised against everything that stands in his path: hoods, victims, his family, colleagues, the young women, his car radio, Christ, in fact any presence of any kind. The declaration of "police activity" by which, in a darkened staircase, he forbids the entry of a passerby while snorting cocaine up his nose is not only an ironic reversal—it indicates that police activity consists essentially of repressing the entry of the Other, guarding a territory in which the law will reign even better, since it does not bother applying its rules to itself. This law is indifferently legal or illegal; its sovereignty triumphs when all is arbitrary. This fury or rage of Ferrara's protagonists effectively manifests what Hegel called the "high-water mark of subjectivity," that moment when consciousness takes itself as law, to the detriment of the world's law.[39]

> It is not the thing that is excellent, but I who am so; as the master of law and thing alike, I simply play with them as with my caprice; my consciously ironical attitude lets the highest perish and I merely hug myself at the thought. This type of subjectivism not merely substitutes a void for the whole content of ethics, right, duties, and laws—and so is evil, in fact evil through and through and universally—but in addition its form is a subjective void, i.e., it knows itself as this contentless void and in this knowledge knows itself as absolute.[40]

The protagonist considers himself as absolute; he is the author of his own law and seeks to impose it on the world. Recall Travis Bickle

(Robert De Niro) in *Taxi Driver* and his notion that the world is a hell that he will set right.[41] In Ferrara, such a figure of subjectivity takes a precise narrative form: the serial killer. And on this point the evolution of his œuvre is especially lucid: this is a case of critical extension. Let us survey the progression of the serial killer in the exercise of his rage, starting with three of Ferrara's early films. The same figure—the paranoiac murderer—is offered in a variety of forms. In *The Driller Killer, Ms .45,* and *Fear City,* revolt is the negation of reality, translating itself in terms of an aleatory but systematic destruction of bodies that are eliminated one by one. From one film to the next, what changes is the nature of the bodies destroyed. Reno in *The Driller Killer* takes New York beggars as his victims—socially invisible characters, like dark masses scarcely discernible in the night, often still asleep, anonymous and sexless figures without distinguishing traits. Thana, the angel of vengeance in *Ms .45,* aggresses male bodies that are libidinal, vigorous, identifiable, and even powerful (such as the Arab sheik). Complementarily, Pazzo (John Foster) in *Fear City* erases the voluptuous bodies of female strippers. This marks a deeper progression towards the public, political character of the serial-killer figure: murder becomes crime, and the corporeal outrage that once targeted the flesh (the skinned rabbit in *The Driller Killer*) metamorphoses into political aggression, taking as its primary object morality, and then the very question of humanity.

*Fury: A Guide to Its Evolution*  In *The Driller Killer,* Reno takes out his anger on himself. This is a case of mental aggression: the film rests on an analogy between the stabs of the paintbrush and the stabs of the drill, savagely exteriorizing the affective torment linked to creation. The phantasmic character of the bodily attacks is underlined on their first occurrence: a series of oneiric inserts—shots of paintings, slow-motion shots, obsessive sounds, mental anticipations, nightmare imagery—makes explicit this transition between inner and outer, between creative agony in the ravaged loft and physical torture in the rundown street. This sequence clinches something seminal. The Ferraran problem par excellence is posed—the transfer between mental image and concrete image—but its solution remains to be found. Henceforth, this solution will consist of confusing the two image-regimes in a disturbing economy of somatization.

In *Ms .45*, Thana, raped twice at the start of the film, takes out her rage against the Other (the male). What starts out as a private revenge changes direction from a seemingly "legitimate" act of self-defense (she kills her attacker and then the slasher), Thana drifts towards a collective massacre—erasing all masculine bodies suspected of sexual aggression, then any man whatsoever, and finally, in the bloody masquerade ball, every kind of body, whether male, female, or transsexual. With Thana, the serial killer passes from singular to general and, through the insistence on the homosexual and even transsexual identity of the final victims, allows maximum extension to the "serial" nature of the killing.

In *Fear City*, Pazzo takes out his fury on an abstraction: urban corruption. He reincarnates the figure of Jack the Ripper; *Taxi Driver's* Bickle is possessed by the same project. It should be noted that this paranoiac figure is also a health freak, certainly on the physical level (exercise, bodily control, and gymnastic virtuosity). The sick character in this story is the hero, Matt (Tom Berenger), whose inner torment is embodied by Pazzo. With *Fear City*, the victim-object thus undergoes a qualitative leap, passing from the general (all material bodies) to an abstract entity (urban depravity). This modifies the nature of the serial killer's enterprise. Where Thana still killed in an empirical manner, seized by the catastrophe of random encounters, Pazzo is driven by an overall project (to clean up the city) within which premeditated assassinations register only as a necessary, fatal consequence.

*China Girl* makes another qualitative leap: criminal logic is no longer confined to a sick individual but belongs to an entire economic system. Beyond the two heroes, Tony (Richard Panebianco) and Tye (Sari Chang), almost every character is a criminal, and the film charts their hierarchy: henchmen, gang leaders, and clan leaders. The arrangement of the apparent antagonists is organized similarly. The Italian Mafia and the Chinese Triad are structured in the same way: they share the same interests (to enforce social obedience so as to guarantee their economic prosperity); their members dress as elegant businessmen, meeting up for ostentatious, high-security dinners. Far from fighting each other, they eventually join forces to perpetuate their power. In such pyramidal structures, the henchmen (physical criminals) represent the proletariat exploited by the godfathers (the real criminals). The real conflict is displaced—it no longer concerns the Mafia and the Triad but parents and children, rich and poor. "We're just poor Chinese kids," explains Tsu (Joey Chin) to his cousin Yung (Russell Wong), who has been ordered to bring him down. The real crime is the inoculation of hatred between brothers, cousins, and friends. "Big brother" Yung emerges as the film's hero because he refuses the code of criminal obedience. Instead of killing to insure his ascension in the Triad, he dreams of heading off to Hong Kong with Tsu. The avid Tsu represents, in terms of material desire, what the angelic Tony and Tye represent in terms of sexual desire: deviant beings whose drives transgress traditions, putting in peril the division of territories, riches, and symbols.

While Tony and Tye dance and embrace, Tsu, at the bottom of the criminal pyramid, strikes out in the streets with his choreographies of death. Tsu and the young rebels live in the underground, surviving and killing like a punk lumpenproletariat. *China Girl* transforms the racist clash between two ethnic groups into a generational struggle, showing how the logic of profit can confiscate children's feelings and desires, even their lives. Crime is dissociated from the gesture of the murderer and returned to its source, the established economic order. When Tsu kills Tony and Tye at the end of the film, his act seems almost absurd in terms of the relations between these three characters. There is no need for him to shoot the lovers. The act must be read in two contradictory ways. On the one hand, the desire of young people—whether pure or impure, altruistic or self-centred—has no official status in this criminal world. Hence, they are reduced to rubbing each other out. On the other hand, Tsu represents the avidity principle in its wild, irrepressible state, no longer under the thumb of Mafia control, but irrigating every level of power, as a poison spreads through a plant's veins. The return of Chin in *King of New York* as the cruel Larry Wong, head of his Triad and an informed cinephile (he watches Murnau's *Nosferatu* [1922]), underlines this second dimension of Tsu Shin's character.

Frank White in *King of New York* is possessed by the same mission (and in the same city) as Pazzo in *Fear City:* to eradicate crime. He has the same self-control, lethal calm, and hallucinatory tendency. But—the decisive difference due to the change in scale of operations—Frank pits system against system, criminal machine against criminal machine. The kingpins he eliminates one by one no longer represent random obstacles; they constitute true rivals on the economic, ethnic, and even ethical levels (he reproaches one of them for exploiting his compatriots). Because *King of New York* effects a passage from (bad) individual morality to a political enterprise, the manifestation of rage duly alters. Frank causes a revolution, bringing about the universal reversal of negative into positive. He has no need for random, exterior gestures of anger like those committed by Reno in *The Driller Killer*, L. T. in *Bad Lieutenant,* or Mercury in *China Girl.* When Frank kills—for instance, the revenge he wreaks at the military funeral upon the cop guilty of the death of Jimmy Jump (Larry Fishburne)—he glides into frame, the window of his limousine opens automatically, he fires on the blameworthy cop (who has imitated the underworld's dirty procedures), the spurt of blood is instant and seems more mechanical than organic, the window closes automatically. White spares not a moment's glance for the corpse; the implacably fugitive nature of his gesture attests to the indifferent character of the act. It is no longer the occasion for any kind of satisfaction (expressive liberation for Reno in *The Driller Killer,* symbolic compensation for Thana in *Ms*

Chinatown in *King of New York.*

Christopher Walken in *King of New York*.

.45, physical fulfillment for Pazzo in *Fear City*), just a simple, logical consequence. Murder no longer comes wrapped in the form of a death ceremony or a sacrificial rite. What eliminates the foolish cop is less Frank's bullet than the insolent elision with which the film depicts his execution.

Frank has no need to externalize his anger; he is filled with rage, possessed by his subjective project. The film suggests the hypothesis of a physiological poisoning via the cop's allusion, "I heard you got AIDS gettin' dicked up your ass in prison." What he really "got" in prison was politics. This is the first of Ferrara's characters capable of holding forth with a discourse on economics and passionately delivering it to the only character, the rule-abiding cop Bishop (Victor Argo), worthy of hearing it. Frank unmasks the clandestine functioning of the American economy and its consequences: the political institutions, generalized corruption, and civil wars it allows to proliferate (the kingpins are less gang leaders than monarchs of their ethnic group).[42]

*Body Snatchers* explores new and more radical ways of generalizing and abstracting the serial-killer metaphor. First, there is the passage from serial killer as individual to serial killer as species, the premise of the *fantastique* fiction, an (extraterrestrial) species that seeks to devour another. Second, there is the passage from the local (New York) to the universal: the military camp is treated not as a real space but as the allegory of a gateway into human hell. This is the film's political dimension—the comparison between industrial and military order and physical and mental pollution. Third, there is the passage from murder to metamorphosis: crime works by replacement. The dichotomous construction of *The Driller Killer* is intensified; this time the human substance seized and penetrated is a complex of flesh, fantasy, and anthropological history. Murder-by-snatching is no longer a disappearance but, on the contrary, a deployment of the body. It is as much an investigation into the interiority of the body as a verification of its belonging to a species. Snatching evokes simultaneously the transformation of the adolescent body wracked by the refusal of its organic, biological destiny and the mutation of the human race as a whole. This time, confrontation with the unlimited takes the perilous form of a face-to-face encounter with what should, in principle, offer a concrete, describable, finite basis for human experience: the organic nature of the body, completely reworked as a field of somatization.

*The Addiction* takes the formal work of generalization and abstraction still further, adding new initiatives on the level of speculative invention. Kathy constitutes a new, *fantastique*-style occurrence of the serial killer. She ends up devouring everyone she meets, including the poor silhouette who tenderly rushes up to help her, as well as her horrified best friend, Jean (Edie Falco). But Kathy represents a metaphysical figure of fury, overwhelmed and torn apart by the evidence of man's inhumanity transmitted (inoculated) into her by the documentary images of the Holocaust. The film thus devotes itself to a triple extension of the operative field of its central figure. First, there is the passage out from contemporary politics to history. *Body Snatchers* is a film about Hiroshima as the emblem of a democratic-capitalist regime's activity; *The Addiction* is a film about all slaughters. If the Hiroshima catastrophe obliges us to treat the body from the viewpoint of its volatization (the figurative economy of the silhouette, the trace), the disasters treated by *The Addiction* (Vietnam, Nazism, drugs, AIDS, poverty, and cowardice) necessitate a return to the concrete body—an organism definitively damaged, as objectified in Kathy's inner leprosy (she loses her teeth and hair, tears out the ends of her mucous membranes, spits out her own flesh). Second, there is a passage from the universal collective (the human race) towards the metaphysical. It is no longer only a matter of the physical corruption caused by industrial society or the civil corruption caused by the militarization of minds. *The Addiction* confronts an essential reversal: what if evil came first? The question from that point is no longer one of corruption but of inhumanity. Kathy's horrifying discovery is that there has never been anything to corrupt because there has never been anything that is integrally human; the only integrity is that of evil. Third, there is a passage from mental image to documentary image. *The Driller Killer* and *Body Snatchers* treat the image as a fantasy and thus as a private, dematerialized phenomenon whose power nonetheless structures human existence. By contrast, *The Addiction* presents the image as exterior, objective, public, and documentary. The film thus questions the status of the image within an economy of horror. The image records evil, projecting it into the public sphere (the classroom slides of Vietnam, the museum exhibition about the extermination camps, the television report on the Serbian massacre) and thereby also propagates it. Kathy, absorbed by these images, in turn absorbs them and retransmits them via her vampiric acts. The kernel of this problem can be seen in *King of New York,* when the underworld lawyer hides grisly photographs of corpses inside a folded-over copy of the *Wall Street Journal:* at the origin of "market progress," there is the blood of economic victims. The illegal drug economy only makes explicit the violence of the general economy.

In a double movement, *The Addiction* effects a trajectory that is the reverse of such shady dissimulation. Kathy introjects and mentally internalizes the image-information. Then she objectivizes the psychic torment caused by these images of disaster, rearing up as a vampire in their light and "taking them on," like L. T. in *Bad Lieutenant,* who, in his own way, devours the world to the point where evil consumes and annihilates itself. In the final orgy in *The Addiction,* Kathy exhausts herself by absorbing evil until she refinds the sonic reminder of the initial trauma: a Vietnamese lullaby whose poignant sadness floats up through the panicked murmurs of history's victims. The image of Kathy transported on a stretcher under the sound of this little song, according

Lili Taylor in *The Addiction.*

(as ever) to an anamorphic structure, exhumes the image of the pain she felt on seeing the slides at the film's start.

Is it possible to go further in the treatment of the universal? Such an extension occurs in *New Rose Hotel*. *The Funeral* represents an interim work, a film of debate, explicit and rational meditation upon the hypothesis of the "First Evil." *The Funeral* formulates three propositions: evil can be talked about, not merely somatized (the nocturnal theological discussion between Ray and Jean [Annabella Sciorra]); we must return to the experience of family to observe what the originary experiences of evil's transmission concretely comprise—namely, filiation and fraternity; and finally, we can conceive a positive resolution to the logic of destruction. Hence Chez's demented but affirmative gesture, erasing the principal members of his criminal family. The Tempio brothers represent three complementary forms of anger. Chez's anger is intimate, private (taken out in the everyday on his wife), fraternal, and chaotic, belonging to the register of psychic dementia: bringing death to everyone, including himself. Ray's anger is familial, clannish, filial, and orderly, belonging to the register of the small-time death machine: he organizes crime with respect to the customary rules and will ultimately be executed. Johnny's anger is collective, public, political, critical, deeply rooted, and even socialist, since (and this is an unexpected initiative for Ferrara) it works itself out in the institutional, political context of the Communist party. This last form of violence is stillborn at the film's opening. At the outset, the attempt at a politically organized violence is depicted as shorn of any future, condemned, but it remains important, signifying that critical anger can raise itself to the level of historic reality. The counterworld of Pazzo (*Fear City*) or Frank (*King of New York*), by contrast, can only belong to the kingdom of the mad.

Two traces of the serial-killer figure persist in *The Blackout*. With the same gesture of strangulation, the drunken Matty kills Annie 2 physically and Annie 1 symbolically ("Annie 1" evokes "anyone," any woman at all). The film then unfolds a series of hypothetical "shots" on the subject of murder. Mickey practices murder in the erotic, symbolic form of sadism, surrounded by images of sexual ceremony where death always lurks. His main problem consists of staging a real murder that would function as the reprise of the fictional murder. He is the character who creates the serial effect, who propagates "video nasty" images.

*The Blackout* concentrates on the projective process that informs *The Addiction:* it abandons the terrain of history but intensifies the question of the psychic powers of the image. Mickey belongs to the realm of the material, collective, public image. He has built a counter-empire, a counter-Utopia (the traditional iconography of the island appears across his studio, the pool scenes, and the palm beach). In his world, sexual, political, and iconic laws are organized according to an unprecedented economy in that they are not submitted to any censorship. By contrast, Matty belongs to the realm of the mental image. He lives the image as memory and inebriation as anamnesis.

The film traces the dialectic between these two regimes of the image: radical censorship (Matty) versus its total absence (Mickey). At first glance, the regimes seem equivalent: all the images are scandalous, and all are associated with bodies (murder images for Matty, sexual images for Mickey). On closer inspection, they differ: Matty's images turn out to be fragile, treacherous, indecisive, and ambiguous at the level of their psychic status (memory, dream-screen, volition, reconstitution, and hallucination), while Mickey's images are spectacular, triumphant, dominant, inscribed within an objective history (the history of cinematic forms), and, like clichés, infinitely reproducible. Ultimately, the film articulates the interrelation of these regimes: the murder committed by Matty has been, de facto, staged by Mickey; all the images are fragmentary, insufficient, flickering, and superimposed; and the missing image that Matty seeks turns out to be not psychic but concrete, video-graphic, and documentary. The true "couple" in this story is not director and actor, but director and psychoanalyst: both use video, both "direct" Matty, and both, in their own ways, lead him to death.

*New Rose Hotel* offers an audacious synthesis of the most advanced ideas formulated by the previous films. Sandii updates the archetype of the universal killer, Pandora (already prefigured in Peina, king of vampires in *The Addiction*). Sandii is responsible for all ills; because of her, human DNA is destabilized and everyone is struck down and killed. But she also destabilizes affective relations. Her illusion devours experience and everything that experience holds intimate. Not only do images now lack all origin (documentary images endlessly appear on screens, already viewed and edited, with no sign of how or by whom), not only do actions reduce themselves to preparatory fragments and indications of failure, but

Sandii herself ends up deprived of her protagonist status. She no longer constitutes an origin or an explanation. Sandii is the reverse of Kathy in *The Addiction,* with whom she forms a diptych. Sandii spreads ill with the blind pride of a creature who seems unaware of what she is doing, while Kathy appropriates and rationalizes guilt to the point of death. Sandii appears among the three enchantresses—or, in mythological terms, Keres, the goddesses of punishment—from whom she cannot initially be distinguished; she might be just any other girl, undiscernible among her bookends, and inaccessible to any form of human discernment. With her, the distinctions between illusion and truth, cause and effect, and ignorance and duplicity are abolished. It can no longer be fathomed why vengeance must be wreaked, or for whose profit. There is no longer even room, in this godless night, to pose the question. The irresistible Sandii thus represents the triumph of the serial killer, destroying at once the human race and the possibility of making sense of that destruction. With a crazed audacity, *New Rose Hotel* tackles not only the sense of disquiet but also the sense of unlimitedness that eats men away.

Henceforth liberated from the notion of God, infinity appears less a force of movement than a corrosive, dispersive energy. Infinity no longer organizes existence according to its negative law; it disorganizes existence and remains itself beyond organization. *New Rose Hotel* thus multiplies the forms of what is unlimited: the incomplete (the protagonist's situation), the unsolvable (the final smile), the fragment (the treatment of the action scenes), the excessive detail (the lost keys), reassessment (the hero's hotel meditation), the heterogeneous (the shots of paintings, which resemble rushes from Dario Argento's *The Stendhal Syndrome* [1996]), and the suspended (the world seems forever on another level from that within which the characters dwell and lingers only as glimpses refracted in screens or windows). After Kathy's liquidation of the self in *The Addiction,* Sandii (the figure of identity-simulacra) saps the foundations of our intellection. In terms of the film's scenario, that means scientific expertise but also, more profoundly, understanding, direct knowledge, and even intuition—hence X's final recollection, incapable of synthesizing his adventure or of understanding whether this young woman loved him at all for even an instant. Sandii radically reverses a Hegelian proposition: she is that infinitely practical idea in relation to which every form of knowledge disorganizes itself.

The three principles of the serial killer's evolution in Ferrara can be summarized as follows. First, he is made the object of a conceptual extension that is asserted with ever-increasing force. Second, he authorizes a critical work that becomes steadily more violent. The state of permanent revolt attached to the refusal of the human condition as finitude thus far has received two Ferraran solutions: integral destruction, or the proposition of a counterworld, the nature of which seems to be indicated by scenes of orgiastic abandon (in *King of New York, The Blackout,* and *New Rose Hotel*). Third, the serial killer's action is exercised, initially and classically, upon politics, and then, in a profoundly intensified way, upon the economy of images in our apprehension of the world and, consequently, upon new forms of ethical negativity.

'R Xmas completely reverses the general narrative postulate. There is no serial killer in this film, since crime has become the normal state of human relations. The parents live from drug trafficking, the mother redirects the money that the son has paid, the cop is arrested for perjury and withholding collected money, and the father tries to bribe the saleswoman in a toyshop to get a doll: each act, whether big or small, manifests only corruption, betrayal, and wrongdoing but is nonetheless experienced as normality. The cops lean on the dealers for the purpose of extortion, while the dealers gently administer their good works (financing the education of impoverished Dominicans). Money has destroyed not only institutions but also those human relationships held most sacred (such as family life)—a fact that no longer seems to bother anyone. In 'R Xmas, following Fassbinder's formula, "everything should be declared criminal."[43] Now the whole world is a serial killer. This immoral, scandalous condition provides the countershot against which Ferrara's protagonists pit themselves.

### Abel, Zoë, and Edouard: Intellectual Context and Radical Politics

*Introduction to the Work of Edouard de Laurot*  Ferrara's films provide plain evidence of his political radicalism, but further evidence is provided by the real-life encounter between Ferrara and a magic couple in cinema history, Zoë Lund and Edouard de Laurot (perhaps less famous but no less precious than Rossellini and Ingrid Bergman, or Godard and Anna Karina). De Laurot remains one of the most fascinating and least well-known figures in contemporary cultural history. This is how Lund, his companion during the 1980s, summarizes the major trajectories of one of the most exemplary filmmakers of the last century:

> It's almost impossible to believe that all this happened to one man. He was there at almost every important moment of the last sixty years. It's incredible! The Polish underground, the French underground during the war, Andy Warhol—and everything else in between, the "wherever" underground! He was also in the British Green Berets. It's astounding to contemplate all that; even me, when I met him the first time, I found it hard to believe. But everywhere in the world I've met people who tell me "it's true," "it's even worse," or "it's even better"—usually those last two descriptions in the same breath![44]

As an officer in the Polish army, de Laurot participated in the defense of Warsaw; after its fall, he spent the rest of the war working for the British Secret Service. In 1950, he obtained a diploma in English studies from Cambridge University. Then he moved to Paris, studied at the Sorbonne (philosophy diploma in 1953), then at the Institut des hautes études cinématographiques (diploma in 1955), and returned briefly to Lodz to finish his education. Throughout this period, he served as an assistant to Jacques Becker in France on *Rendez-vous de juillet* (1949), then much later to Peter Weiss in Sweden on *The Mirage* (1960) and Federico Fellini in Italy on *Juliet of the Spirits* (1965)—not to mention Orson Welles on *Don Quixote*, the filming of which began in 1957. He wrote the first draft of the script of Henri-Georges Clouzot's *The Wages of Fear* (1952), based on Georges Arnaud's novel—which David O. Selznick rewrote because he found it too politically confrontational—and translated dialogue for films at Columbia in the mid-1950s, including Alessandro Blasetti's *Lucky to Be a Woman* (1956).

In 1955 de Laurot cofounded *Film Culture* magazine with Jonas Mekas and contributed to it until 1962. His writings include the first essay in the first issue, "Towards a Theory of Dynamic Realism," a number of subsequent theoretical texts, and interviews with Boris Kaufman and John Huston. De Laurot eventually distanced himself, for political reasons, from *Film Culture*. He founded the Cinema Engagé group and, in the magazine *Cineaste*, published his major theoretical manifestos: "From Logos to Lens: From the Theory of Engagement to the Praxis of Revolutionary Cinema," "Production as the Praxis of Revolutionary Film," "Composing as the Praxis of Revolution: The Third World and the USA," and "The Public as Vanguard of the People."[45]

De Laurot founded the cinema department of the Free University of New York in 1965–66. He directed several shorts for John F. Kennedy's presidential campaign in 1960. The same year, in Italy, he codirected the satirical short *Un altro Festival* with Andrzej Munk. As a militant he made two masterpieces of Cinema Engagé: *Black Liberation* (a.k.a. *Black America* and—after censorship—*Silent Revolution* [1967]), in collaboration with and in support of the Black Panthers; then *Listen America* (1968), a prophetic film about American society as a paranoiac system of control. In 1968, he also wrote a short, *The Wager,* about the self-immolation of several American citizens in front of the Pentagon during a siege of the United Nations to protest the Vietnam War. In the 1970s de Laurot filmed, from day to day, a series of psychedelic and erotic experiences in sixteen millimeter; the footage exists but remains unedited. Also left behind are the rushes of a fiction film featuring Ben Carruthers from Cassavetes's *Shadows* (1959). De Laurot was a friend of James Baldwin, Jonas and Adolfas Mekas, and Pier Paolo Pasolini. He was branded an activist, and Lund alleges that he was assassinated by the CIA in his hospital bed. He was buried in Warsaw's military cemetery.

De Laurot's cinematic style bears no resemblance to Ferrara's. De Laurot chose the documentary tract or pamphlet form. His films belong to the Grand International Revolutionary Style that began with Dziga Vertov's films, passed through Chris Marker in France, and nourished the works of Santiago Alvarez in Cuba and Fernando Solanas in Argentina (*Cineaste* published Solanas and Octavio Getino's crucial manifesto, "Towards a Third Cinema"),[46] the Newsreel group in America, and the Dziga Vertov and Cinéthique groups in France in the 1960s and 1970s. *Black Liberation,* inspired by *Les Statues meurent aussi* (1950–53) by Marker and Alain Resnais, today looks like one of the most assertive and innovative works made about the Black Panthers. A condensed, staccato montage of shots and stills, cut to the rhythm of whiplashes and African American music, this collage of speeches by Malcolm X and Black Panther leaders (read by Ossie Davis) is a pure call to revolt and urban guerrilla activity.

De Laurot's manifestos illuminate a number of preoccupations that overlap with Ferrara's work and help fill in its intellectual context. I will concentrate on two fundamental, common points: an existential conception of engagement, and the necessity of creating an "American fresco."

*Revolution Is Morality in Action*  De Laurot retells (with a strong novelistic flourish) his first encounter with cinema as follows:

> The first time that I had a camera in my hands was at the end of the war when I was a young teenager. We captured a German tank, entered it, and found—aside from the usual tank accoutrements—the first combat 35mm Arriflex! So we told the soldiers that we would let them live if they instructed us how to operate the camera. There was an Austrian gunner shaking and not really believing that we would let him live. We did, and he instructed us.

This biographical knot between camera and combat would never be untied. For de Laurot, the camera is a weapon; he will never cease defending, theorizing, and illustrating what he calls *cinema engagé*. This conception of engagement comes from Jean-Paul Sartre's existentialism:

> Engagement for us is, in the first place, not propaganda, as Sartre's conception was often misconstrued to mean. Rather, for us engagement is the tending through artistic creation to achieve as much as possible a *unity between consciousness and conscience*. As a second definition, no artist who is endowed with a conscience will express less than his consciousness embraces. It's almost axiomatic. Nevertheless, the deep creative need is personal. Again, I want to make the distinction—personal, not private. He personally feels that because such or other aspect of life or truth has not yet been cogently conveyed to the world, and because in a certain sense he is the sacred, unique owner of that truth, truth must be out—and out in the way he personally sees it. . . . The larger the consciousness, the personal truth, and the personal anguish of the artist, the more universal will be his art. From the point of view of his personal ontology, that is to say of his own becoming—which he achieves in the process of creation—one can say that *engagement for the artist is the possibility of transforming, through his art, personal anguish into history.*

Such an existentialist ideal of engagement—along which de Laurot followed the same political evolution as Sartre, from humanism to Maoism—opens up a dimension that he develops in a privileged way in all his texts. This dimension relates directly to Ferrara: the exacting demand for a moral and spiritual perspective within political struggle. In "Prolepsis," a statement recapitulating his convictions, de Laurot argues the proposition that "revolution is morality in action." While pledging his faith in Marxist-Leninism and its logic of the "concrete analysis of a concrete situation," de Laurot makes clear that only spiritual, moral, and ethical convictions can legitimately determine political struggle. This marks a fundamental divergence from the Chinese and European versions of Marxist-Leninism and clinches de Laurot's connection to Ferrara.

Most American radicals and the Analysts, lacking a moral dimension, reject ideological, philosophical, ethical, "religious" words such as: spirit, morality, salvation, divinity in man, Logos, man's essence, destiny, mankind, eternity, becoming, transcendence, etc. Why do we Americans fear—yes, fear—the use of these words and words like ultimate, absolute, etc.? Even as a Marxist, one must at this point cry out, "Eli, Eli, lama sabachthani"! Just as we have rejected the ultimate meaning of such words, we risk rejecting Revolution's ultimate goals. For, such words did not originate with Engaged Cinema. Marx, Lenin, Ho Chi Minh, Mao, Guevara, Fanon propose the same vocabulary, the same consistent moral thrust, the same ultimate objectives.

From that point, what characterizes de Laurot's theoretical and screenwriting output (notably the script "Promethea," never shot, on a South American revolutionary), as with that of Lund (the screenplays for *Bad Lieutenant* and *Kingdom for a Horse,* as well as an unfinished trilogy of novels, "490"), not to mention numerous Ferrara films (*King of New York, The Addiction, Dangerous Game,* and *Mary*), is the reinvestment of Christian imagery into revolutionary values. This approach descends directly from Pasolini's depiction of Christ in *The Gospel According to Matthew* (1964) and also his modern transposition (written in 1968) of the life of St. Paul into Paris, Rome, and New York.[47] De Laurot continues: "That brings us to the difficulty the analysts had comprehending 'Christian imagery' in our scripts. They must understand that the task is to de-mystify alienated human aspirations, transform and replace them with real revolutionary values, and thus fulfill the conditions of necessity in man."

The goal of revolution is not only to redistribute bread but also to give a "different taste of bread," as Malcolm X states at the end of *Black Liberation*. This is why the ultimate revolutionary act, fused with the high road of morality, is self-sacrifice. The Christian figure allows a synthesis of all the contemporary revolutionaries to whom de Laurot and Zund refer: Fanon, Guevara, Martin Luther King, Malcolm X—and we can add Amílcar Cabral, murdered liberator of Guinea-Bissau and Cape Verde. In *The Wager*, a filmic essay on Americans who immolated themselves in protest, Mrs. Norman Morrison, the wife of a thirty-one-year-old Quaker who doused himself in gasoline and ignited himself in front of the Pentagon on 2 November 1965, explains that her husband sacrificed his life "to express his profound dismay in the face of the suffering caused by the Vietnam War." Mrs. Morrison also appears in the episode of *Far from Vietnam* (a collective work organized by Chris Marker in 1967) titled *Ann Uyen,* where she again describes the reasons for her husband's gesture: "The incongruity of our wealth compared to the suffering of the Vietnamese people, knowing that in a way we are responsible for this." *The Wager* also deals with the case of Celene Jankowski, a twenty-four-year-old who attempted to immolate herself at South Bend, Indiana, on 10 November 1965. "She declared to her husband that she wanted to persuade him to follow her into death: 'All the world's problems are my problems.'"

Such sacrificial gestures explain *The Addiction*'s choice of My Lai images to precipitate the moral crisis that leads Kathy to the point of death, devastated by "all the world's problems." For Ferrara, St. John, de Laurot, and Lund, the "sublime of human experience" (de Laurot) guarantees the fusion of morality and revolution and constitutes the horizon of all action, representation, and meaning.

Ferrara pursues his mystical realism in minimalistic forms—and in this respect he is much closer to European than American filmmakers. When Scorsese tackles Christian imagery and the Gospels head-on in *The Last Temptation of Christ* (1988), he transforms the Passion into a tour through cinematic styles: a neo-realist sequence, a psychedelic sequence, a Griffith-style sequence, a Pasolini-style sequence. The film becomes a veritable general treatise on imagery. When Ferrara directly confronts the Gospels in *Mary*—in which he uses as a guide the character of Mary Magdalene, who initially was to be played by Barbara Hershey, the same actor who incarnated her in *The Last Temptation of Christ*—he purifies the fable and entirely devotes himself to deepening the gesture of comparison. The Christ figure here serves as a critical lever, a way of establishing a parallel between the military repression in Palestine's Gaza Strip and the police repression in the Bronx. In this sense, Ferrara is a true theologian of imagery: he recognizes that the great speculative force of Christianity, beginning with the division of Old and New Testament, involves inventing and knitting relations between the literal and the figural. It is on this terrain that Christianity interests the cinema: for its figurative power much more than for its themes, precepts, and reflexes.

*Mary* interweaves three investigations into Jesus. The first could not be more conventional: a television program presenting a series of interviews with experts conducted by Ted Younger (Forest Whitaker). The second could not be more archaic: a pilgrimage to Jerusalem undertaken by Mary the actress (Juliette Binoche). And the last could not be more demented: a film in the process of being completed by Tony Childress (Matthew Modine), the release of which raises the ire of Christian groups—as Scorsese's film and Godard's *Hail Mary* (1985) did in their day. The demonstrations held by fundamentalists at the release of Godard's film were, moreover, filmed by Shirley Clarke outside the Bleecker Street Cinema (run by the filmmaker Jackie Raynal), and one can sense a trace of the violence of these documentary images in *Mary*'s final sequence, in the course of which Tony combats journalists, cops, and spectators so that the images of his film can finally be projected onto a screen. Confronted with a crowd, a police force, and even a projectionist who all refuse to watch his work, the filmmaker begins the screening by himself. Ferrara closes *Mary* on these images of grace, joy, and beauty that no one wants to discover.

*Mary* addresses a major issue—the real, historical, concrete suffering of the oppressed—and, through its three main characters, a particular subject: the pathetic ways in which the psyche re-creates and upholds the individual. The three protagonists represent three stages on the path to peace—and the path that remains the most distant, shut in on itself, crazy with grief in the cabin of its own despair and idealism is that of the filmmaker.

*The American Condition*   The second area common to Ferrara and the Cinema Engagé group involves the necessity to create a critical fresco covering what de Laurot called, in an ironic twist on André Malraux's *The Human Condition,* "the American Condition." In 1968, the New York unit of Cinema Engagé announced the launch of a dramatic fresco, in thirty-five-millimeter black-and-white, titled *La Condition Américaine.* Its subject would be the relation between the individual and the social within a context where the atrophy of spiritual values reigns.

> The filmmakers intend to illuminate actual centers of power and lines of forces which determine the development of both personal and socio-economic realities in the United States. By thus showing the relation-ship between the objective social conditions and their overt and covert impact upon the individual, and by dramatizing the atrophy or absence of certain feelings and values, the profile of the American *qua* American merges—the American as an individual, yes; but also as a by-product of his society, as a being conditioned by America, a being who will affirm what infirms him.

De Laurot quoted, with particular irony, his own script for *Promethea:* "How can I talk to them about Morality and Revolution if, as I speak to them as revolutionaries, they'll listen to me as Americans?" Such a vision of the American Condition informs the scripts for *Dangerous Game* and *The Funeral,* both by St. John. The latter, in particular, presents itself explicitly as, in Johnny's words, a fable on "the tragedy of bein' an American in the twentieth century," that is, the tragedy of avid, criminal, imbecilic materialism forever in search of self-distraction ("we need somethin' to distract us"—cinema, radio, drugs) in order to forget, for a moment, the emptiness and shame.[48]

*Love on the A Train,* a short film written by Marla Hanson and directed by Ferrara for the HBO anthology film *Subway Stories: Tales from the Underground* (1997), mounts in eight minutes a trenchant attack upon the spirituality of the ordinary American Condition. John T. (Mike McGlone), an emblematic, married young urban professional with his broad-shouldered suit and decorative briefcase, takes the A train to work each day. There he encounters "the girl" (Rosie Perez) who sexually excites him. Every morning he finds her on the same train; without ever exchanging a word, he touches her and makes her come—an act shown in kinetic superimpositions that represent, in Ferrara's work to date, a height of plenitude, a sensual extension of the scenes of caressing between Frank and Jennifer (Janet Julian) in the train in *King of New York*.

An eroticization of the everyday, *Love on the A Train* explores a reversal of appearances. Seen from outside, a man fondles a woman's body, recalling the customary scenes of harassment that elicit rage in *Ms .45* and *The Addiction*. But in reality a woman makes use of a man's body for her own pleasure; on the day that he attempts to speak and thus exit this realm of the senses, she pushes him away and vanishes. But one morning, the man, in the company of his pregnant wife (Gretchen Mol), crosses paths with the young woman at the train-station entrance: they recognize each other, and the troubled wife demands to know who this stranger is. Three times over, the husband denies knowing her: "I don't know . . . I don't know. I don't know who that was." Suddenly this modest urban adventure reveals its biblical dimension: the husband is like Peter denying Jesus three times before dawn. *Love on the A Train* completely hollows out the American yuppie: unfaithful to his marital vow and to all his promises, he betrays his wife for the duration of her pregnancy; unfaithful to his own pleasure, to the body and its ruling drives, he denies the very existence of sensual joy. He governs the economic world but possesses nothing; he embodies the model of social success but amounts to only a disastrous figure of miserable betrayal.

The two principal differences between Ferrara's works and the conceptions of Cinema Engagé are as illuminating as the similarities. For de Laurot, the artist's task is proleptic in the sense that he possesses "the power to *perceive futurity within the present*," opening onto a moral creation of the world. "The artist then transforms the world in the most profound sense, for he acts upon consciousness: in creating art he at the same time morally creates reality": this is the principle of dynamic realism. No trace of such positivity can be detected in Ferrara's work; it is entirely devoted to a description of the negative without the slightest utopian or messianic appeal. In this sense it is much closer to the purely critical positions of Adorno than any version of Marxist-Leninism. De Laurot and Lund, following the Vietnamese, Cuban, and African American models, were fascinated by clandestine forms of liberation wars, guerrilla warfare, and secret subversion. This is what de Laurot called the Second Front, an opening onto the American territory comprising activist groups (official or clandestine, civil or military) modeled on Third World revolutionary parties to combat American imperialism from within. So far, no trace of this guerrilla imaginary can be found in Ferrara's work. It can instead be found in John Carpenter, at his best (*They Live;* 1989) and his worst (*Escape from L.A.;* 1996). However, one of Ferrara's projects, announced in 2000, shows his interest in the activist dimension of critical activity: seemingly a transposition of Lund's life, it is titled (in French, as if in homage to the French revolutionary vocabulary dear to de Laurot) *Coup d'Etat:* "In a parallel universe, where independent filmmakers literally wage battle against the studios in a war-torn Hollywood, a 24–year-old former indie actress cum underground war hero decides to join the studios to direct her first film."[49]

Zoë Lund at the Cinémathèque Française in February 1997. Photo by Daniel Keryzaouen.

*On Political Passion*  In 1993, Zoë Lund found herself at the Rotterdam Film Festival. To thank the organizers for their kindness and hospitality, she jumped at the offer to write, perform in, and direct a film in three days. The result, *Hot Ticket*, was included in a collective feature, *Scenes from Rotterdam* (assembled by Mijke de Jong), and is now available on the French DVD of *Bad Lieutenant*. *Hot Ticket* lasts barely over a minute and a half. Like all films that use a short form to achieve intensity, it displays particular ingenuity.

*Hot Ticket* unfolds in two shots. The first is brief: Zoë, dressed entirely in black, a large black hat in her hand, finds herself in the foyer of a cinema decorated in red velvet. She moves towards the camera, as if leaving a screening. A sequence-shot follows: Zoë, now wearing her immense hat, descends a staircase and heads towards the cinema's ticket box. Instead of money she slides a full syringe under the glass. The cashier gives her a ticket, which she pockets. Then, a little edgily, she asks, "Am I too late?" "No," answers the cashier. "No, you just made it. You can go in now." At once relieved and resigned, Zoë sets forth, moves towards the camera, leaves the cinema, and ends up in the street. It is dark. The camera pulls back to show her in wide shot, utterly vulnerable out in the world. Then it pans away from her to show the façade of the cinema (the Luxor), while her voice-off utters: "That which is not yet, but ought to be, is more real than that which merely is." The camera pans back to her. Distraught, she glances right and left and then looks directly into the camera. Adjusting her enormous hat, she turns around, moves slowly away to the right, thrusting herself down the paved street that is illuminated by commercial signs, until she disappears among the passersby.

*Hot Ticket* constitutes a visual apologue. Like everything Lund has created (including her performance in *Ms .45*, the script of *Bad Lieutenant,* and her unfinished novel trilogy, "490"), it returns us to the most naked and vivid state of existential necessity. At the start of the twentieth century, the first theorists of film, fascinated by the analogical properties of this new medium, imagined how the cinema might reach its fulfillment. The public would enter the theater, at the front of which would be set not a screen against a wall but a transparent window through which spectators could directly watch the real-life spectacle of the street. It would take a century for someone to think of traversing that great, theoretical film theater, passing through the glass and describing candidly what is to be found in that street: a pure experience of anguish, solitude, and destitution that demands, moment by moment, an experimental bravura.

But what is this "hot ticket" that guarantees the inversion of entry and exit, theater and world, birth (the red, uterine ambiance of the Luxor) and death (the anguished eviction into the night), cinema and reality? Or, in eminently concrete terms, what makes us live, what is it that flows in our veins and allows us to stand tall? What do we believe in, and what are we addicted to? To heroin? To love or courage? To creation? To ourselves? *Hot Ticket* answers radically. The inversion between theater and world is not simply a neat twist; it signifies a revolution. The proposition spoken offscreen by Lund—which appears in a different form near the start of de Laurot's "Prolepsis" manifesto ("the capacity to perceive that which *is not* as more real than that which *is* . . . the need to exact what *ought to be* rather than what *is*")—offers the essential formula of ethical exigency: it founds all culture of protest with its revolutionary imperative; it is the vigilant safeguard of hope.

From Vietnam to the civil rights movement through the aesthetic of struggle advocated by Abbie Hoffman, the activist works in the name of a world that will one day be more just. In "490," Lund offers her self-portrait as a black militant ("She is black. She is a junkie. She is incredibly sexy and doesn't apologize"), capable of sacrificing her life to her ideals in a gesture that is neither romantic nor exalted but logical and efficacious. What we are addicted to, what replaces the syringe, is a belief in the possible fullness of life, in the absolute intoxication of the true or, rather, the real—for Hegel, "The True is thus the Bacchanalian revel in which no member is not drunk."[50] *Hot Ticket* offers the best possible introduction to the work of Ferrara, since his work echoes the same principle: an attentive conservation of fundamental ethical values. Ferrara places these values under the aegis of Patrick Henry and his celebrated declaration of 1775: "Give me liberty or give me death."

Life truly lived is a dangerous, violent, and bewildering experience. In the real world—meaning the inverted world of injustice and mutilated existence—it can scarcely be lived other than as a passion. The separate and collaborative works of Lund and Ferrara arise from the same tragic conception—fierce attachment to the realization of the true in spite of all concrete historical evidence, a conception of life as political passion.

This idea was admirably illuminated by Antonio Gramsci in his *Prison Notebooks* of 1931–32: "One may speak . . . of 'political passion' as of an immediate impulse to action which is born on the 'permanent and organic' terrain of economic life but which transcends it, bringing into play emotions and aspirations in whose incandescent atmosphere even calculations involving the individual human life itself obey different laws from those of individual profit."[51]

The critical preservation of the fullness and Dionysian intoxication of life; a sacrificial imaginary; a technical analysis of everyday hostility; the constant of an irremediable inner fragility; a conceptual guerrilla act—in ninety-six seconds, *Hot Ticket* reminds us that, in the name of these values, even if the moment has always already passed, we can never be too late. When at the end Zoë disappears into the night while the neon advertisements remain, it leaves us with an essential lesson, a visual talisman representing the vanishing point of all political action, which finds its literary expression in a letter from Adorno to Benjamin: "The goal of the revolution is the elimination of anxiety."[52]

### Where Does All This Evil Come From?

In human nature, according to Hobbes, there are three principal "causes of quarrel": competition, diffidence, and glory. They necessitate three modes of behavior involving the use of violence: for gain, for safety, or for reputation.[53] These three initiatives correspond, in the same order, to Frank White's gestures upon leaving jail: to rob (ransacking the riches of King Tito [Ernest Abuba] and Emilio Zapa [Freddy Howard]); to seek refuge (the luxurious fortress at the Plaza and the reunion with his gang members); to show himself in public (the restaurant appearance and the reunion with his lawyers). This strategic division clears up an apparent script incongruity: Jennifer, Frank's fiancée, is not waiting at the jail when he is released nor at the Plaza when he returns; in both cases she is replaced by two female bodyguards. Jennifer enters at the Glory level since, as a lawyer, she is associated with neither gain nor material safety but reputation.

The restaurant sequence that introduces Jennifer is decidedly odd. Frank enters, looks to the back to find his fellow diners, crosses a mezzanine and descends a staircase—but to join his friends, he must again climb stairs. The space seems aberrant. The building's façade, adorned in neoclassical columns, promises a polysemic site: temple or law court, it is in fact a restaurant where no one eats. It is populated by three social types: glamorous women, specialist officials of high society (from the milieux of law, the press, and publishing—or *publicity* in its primal sense of "making public": "Wait for the paperback," advises Pete Hamill as the journalist who writes about Frank's exploits in his columns), and specialists of economic power (businessmen, women of the world, Frank and his entourage, all dressed the same way). The sequence establishes the relations between these three instances—in this case, their modes of complicity. There are five orders of complicity: subordination, connivance, collusion, attraction, and embrace.

Subordination: professional justice is in the service of crime, the two lawyers are in Frank's employ, and an anonymous judge salutes the assembled group, compromised by his friendly presence alone. Connivance: "You know Frank," his lawyer-lieutenant, Abraham (Jay Julien), indicates as he points out the guests, with no need to make further introductions. However, this familiarity is shot through with oddities, such as the young blonde woman who has never met Frank ("I've heard a lot about you. And it's all bad"). Whether or not these people have met is unimportant; the most important thing is their reputation, abolishing any difference between public and private: a private conversation occurs like an interview ("What can we expect from the reformed Frank White?"), and, symmetrically, the more that people know each other, the more distant they seem. Thus, the exchanges between Jennifer and Frank occur in shot/reverse shot, and their spatial and emotional distance (in a very Hawksian way, Frank launches into reproaches without even saying hello) is gradually charged with affects and turns itself into intimacy. This phenomenon leads to the third relation of complicity: the collusion of interests between capitalism, justice, the press, and the criminal world. Their respective representatives cohabit the same space. The carefully monitored co-presence of all these parties suffices to signify their secret, illicit, and fraudulent agreement—by virtue of the uniformity of their gestures, costumes, and sound, and by virtue of the affective nature of the shot/reverse shot cutting between Frank and Jennifer (the more distant they are, the closer they become; the more they speak of business, the more it becomes a question of desire). Attraction, the fourth order of complicity in this scene, relates exclusively to Frank:

he enters in a low angle, the extras move towards him, an awestruck woman gets up out of her chair as he passes, another points at him, and murmurs surround him. This is the great criminal as superstar, emblem of a society that idolizes one who proves himself most capable of avidity and cruelty. And finally, embrace: the scene opens abruptly on the word "sex" uttered by Pete and ends on Frank's sexual proposition to Jennifer. In between, women writhe in desire for him (mimicry, winks, and hints). In short, the world of affluence, appearances, and "glory" is the world of complete civil corruption, which renders all relations rigged, bought-off, and tainted.

Frank enters this world as a great criminal, but only to suddenly assert himself as a reformed lawman, a future mayor, and a converted hero. To reverse the corrupt world, appearances must be reversed; this is why the space is unbalanced and the images topsy-turvy. To this point, the film has followed the traditional iconography of criminality (violence, murder, drugs, prostitution, the lower depths, the underworld). Here, everything is reversed: the real criminals are the suave, serene, elegant members of the political, economic, and legal establishment—the most despicable of all being the silent, scarcely glimpsed judge. In the midst of this privileged sector, Frank is the only character who stands for the temptation of good. The "glory" scene effects a true reversal of cinematic syntax and figurative values: what is high is really low, what passes for clean is actually dirty, what seems legal is criminal, what seems separate is intimate, what is unknown is known, and what is respected is infamous. The scene describes, in a strictly cinematic way, what the responsible communist's discourse in *The Funeral* makes explicit. In an early version of St. John's screenplay, this figure justifies the election to political office of a character named (in an extremely coherent and systematic way) White: "The election of comrade White, a convicted political criminal and target of fascist surveillance, proves, they say, our dedication to anarchy and amoral ideology. But I want to explain to you tonight that it is *only* the criminal, the criminal in *their* eyes, that is, who can best lead the country from the corruption and shallowness of their greedy and dying capitalist mentality."[54]

Forever ironic and elegant, Johnny translates these terms to his accomplice, the very secondary and aptly named Ghouly (Paul Hipp), as follows: "Cut the shit, you fuckin' idiot, you heard what he said, only criminals can be real leaders—you finally got some ontological valida-tion." *China Girl, King of New York, Body Snatchers,* and *The Funeral* describe, step by step, how the Mafia and capitalism, far from being two rival universes, represent two versions of the logic of invidia. In Ferrara's work, the Mafia represents all at once the past, future, and truth of capi-talism. The Mafia is the combative faction, and capitalism is the victori-ous faction; their reciprocal fascination ("glory" in *King of New York*) and objective collusion (the Spoglia family in the boss's service in *The Funeral*) indicates that the only difference separating them is their rela-tion to the state—which supposedly represses one in favor of the other. Fables of the Mafia, an openly criminal secret organization, allow the description (in novelistic terms) of how capitalism functions—a secretly criminal open organization. Radically, *New Rose Hotel* effaces all differ-ence between industrial group, criminal network, and state ministry.

Augustine asked, "Unde hoc malum?" (Where does all this evil come from?). *The Funeral, Dangerous Game,* and *'R Xmas* (like Scorsese's *Casino*) look for the point at which, in the American Condition, avidity hollows out all human relationships. They seek to understand how the capitalist subject ruled by economic violence—far removed from the nation's initial myth, founded on a belief in prosperity and the fructifi-cation of riches—is a subject of destruction and anxiety. The Ferraran corpus devotes itself to describing how such corrosion reaches into the soul. This is the principal subject of the marital disputes in his films. In *Mother of Mirrors* (the film inside *Dangerous Game*), Russell (James Russo) throws this in the face of his wife Claire (Madonna): "I didn't marry the Virgin Mary. I married you. And together we lived as far out as the suburban American society would let us. Infidelities, drugs, alcohol, personal debt, consumerism, all-night binges. . . . Everything to keep the absurdity of our lives off our backs. Everything exciting that distracts the middle class from taking the gas pipe."[55]

In *The Funeral,* Ray yells a similar sentiment at his wife Jean: "If I do something wrong, it's because God didn't give me the grace to do what's right. Nothing happens without His permission." Russell and Ray reformulate, in their angry, American words, what Walter Benjamin once hurled onto the page: "Capitalism is probably the first instance of a cult that creates guilt, not atonement. . . . The nature of the religious movement which is capitalism entails endurance right to the end, to the point where God, too, finally takes on the entire burden of guilt, to the point where the universe has been taken over by that despair which is actually its secret *hope.*"[56]

We shall now see how passion in Ferrara's cinema demands exactly this passage through guilt, in an effort to find the means not to surpass but to transgress the negative.

## "Going to the End of Being"

### Death and Its Archaic Resonances

Death constitutes the principal material of Ferrara's cinema. Giving it, taking it, giving it to oneself, giving it again to someone who is already dead (the hoods in *King of New York* fire on corpses, and Chez shoots a coffin)—this is the essential activity of his characters. Is it a morbid predilection? On the contrary, it can be argued that Ferrara's films attempt to give meaning to the irreparable nature of death. In this light, they invent fictions of abandonment, disappearance, and anxiety that work unrelentingly to find the means of symbolically conjuring physical, affective, or moral absence. Eddie (Harvey Keitel) explains to his actors in *Dangerous Game:* "For all of us, abandonment is death."

*Solitude/Fusion* "[E]ach being is, I believe, incapable, on his own, of going to the end of being."[57] The great Ferraran figures try to go all the way to that end, to take this voyage; they never renounce this mission. They are beyond being to the point of becoming phantoms, angels, or shadows; they exhaust all forms of alteration rather than remain fixed in their identity. Such is the existential imperative: in *Dangerous Game,* the director demands of his actor, "I need you to dig down into fuckin' hell!" Risking every danger, the Ferraran protagonist must venture forth alone.

Profound solitude characterizes most of Ferrara's heroes. Thana's solitude in *Ms .45* is marked by her muteness; Reno (*The Driller Killer*) cannot bear his neighbors and brusquely pushes away his partner; Frank is a king in New York, a unique being whose metaphysical sovereignty isolates him from everyone; L. T. in *Bad Lieutenant* is solely responsible for the bets he places for his colleagues and is accountable to no one, especially not his creditors; Marti—whose surname, Malone, blends "evil" (French: *mal*) and "alone"—invents for herself a fable of total world destruction to rid herself of her family in *Body Snatchers;* Kathy in *The Addiction* devours her comrades and ends up being devoured by her peers (the other vampires); and in *The Funeral,* Johnny Tempio is dead, Chez is crazy, and Ray rules over a family from which its members only wish to escape. Eddie in *Dangerous Game,* who needs to destroy his family to make his film, is so unsure of his status that, before leaving for work, he whispers in the ear of his sleeping son, Tommy (Reilly Murphy, the same child from *Body Snatchers*): "Don't forget me, kid, I'm your Daddy." Matty (*The Blackout*) finds himself isolated due to his star status (a pagan form of sovereignty); he is abandoned (by Annie) and in turn abandons another (Susan). Fox in *New Rose Hotel* ends up so abandoned that he is not even sure whom he really met (the polymorphous Sandii).

In 1988, for the producer Aaron Spelling, Ferrara made the pilot for a television series with a truly programmatic title: *The Loner.* This loner is Michael Shane (John Terry), an extremely rich and rather Oedipal New Yorker who decides to become a cop in order to mingle with villains. (He only manages to find the underground with the help of his best friend, a sort of fallen Beat poet.) Michael constitutes the upperclass, melancholic, loquacious version of L. T. Brad Stevens describes his introduction well:

> Approximately eleven minutes into *The Loner,* Ferrara's camera tracks past a painting showing two distorted faces, one of which appears to be screaming, and finally comes to rest on Michael Shane, who is nervously shaking a wine glass. This image precisely sums up Shane, a man so torn by internal conflicts that he seems barely distinguishable from those painted faces with which he is juxtaposed. As the shot continues, Shane's mother approaches and asks, "What is this mission you have in life to make yourself and everyone around you miserable?" to which Shane can only reply, "I don't know."[58]

*'R Xmas* follows this path but reverses it: the wife cannot be alone; rather than abandon her kidnapped husband, she tries to buy him back by every possible means. And she gets him, as well as a doll for her

daughter. But in Ferrara's work, recuperation is not reparation, so this wife recuperates either too much (three dolls instead of one) or not enough (her husband returns, no one understands how or why, just in time to hand out the Christmas presents).

Above all, these fictions of solitude favor psychic odysseys. After the rage against the outside, the second form of revolt against the limitation of being oneself, of "never being other than a man," consists in living individual singularity as a death experience. In Ferrara, death is not primarily a matter of crime, murder, and vengeance; it is the test of the limit of being only oneself, that is, the inability to be the Other, to reach a level of communion and fusion. That is why his characters only reach communion at the very heart of death.

This supreme event has so far taken three forms in Ferrara's work. First, death allows access to fraternity. As Thana dies in *Ms .45,* she utters her first word, "sister." Johnny Tempio becomes a permanent interlocutor for his brother Ray in *The Funeral* because he lies in a coffin; while Chez's act in the same film—firing three times at the corpse, Ray, and himself—guarantees the reunion of all three brothers in death. Second, death allows access to the universal: the dissolution of *Bad Lieutenant's* L. T. within the crowd; the expiry of *King of New York's* Frank in the middle of a traffic jam; Kathy's agony in *The Addiction* as she bathes in the collective blood of vampires and victims past and present, like a great river of blood from the depths of history. Finally, death allows access to self-fusion: Matty's ghost in *The Blackout* re-finds the ghost of Annie 2, who represents at once a very young woman, his victim, his lover, his wife, and his mother, a being from whom it would be desirable never to be separated.

*The Journey* So what does "going to the end of being" (Bataille) or "digging down into hell" (Eddie) really mean? Not the solitary accumulation of extreme, transgressive experiences but the transgression of the experience of solitude, of this despair of never being other than a self. L. T., for instance, finds himself in a vertigo of transgression that leads him to explicitly breach numerous limits. It is impossible to count how many times he snorts cocaine (often on the move, as when he paces about in a Korean grocery store after sending away two hoods), but it is possible to count how often he crosses a barrier—specifically the yellow strip declaring "Police Line—Do Not Cross." This happens three times: at the crime scene, when he inspects the car containing two female corpses; in the church, when he inspects the fallen statue of the Virgin (which then becomes an icon not only of the raped nun but also of the two dead girls); and in front of the bus terminal where he will pardon the two rapists, when he arrives, passing around the barrier (now metamorphosed into a yellow cordon), and when he leaves, passing under it—both gestures of humility. The effect is the same for Frank in *King of New York* crossing the doors and grills of the train station. A gesture that could hardly be more ordinary (entering a station, leaving the subway) is transformed into a metaphysical passage because it is not merely a matter of changing spaces but changing existential status: to cross the limit of rational resignation, according to which, undoubtedly, I am only myself, and acceding to another state, where the subject is no longer bound by finitude.

The treatment of death opens up several forms of infinity, and it is essentially through these that Ferrara's work renews and deepens itself to the point of absolute intensity. Four such forms of passage to the limit will be considered: death as touchstone, as the "failure ball," as sacrifice, and oceanic death.

*Death as Touchstone*   The ethical stakes of the treatment of death manifest themselves most clearly in Ferrara's depiction of extras—those minor players who usually figure in cinema as mute, background bodies. In Ferrara's work, the relationship to the corpse, to human remains, manifests a crucial link to humanity that is of a quasi-anthropological order. In *King of New York* the gangsters talk to corpses, give them newspapers to read, and take trophies from them (the glove of King Tito [Ernest Abuba]). The dead are partners, whereas the hooded cops who stage a massacre in Frank's lair turn corpses into human spinning tops and push them around negligently as if they were dolls. Note, moreover, that in Ferrara's re-editing of *King of New York* done a year later for Schoolly D's music video of the same name, the shots of Tito's murder by the hoods (the corpse considered as subject) and those of the murder of the criminal sidekicks by the cops (the corpse considered as object) are assembled side by side. Ferrara's gangsters have a "person-to-person" relation with corpses. As brothers to the dead, they know that, at any

David Caruso and Wesley Snipes arresting Larry
Fishburne in *King of New York*.

instant, they too may die in their turn, regardless of their weapons or
battle positions. Immersion in crime is fundamentally the creation of a
constant relation to the mortal truth of man.

The initiation ritual in *The Funeral* directly develops this principle.
At the age of thirteen, in order to become a man, Ray must execute a
man tied to a chair in the depths of a subterranean depot to which his
father takes him. The scene presents itself as a memory twice over. It
constitutes an autobiographical flashback: Ray remembers the night of
his initiation and what it meant. Ray's father explains to him, "He has
to die because life doesn't allow enemies to live side by side forever. If
he leaves here alive, he will return eventually to kill, because he'll be
driven by the fear that one day we'll change our minds."

It is thus not a matter of "kill or be killed" (an animal and military maxim) but "kill or be threatened" (preventative murder, a Mafia
maxim). Crime no longer arouses a vital reflex of the primitive brain
but unfolds the perverse reasoning of a twisted speculation. According

to *The Funeral,* Mafia logic follows from this screwed-up codification of a paranoiac reasoning.

The scene is also a cinema memory, on two levels. On a minor level, the music that punctuates it is similar to that which accompanies the finale of *King of New York*—a phenomenon of "sonic echo" announced and reinforced by the soundtrack that makes Ray's inaugural gunshot resonate strongly. Thus *The Funeral*—according to this exigency of critical reprise characterizing Ferrara's work—leads us to retrospectively reconsider Frank White, the idealist who wished to create a reign of goodness in the world despite the world itself and who erased everything to arrive at this end ("Ain't nobody left!"). The murderous little boy in *The Funeral*—because of the similar music, and because of the same actor (Walken)—is also the young Frank, the origin of his demented reasoning, something *King of New York* totally ignores in order to preserve only the sublime aspect of Frank's ethical project. (This "return" of Frank also hints at Ferrara's oft announced desire to make a prequel to *King of New York.*)

On a major level, the treatment of the victim directly refers to the torture scene in *Rome Open City:* the same language (Italian), the same dramatic lighting on the victim tied to a chair, the same transformation of the supplicant body into a living sculpture (in Rossellini's case this is no metaphor, since the victim's wounds were actually fashioned by a sculptor), and, above all, the necessity for a moral debate around the figure of the martyr. In Ferrara the Mafia lesson transforms itself into an investigation into the faulty powers of reasoning; in Rossellini, the Nazi officer gives himself over to a delirium of lucidity, describing the future of the world after Hitler's conquest as an immense military camp in ruins—the burning camp in *Body Snatchers* offers a visual version of this. In both cases the relation to the martyr overturns our humanist benchmarks. In man there is first of all cruelty, predation, indifference, invidia, will to power, and a boundless taste for death. Such is humanity; the task for philosophers is to find what there is in this humanity that could possibly deserve respect.

*Death as the "Failure Ball"* Ferrara's work cultivates bloody balls: a dance transformed into a massacre (*Ms .45*), a massacre transformed into a party (*King of New York*), a permanent party that is a permanent source of anguish (the rehearsals and performances in *The Driller Killer*), the world of night and dance treated classically as the lower depths (*Fear City*), and a university ceremony swinging into a vampiric orgy (*The Addiction*). Even though, in anthropological terms, the ball represents a fusional event, the major occurrences of this classic topos of the *film fantastique* in Ferrara celebrate the inaccessible. Thana in *Ms .45* utters a word of communion, "sister," at the very moment of dying; Reno in *The Driller Killer* translates the sound of the music played by his neighbors and their girlfriends into the vibration of his murderous drill.

The orgy in *The Addiction* undoubtedly constitutes the most profound instance of this category. Kathy's thesis defense is depicted in a lateral tracking shot punctuated by natural zones of black that are part of the set—zones of black symmetrical to those that, at the film's start, monumentalize the motion of the slides and make us pass from the real (the class on Vietnam) to the vampire allegory (the nocturnal encounter with Casanova). But the thesis scene's tracking shot is more radically invaded by such dark transitions, ending in pure blackness. The post-award party, supposedly celebrating the fasting demanded by reason and the successful completion of this task, is metamorphosed into barbarity: the guests are transformed into sheep or wading birds, the vampires become a horde of hyenas, vultures, and other carnivores tearing the bloody flesh from their still palpitating yet already dead prey. To exercise reason—to comprehend evil, to fully embrace it (the encounter with Casanova), to look it right in the face (the encounter with Peina)—leads to this experience of pure abomination. But even if this scene represents the total failure of reason in the face of evil, this cannibalistic return of the animal in man does not simply amount to a desertion of the speculative faculty.

*The Addiction*'s party corresponds to a form of wisdom: the negation of the world by a consciousness that the animal incarnates. In a magnificent paragraph (which obviously inspired Bataille's *Theory of Religion*), Hegel describes animal devouring as despair in the face of the real:

> Even the animals are not shut out from this wisdom but, on the contrary, show themselves to be most profoundly initiated into it; for they do not just stand idly in front of sensuous things as if these possessed intrinsic

being, but, despairing of their reality, and completely assured of their nothingness, they fall to without ceremony and eat them up. And all Nature, like the animals, celebrates these open Mysteries which teach the truth about sensuous things.[59]

This devouring wisdom of beasts constitutes the natural model of a relation to the true, expressing violence and the sacred dimension. Here we come close to Pasolini's conception of barbarity. This explains *The Addiction*'s superimposition and multiplication of the vampire, no longer treated as a spiritual figure but as a nocturnal beast. Observe how the doctoral student reaches truth: reason has found its logical outcome, the organic, absolute, and festive identification with despair. To seize the real in its truth amounts to this total despair. Once the party is over and the animality has passed, Kathy can encounter the non-natural forms of nothingness, the three forms of going beyond the evident: the extreme unction given by the priest; the extreme conclusion offered by Casanova, the initiatory vampire ("We're not evil because of the evil we do, but we do evil because we *are* evil"); and the self-destruction affirmed by Kathy herself ("self-revelation is annihilation of self"), who exits frame as an unappeased phantom, thus perpetuating this self-annihilation.

*Death as Sacrifice* Sacrifice is the simplest way of giving death a meaning. L. T. in *Bad Lieutenant,* Frank in *King of New York,* Kathy in *The Addiction,* and Chez in *The Funeral* represent variations on the same sacrificial theme, in an œuvre that often returns to the motif of the Crucifixion (the art dealer Briggs [Harry Schultz] splayed on the door in *The Driller Killer;* L. T.'s arms in a cruciform between the two hoods in the grocery). Ferrara has remarked, "At the end of *Bad Lieutenant,* when Harvey is in the car and has let the boys go, after that he sacrifices his life for the children who were menaced, and I wanted to film a close-up. . . . But even if Harvey was capable of acting this close-up, I leave it to Scorsese or Pasolini."[60]

Ferrara is being modest here, but his film retains its logic. L. T.'s death in his car, in wide shot, guarantees the direct passage from the unconscious (obtuse singularity, immersion, paranoia) to universal consciousness (dissolution of singularity in the crowd, prepared for by the anonymous status of this character who has no name). The wide shot guarantees that the villainous execution is a successful sacrifice. By the same token, Ferrara had already shot such a close-up more than once. But in the case of *King of New York*'s finale there is, crucially, an irreducible opposition between Frank and the rest of the world. Outside, in log-jammed Manhattan, uniformity reigns in the repetition of gestures and postures (the cops advance along the cars, position themselves, aim their weapons), lights, shots, and motifs. Outside is the human community; inside, in Frank's taxi, the irreducible singularity who wanted to change the course of the world and could only manage to suspend it for an instant agonizes in close-up: the traffic jam is a suddenly sublime figure.

*King of New York* and *Bad Lieutenant* end on the same event of death in a car halted in the dead center of Manhattan, but with exactly opposite meanings. Frank remains the character of contradiction against the law of the world, shut up in himself, dead for an ideal that the world (emblematized by the neon Coca-Cola sign filmed in extreme close-up) did not want to recognize. L. T. dissolves his singularity within the universal flow of the world and implements the conversion that Frank could not accomplish ("It All Happens Here" on the façade of Trump Plaza, Donald Trump being one of the models for Frank White).

The time frame of *The Funeral* corresponds to an all-night wake around a corpse. From a narrative viewpoint, all the characters implicated in the murder intrigue are dead by the end of this night, plus a few more: Johnny the victim, whose only fault was to have humiliated his future killer in front of friends; Gaspare the wrong man, coldly executed in front of his family, whose only fault was to have been suspected; the true killer, an obscure mechanic treated by the film more as a problem than as a character (what was his motivation?), personified simply to trigger the pathology of honor. But all that is not enough to liquidate the narrative itself. An unexpected massacre occurs at dawn, converting the morbid approximations of Mafia logic (kill no matter who, no matter how, no matter why) into a rational sacrifice. After indulging himself in a sentimental meditation in his bar (he relives, in flashback, a happy moment with his brothers), Chez leaves to bury the remains of the mechanic. Then he goes to Ray's house, where he successively kills two bodyguards, fires into Johnny's coffin, shoots Ray, and then puts a bullet into his own head, to the accompaniment of entreaties and cries uttered by the assembled wives and fiancées. Completely deathly, this ending nonetheless declares itself to be profoundly optimistic.

Chez is the character of unconsciousness, the "idiot"—a minor, profane version of L. T. in *Bad Lieutenant*. He is crazy (his wife wants to send him to Italy for treatment); he is the manager of a bar, thus associated with inebriation; he is ecstatic (his hysterical song); and he is a Mafioso in the sense that the film gives to the term—a creature blinded by vanity, he confuses honor with interest. This completely disgraced character erases the logic of death and destroys destruction. He does this through *amour fou,* in the name of brotherly fusion. His act liberates the forces of life and reasoning—the women. At the rock bottom of enraged madness, the human being is shown still to be capable of acting upon a human principle, radically putting an end to a morbid economy. *The Funeral* describes the burial of a particular logic—the necrophilic celebration induced by organized crime. The film's final sacrifice represents, across the range of Ferrara's œuvre, the apogee of good, the affirmative "happy ending" necessitated by the tragic nature of the filmmaker's enterprise. But the final shot immediately modifies this perspective. The excessively close image shows the coffin cover being closed over Johnny's dead, serene face. But no one has been shown reopening the coffin—on the contrary, Chez metaphorically "seals" the lid by seemingly casually firing two bullets into the coffin. Thus the final image suggests that the entire film might have been the dream of a corpse.

But there is still more going on, at a formal level, at the end of *The Funeral.* The treatment of Chez's murderous act doubtless constitutes the film's most brilliant invention. This act benefits from a double elision. The first elision involves the factual information about the revenge— no one has explained to Chez whom to bury, where, or why. All this information belongs to Ray; the fact that we find Chez with a mattock before the mechanic's corpse guarantees the empathetic, magical effect of one brother's substitution for the other, as if a result of the euphoric memories of brotherly fusion relived by Chez in the bar. In Ferrara's films, visions (desires, memories, reveries, or hallucinations) constitute the principal driving force. The second elision involves Chez's decision to perform the act. Nothing announces the final massacre; it is experienced by the characters and spectator alike as a shocking surprise. To put it another way, Chez's decision is treated less as a conviction than a practical necessity, "beyond" mere fury. The narrative mismatches create a climate of categorical imperative—suddenly, there is no longer any information in a film characterized by everybody looking for information all the time, and there is no more deliberation in a film that has contained a lengthy moral dispute.

The Ferraran genius hones itself on the representation of psychic processes. His other films develop the categories of disquiet, doubt, torment, and thus sacrifice under the umbrella of somatization. In *The Funeral*, the brutal passage to Chez's act allows the complementary representation of necessity and certainty and shows that they do require narrative forms no less deranged than in the other films.

*Oceanic Death*  To render finitude infinite, *King of New York* suspends the flow of the world, *Bad Lieutenant* dissolves the singular in the universal, *The Addiction* works out a double passage to the limit, divine mercy and resurrection, then in a terrible movement of confiscation immediately turns resurrection into a register of nothingness, *The Funeral* destroys destruction and suggests a "virtual" ray of hope (the potential "becoming" of the women now liberated from Mafia rule). With *The Blackout*, it is no longer a matter of figuring a beyond-death; death itself has become unlimited.

Freud described the infinite feeling of imagining oneself harmoniously plunged into the world as "oceanic." The end of *The Blackout* elaborates a literal image of the dysphoric version of that same sensation. Matty discovers the truth about his own crime, a truth recorded on videotape by Mickey: he strangled not his partner Annie, as he came to imagine, but a young waitress (Annie 2) whom he randomly encountered. Burdened with desperate remorse, he goes to a beach, where he runs into his new partner, Susan. He declares his guilt, pushes her away, and hurls himself into the dark sea. He swims out to the depths until he is exhausted while Susan sobs, prostrate on the sand, unable to follow him. A series of shots linked by fades-to-black trace Matty's trajectory towards engulfment; in the same way that he swims until exhausting his energy, the film seems to want to exhaust the plastic qualities of darkness. A final superimposition, set against the darkened sea, emerges slowly. Annie 2, upright and naked, greets Matty with these words: "Did you miss me?" In a movement at once of sorrow and adoration, Matty bends towards her, tracing the gesture of touching her stomach. A song fades up, performed by Gretchen Mol (who often plays fiancées or wives in Ferrara's films); the song, "One Fateful Day," begins with an address, almost an interjection: "Mother!" Then the end credits roll.

This black ending in *The Blackout* responds to the red ending in some prints of *The Driller Killer*. Over a shot of pure red monochrome, we hear the voice of Carol (Carolyn Marz) calling her husband, whom we know has been replaced in bed by Reno; Reno creeps towards his "bride" and prepares to bump her off. The red monochrome has at least five functions: it is the propitious screen that covers up the scene in the way that bedsheets cover bodies; it is the blood-soaked sheet that serves as a superlative to the murder that is about to take place; it is the final painting, realized by Ferrara in Reno's place; it offers the abstract allegory that can replace any gore scene; and it is the vibrant visual suspense that transforms the ordinary situation into a nightmare and projects it into the framework of reality (at every moment, in marital beds everywhere, husbands crazy with love are susceptible of becoming killers).

The figurative allegory that concludes *The Blackout*—fragile silhouettes imprinted on a gleaming black background—reverses this proposition. The murderer crosses an ocean of lack to return to the point of adoring the beloved. Lack has invaded everything, becoming the very substance of things: lack of the Other (Susan's cries on the beach as she sees her lover and the father of her child disappear—she has come to tell him that she is pregnant); lack of oneself (suicide prompted by an unbearable self-image); and a kind of total, cosmic lack (the only possible communion with the beloved occurs in absence, "Did you miss me?"). This time there is no reversal. The end of *The Blackout* guarantees an invasion of the negative without the slightest possible reparation. Contrary to the treatment of death via ellipses or metonymies typical of other filmmakers, Ferrara represents death and the abandonment complex—painful absence as a plastic plenitude. The final movement of veneration manifests the heartbreaking tenderness through which lack perfects its empire.

*Larval Fictions*  Death, according to Ferrara, is neither a narrative end nor an ethical solution but the unlimited expansion of torment. Peace never finds a place in Ferrara's universe. Casanova explains to Kathy on her hospital bed, "To find rest takes a real genius." So the frontier between life and death has no real meaning; this is what could be called the principle of larval fictions—the larva as that little unappeased phantom who continues to haunt the living.

This concept relates to Ferrara's fables about vampires (*The Addiction*) and extraterrestrials (*Body Snatchers*), but also to all those films that display a cadaverous construction. *The Funeral* is structured around a night of mourning. The ghostly protagonist of *King of New York* comes "back from the dead" and then re-finds this environment everywhere (prison bars/train station bars) during his sojourn in the economic world. *Bad Lieutenant* unfolds between two car-tombs in Manhattan, one containing the two young women's bodies and the other holding L. T., as if the entire fiction that develops the anxiety remains foreclosed within the view of those women. In Ferrara, death gives narrative form to the suffering that accompanies thought. To experience an emotion means dying of sorrow; to reflect amounts to dying a thousand deaths; to repress anxiety means that it will instantly reorganize itself into horrifying deathly scenarios. Whether cops, vampires, or Hollywood stars, Ferrara's protagonists are made of the same stuff: infinite sensitivity.

*The Tradition of Hubris*  Reno (*The Driller Killer*) locked in his creative torment, Thana (*Ms .45*) in her muteness, L. T. (*Bad Lieutenant*) in his blindness, Frank White (*King of New York*) in his plan of reform, Kathy (*The Addiction*) in her moral torment, Matty (*The Blackout*) in his affective torment, Eddie (*Dangerous Game*) obsessed with his film—the normal state of such characters evokes an impassioned bondage. Burdened by infinite disquiet, they are all figures of excess. Ferrara's œuvre grounds its psychic investigation in the mythology of hubris, which takes at least two forms. Immoderation through excess is embodied in figures with paranoiac tendencies (Reno, Thana, Matt in *Fear City*, Frank in *King of New York*, L. T., the protagonists of *Dangerous Game*, Mickey in *The Blackout*). But Ferrara adds an immoderation-by-default to this classical manifestation of hubris in Kathy, whose psychic journey proceeds by reduction and ablation, by loss of energy and (literally) pieces of herself. The leprousness of this ever weaker and more damaged figure evokes a hubris of self-destruction.

The principle of hubris possesses profoundly archaic resonances, since it can be found at the very origins of the motif of human revolt. We can refer to Hesiod, whose archetypes suffuse Ferrara's figurative invention, beginning with the myth of Pandora as well as that of the Titans, whose overweening pride seeks to instigate a sovereignty of disorder, like Frank in *King of New York*.[61] Hubris is another name for revolt, considered as senseless, against the gods, the laws of nature, and the human condition; it invites failure and is always punished by the Olympians. But what happens when everything is in a state of revolt and there are no longer any gods to punish the rebels? Either characters become gods themselves (Frank the "fucking king"; Peina in *The Addiction*), or they become the king of demons (in the profane kingdom, demonic creators like Reno, Mickey in *The Blackout,* and Eddie in *Dangerous Game*). Or they choose to become nothing, tending either towards a state of pure nothingness (Kathy and L. T.) or totally drowning in lack (Matty in *The Blackout*).

*The Unliveable: Conditions for the Emergence of an Ethical Principle* The ending of almost every Ferrara film comes up with an astonishing representation of death: the loquacious death of the mute in *Ms .45;* death as a universal vocation for the autistic L. T. in *Bad Lieutenant;* a death capable of freezing the whole world for a moment in *King of New York;* a conceptual immolation for the student in *The Addiction;* an optimistic massacre in *The Funeral;* a posthumous oceanic remanence for the characters in *The Blackout;* and an enclosed, ritualistic remembrance (this time pre-death) for the characters of *New Rose Hotel.* Such depictions of death represent neither an ending nor a fulfillment but rather a synthesis that marks a beyond. This conceptual overstepping transforms the trajectory of the protagonist into the frantic affirmation of a persistence not of the person but of the ethical design in the name of which that person has disappeared. Death in a Ferrara film is the contrary of liquidation: it allows access to meaning, authorizes the ultimate appearance of ethical correctness, and lays bare the principle that informs (even obscurely) the behavior of the protagonists—for example, the conjugal attentiveness in *The Blackout,* or the "unhappy consciousness" in *The Addiction.*

Such a logical status for death determines particular figurative forms:

deathly unveiling appears as a surplus element, favoring unexpected echo-shots—a coda or filmic surplus in which what is most essential must be detected. There is an increasingly marked separation, in the course of Ferrara's career, between this final surplus and the main body of any given film. This occurs due to the use of fades, black frames, the opening of a parenthesis, a bad editing match, a change in the image-regime—any disconnection whatsoever preserves the fragile emergence of the ethical principle that is truth's violence, not merely a temporary reconciliation. To put it another way, death in Ferrara is never a funereal event but the jagged, intricate laying-out of a proposition concerning what is unliveable.

### The Double 1 and 2: Duplication and Division

A more typical logic of human overflowing occurs not through inner hubris or vertigo but by the equivalence of Same and Other. This abolishes the borders that reinforce the airtightness of people, as well as those borders between the individual and any other entity, engendering complex, autonomous figures of confusion between self and non-self. The decidedly irrational arithmetic of the double offers three elementary forms, which correspond to an equal number of figurative initiatives in Ferrara.

• *The Double as Duplication of the Same.* Formula: $1 = 1 - 1 = 1$. This is the *Body Snatchers* principle. The Same becomes the Other in a dynamic of radical substitution; its only destiny is to be liquidated. In cinematic terms, this corresponds to a shot/reverse shot: the replacement of one shot by its *vis-à-vis*.

• *The Double as Division of the Same into Two.* Formula: $1 = 1 : 1 = 2$. The Same is posed as the paradigm or couple, dividing itself into two complementary figures. This describes the figurative scenarios of *Fear City* or the music video for Mylène Farmer's "California," which proceed via a dynamic of splitting and distribution. This time, the destiny of the Same is to be cleaved. In cinematic terms, this corresponds to the split screen.

• *The Double as Shadow.* Formula: $1 = 1 + 1 + 1 + 1 + \infty = -1$. The Same proves to be a source of replicas that hollow out their origin. Beyond the pure alterity of duplication (first formula) or simple doubling (second formula), this third formula inaugurates dynamics of redoubling and approximation. In cinematic terms, this corresponds to superimposition (singular or multiple). The Same becomes impure, frayed, finding itself everywhere in its degraded effigies and able to absorb all sorts of alterities. This time, its destiny is to be residual; the Same lives itself as infinite loss. The scenario of *Dangerous Game* proceeds from such a melancholic dynamic: the actor, a classical figure of hesitation between the true and the false, endlessly travels through different avatars of the simulacrum, challenging the question of the subject to the point of its pure and simple disappearance. In all three formulae, the energy at work mainly involves a logic of projection.

One can easily see the overall perspective of Ferrara's elaborations and how the principle of the double is inscribed within them. The general stake of these constructions is to compensate for, to forget, and to fill up the tragedy of separation between individuals by way of multiple processes of mental fusion. This fusion is sometimes figured as empathy, which engenders intensive fictions of guilt where fusion can reach the point of cannibalistic devouring (as in *The Addiction*). And it is sometimes figured in a circuit of copies and their multiplication, which engenders extensive fictions of the double where fusion can reach the point of self-liquidation (as in *Dangerous Game*).

*The Double as Duplication of the Same, or Abominable Familiarity* Body Snatchers deals with exact substitution of the Same by the Other that is the Same—the alter ego, not the Other of the self but the other self, the Other that reveals the truth of the self. The fable turns around a supplanting of the mother by the stepmother, beginning from which the motifs work to displace and replace in a malefic circuit of ungodly substitution. The cry, "That isn't my Mommy!" is uttered by little Andy, the legitimate son, after it has been thought by the adolescent stepdaughter, Marti—following a process of mental transference, the invasion of an innocent consciousness by the anxiety and anger felt by another. This is typical of the empathetic logics at work in Ferrara (Matt in *Fear City* bleeding for the sins of another; Kathy in *The Addiction* agonizing over the suffering of all). Narratively, Carol is meant to be only the stepmother, but the substitutive circuit proves so rich that there is a return to the source: the stepmother could be the real mother, and her status as usurper would be less a narrative given than a script pretext to wildly fantasize about the figure of the mother. *Body Snatchers* progresses by superimpositions and slippages from one maternal archetype to another. It ends up establishing an extremely rich analytical panorama that responds figuratively to the question, "What is a mother?" This accumulation of stereotypes can be clarified by dissociating three strands.

First, the familial strand: The source of rage in the film can be better understood if one grasps the first duality that presides over Carol's status—not the double status of mother/stepmother but that of mother/ wife. As a wife she appears in the marital bedroom as a nude body, a body posed as improper, suspect, displaced, and menacing. This erotic vision is attributed to the scared little boy on the level of an episode transferred from the great incestuous father/daughter fantasy from which the "family romance" usually draws its energy. Carol thus becomes a mistress since, as a snatched and naked body, she can obviously no longer feign the status of legitimate mother. The second thread belongs to the actress—in the sense of the actor as an artifact, as a lie (a common reduction of the art of the actor that will be explored by *Dangerous Game*). Carol completely exhausts the properties of a performer: she is the perfect actress, a phantasmatically exact substitute of a persona (using the same body, she incarnates another person); she is an "understudy" (as an illegitimate, unwarranted replacement, she avows her fallen, accessory nature by leaving behind her bodily traces in the bed); she is an effigy (her body is false); and she is human remains, a corpse (an image of life but deprived of real life). The third thread is myth, anchoring the film within popular iconography: Carol is Wicked Stepmother, witch, ghost (in her white nightgown, haunting the house with her oppressive presence), ghoul (vampiress), succubus (demoness who comes in the night to be united with a man whom she will then eat), Medusa, enigma (her smile, whose trace reappears in the final shot of *New Rose Hotel*), and, last but not least, she incarnates death.

The principle of discredit that attaches itself to the mother has as its essential goal the transformation of the source of life into the origin of death and the exaltation of individual death as collective death; Carol menaces not one sector of mankind but humanity in general. *Body*

*Snatchers* thus doubles the mother as stepmother and multiplies the stepmother into a veritable gallery of vile figures. But the true origin of infection is the daughter, who is presented as a fresh, natural figure. The film is intent on evoking, without limits, a fantasy of female incest; the alienation triggered by the Snatchers results from the mother's enterprise of alteration, the stake of which is a symbolic murder. To simply kill her is not enough: Marti must degrade, waste, discredit, and disgrace her.

*Body Snatchers* is a figurative torture laboratory where duplication (snatching) serves as an instrument for the proliferation of other kinds of insult; it is a film not of disquieting strangeness but its opposite, abominable familiarity. We could say that, in its family-romance dimension, *Body Snatchers* is a *fantastique* enterprise of figurative defamation.[62]

*The Double as Division of the Same*  According to this eminently traditional structure, the Same presents itself in the form of a paradigm, often organized in the couplet of protagonist and antagonist. Ferrara's œuvre offers two explicit instances of such a distribution of roles: *Fear City* and the video for "California," as well as a less obvious but no less efficient instance in *Ms .45*.

The protagonist in *Fear City* is a former boxer who attempts to control his destructive energy. The character is divided in two: Matt the courageous, tormented law enforcer, and Pazzo the cold, perverse serial killer. The structural opposition is between death-drive (Pazzo) and anguished guilt (Matt); the decorative opposition is between Chinese martial arts (Pazzo) and western boxing (Matt)—a fashionable opposition in genre films of the previous decade, thanks to Bruce Lee's success. Despite these strongly underlined differences, the two characters are more similar than different: both mute, they choose the same object of desire (prostitutes), exhibit the same panic in relation to women, and resolve their problems with their fists. The film declares the single identity of these two protagonists beginning with the bleeding nose scene. In bed, Matt embraces his beloved Loretta (Melanie Griffith), a striptease dancer. In the street, lurking in the dark, Pazzo waits for a dancer whom he eventually kills with a dagger. Matt suddenly wakes up with a bleeding nose. The murder scene clearly replaces the love scene, expressing the unbearable nature of the sexual relation. The blood serves as an anchoring signifier between the two characters, a "quilting point" or sylleptic material: blood flows from the victim/blood of guilt. Eddie in *Dangerous Game* relates to Sarah a wonderfully romantic version of a similar incident: while making love to his wife, he begins to bleed from his nose. He concludes, "I gave her my cum and my blood. . . . I symbolize that with a ruby and a diamond."

Above all, the murder in *Fear City* appears as the hero's dream, as is the case with the nun's rape in *Bad Lieutenant* and systematically within the structure of *The Driller Killer:* Matt bleeds from the guilt of having dreamt such an abomination. Is constructing scenes of murder or rape as anxiety dreams a naïve way of legitimating violence, or rather a way of avowing the jubilatory dimension of fantasy? This problem, which returns us to the concrete questions of figurative deontology, is treated directly in *The Blackout*.

The music video "California" speaks volumes about Ferrara's work. In a parallel montage, it depicts the lives of two couples, one rich and the other from the lower depths (both couples are played by Mylène Farmer and Giancarlo Esposito). The narrative unfolds the encounter of the two couples on a Miami street and the eventual substitution of the wife for the prostitute, whom she replaces on the street—and whose murder she avenges by murdering the pimp. This clip is not merely an anecdotal surplus to Ferrara's work; it elucidates an important aspect of his major hypermoral fictions.

Esposito's presence makes explicit the connection with *King of New York* (in which he had already played a gangster role). Both films are elaborated on the same model of collage, mixing high and low, the society of the spectacle and the underworld, daily ceremonies and Mafia massacres. But in both cases the opposition between the worlds of affluence and misery does not amount to a conflict; the subterranean criminal economy is the truth of the officially policed world (*King of New York*), just as the whore is the truth of the wife. Farmer's character refers to Thana in *Ms .45* but also to Sarah in *Dangerous Game,* whose final murder she (in a sense) avenges, as much through the means of an explosive, liberating montage as with a knife: a pell-mell of the real and the phantasmic, of short shots, flashes, and subliminal shots where (if you freeze the individual frames) shot-ends and clapperboards can be discerned.

As an adolescent, Ferrara hesitated between music and cinema. As is clear from the superb declaration at the start of some prints of *The Driller Killer*—"This film should be played loud"—he never made that choice, preferring instead to adopt every form of alliance not only between music and image but more precisely between song and narrative. He has co-composed numerous songs for his films; made works in the style of live concerts, designed to end in a general riot (*Ms .45*); and played characters such as a high-as-a-kite pop singer who hurls himself into his jubilant audience (*9 Lives of a Wet Pussy* and *The Driller Killer*). He has introduced the music video as a heightened, autonomous "montage sequence" into his major fictions (such as the blue-tinged massacre in *King of New York*, the rape in *Bad Lieutenant*, the concerted return to drunkenness in *The Blackout*, Sandii's song at the start of *New Rose Hotel*, the depiction of the drug dealers' activities in *'R Xmas*); and shown how the video can ceaselessly infiltrate the overall montage (the urban images that automatically occur whenever the hero hears a song in *China Girl*). Ferrara accords a crucial narrative role to songs, whether over the scene (the Vietnamese lullaby in *The Addiction*, "One Fateful Day" in *The Blackout*) or inside it (Sandii's song). His career is punctuated by music-video assignments: for his preferred musician, the Philadelphia rapper Schoolly D, and also The Phoids, Ben Folds Five, Abenaa, and Dead Combo. "California" transforms itself into a visual tract, offering a particularly intense concentration of Ferrara's forms and themes.

In general, the music video as a form represents the advanced point of fetishistic reification within a capitalist regime. It fulfills a secondary "wrapping paper" role, arousing desire by the simplest sensory-motor means (colors, rhythms, and repetitions) as part of a logic that transforms what should otherwise be the freest and most accessible thing in the world (pop music) into merchandise. But the video also fulfills a primary role, causing (with cynical simplicity) the libido's "switches" to fire to the max. The song is thus transformed into a hackneyed tune, where vacuousness rules (to sing within this regime necessitates saying nothing about anything: the triumph of the love song as decoy), and the singer is degraded into a figure of prostitution. The average video accustoms us to the general crudeness of this market relationship and the conversion (assumed to be normal) of desire into invidia (desire conceived exclusively as a desire for possession). "California" strips bare the fetishistic motor of the video form by using the prostitute figure in a completely different way.

Thanks to the parallel editing, the prostitute appears as the banal double of the wife, negative to the rich woman's positive, expressing the truth of marriage as a relationship of economic and sexual exploitation. In some sense, "California" responds to the question, What if the "angel of vengeance" was married? The video could work as the opening session of a colloquium devoted to the life and work of Valerie Solanas, the author of the *SCUM Manifesto:* the notion that marital relations are the fruit of economic domination has rarely been affirmed with such violence. But, going much further, "California" shows—by means of this representation of marital life as sexual exploitation—that, in the world of reification, there exists no more difference between a wife and a whore than between a woman and an advertising billboard. Prostitution here is not simply novelistic iconography but the emblem of a relationship of exploitation that animates many dimensions of existence, from the urban environment to the marital caress, from a society party to a crime headline. In such a world of obscene supply and addicted demand, all bodies are interchangeable, duplicating themselves in nocturnal superimpositions bathed in red and green.

This metaphor-montage enables one of the greatest moments in Ferrara's cinema: the distribution of the same gesture of market seduction over five different bodies, who are beautiful like Andy Warhol's "multiples." A car stops in front of the prostitutes, one of them approaches, another bends in, and the face of another appears at the window; the car leaves, and the young, seductive face is transformed, via a fourth intermediary, into an aged, sickly face. "California" modernizes a classical pictorial schema, the Ages of Life: in the continuity of match-cut motion, it ties together what the pictorial allegory renders as spatially adjacent.

"California" also renders explicit the anamorphic structure of Ferrara's films—this long process of translation that elucidates the scandal latent in an initial image by elaborating, little by little, its truthful, catastrophic version. In a pleasing coincidence, it is fitting that Farmer sings, "In retrospect, my life anamorphoses itself"—suggesting that she is an astute analyst of Ferrara's work. But like *Fear City,* "California" simplifies the process: the video proceeds not by progressive alteration but by a juxtaposition of two regimes. It offers, on this level, a catalog of devices connecting the patent with the latent: parallel editing; encounter by actual superimposition (the reflection of the prostitute in the bourgeois car window); shot/reverse-shot (the exchange of looks between the doubles); the concrete incarnation of duality, when Farmer leaves the toilets dressed as a woman of the world but made up as a whore; and the final flash-montage, which shows everything at once, the two existences, the cruelty that results, and the cinema itself (the clapper and end-shots). "California" thus achieves a general laying-bare, and not only of female bodies: marital relations, commercial relations, the workings of music videos, even the fundamental structure of Ferrara's filmmaking. Naturally, it all ends in a frenetic explosion.

A fiction that proceeds by this kind of actuarial division can be said to possess a lateral organization. According to this organization, a single phenomenon is distributed over two protagonists (or two entities). But in a more singular way, Ferrara's lateral organization operates as a translation or metamorphosis. For example, the political radicalism of *Ms .45* derives from its figurative structure, that is, its subterranean constitution of the Thana-Laurie couple. On one side, we have Laurie (Darlene Stuto), an average worker whose irritation and rage in the face of harassment (sexual or on-the-job) nonetheless expresses itself in a socially admissible way—an expected protest within a regime of instituted oppression. Laurie fights, insulting with words and gestures (the street hecklers, and through them crimes against women in general: rape, domestic violence, economic-political-religious subjugation), and she defends her comrades against their boss. But her firmness and dedication render the situation tolerable. By pushing such aggressions away, she enables them to go on; she arranges the world only as far as she possibly can. On the other side, we have Thana, who represents an exacerbated Laurie, her nightmarish version. Like Laurie she endures and suffers—but she also moves into action. Laurie possesses only one weapon, speech. But mute Thana avails herself of every kind of weapon (body, knife, revolver, costume, and initially the iron—which guarantees the transition between the desolate world of work and the dreamworld of revenge). Put another way, Thana is not at all a psychopath; she incarnates the logical, politically radical response to an intolerable situation—a situation that, in the everyday, we convince ourselves to put up with at the cost of our mental health. Thana is the part of Laurie that will never accommodate to the slightest relation of force or power. Even though, in the course of the film, these two young women never seem close or have a full-blown scene devoted to their interaction, it is clear why it is Laurie who, at the end of the party, wipes Thana out, and why Thana makes the offering (in a slowed-down, spectral tone) of her first spoken word to Laurie: "Sister." By erasing Thana, Laurie bears witness to the gesture—at once castrating (she wields an enormous knife) and protective (without this gesture, society is no longer even possible; it would be the reign of pure violence, Thana's reign)—through which the human creature participates in his or her own enslavement. Laurie kills the adolescence that is represented throughout the film by Thana's bodily mutation. This is an adolescence entirely aligned with rebellion, senseless and clumsy (Thana ends up killing anyone at all). But its worst blunder remains ethically more just than the "arrangements" of socialization. Once dead, Thana can become an adult, that is, servile.

### The Double 3: The Shadow, or Pure Intimacy

*The Double as Shadow* Within the type of form created by Ferrara, the subject loses itself in its multiple versions or images, and the film resembles a ravine, created from violent tremors, into which this protagonist ends up falling. The laboratory of shadows par excellence is the actor. On this level, Ferrara's œuvre offers a spontaneous triptych: *Dangerous Game, The Blackout,* and *New Rose Hotel.* Here the protagonists are professional performers (Sarah [Madonna] and Frank Burns [James Russo] in *Dangerous Game,* Matty in *The Blackout*) or amateur performers (Annie 1 and 2 in *The Blackout,* Sandii in *New Rose Hotel*). The first two films in the series treat the actor essentially on a private level, from the viewpoint of the character's psychic economy; the third places its performer (Sandii) upon the stage of global simulation, according to a logic that allows maximum extension to the very concept of being an "actor"—a similar logic to that which enlarges the serial killer's operative field.

What unites the three films about actors? Other filmmakers make the knight or the wandering soul their figure of predilection; Ferrara and Cassavetes often return their protagonists to the status of performers, as if the actor constitutes the most profound bedrock of all living creatures. Recall the ending of Cassavetes's *A Woman under the Influence*

(1974), in which the characters, depicted realistically throughout the film, suddenly close the curtains of their home as if it were a theater. In Ferrara, acting refers not to theater but to ritual. At the end of *The Driller Killer,* Reno disguises and covers himself with paint in order to proceed with the concerted murders that he now stages, no longer simply committing them in a random fashion on the streets. Thana in *Ms .45* carefully dresses as a nun for the ball and, in a gesture of blessing, kisses the bullets she will later fire. But in the films devoted directly to acting, costume does not matter; as in Cassavetes, actor-characters serve as existential guinea pigs. Through them, the film will revive the investigation of questions of identity, truth, and power. However, in contrast to Cassavetes, for whom the actor is primarily a singular, concrete, tangible body, Ferrara poses his actor-characters as images. Ferraran actors and actresses are icons who, in the triptych, preside over a permanent iconodulia, or worship of images, bolstered by the use of well-known effigies of the global culture industry (Madonna, Claudia Schiffer). Sarah is a (television) star, Annie 1 becomes a star (Mickey proclaims that she is "my star"), and Matty represents a sure Hollywood box-office value ("the six-million-dollar movie man"). Sandii in *New Rose Hotel* has no particular ambition but, because of her multiple identities, develops her aura to the point of gliding above the world—primarily on the strength of her presence (her belly, with its angel tattoo, superimposed on Tokyo), and then of her absence.

Ferrara's three fables about acting embark on an enterprise of idol-destruction—a process that, paradoxically, mythifies the idol even more. A similar narrative movement takes the idol from adulation, to profanation, to execration, and from there, either to crime (*Dangerous Game*), authentic adoration (*New Rose Hotel*), or both (*The Blackout*). In each case, the film invents an apparatus of disappearance that is problematic, even insoluble. Murder elides Sarah in *Dangerous Game;* Annie 1 disappears and then returns in *The Blackout,* but her return does not mend the absence; Sandii in *New Rose Hotel* evaporates but nonetheless returns to provide the final image—merely to offer the "Mona Lisa smile" that, in the West, represents the emblem of feminine enigma, a smile that, paradoxically, the protagonist X (who is in the process of remembering this image) cannot see. In all three cases, it is a matter of elaborating a nightmarish narrative structure that strives to render an account of the abandonment complex: mothers who abort (Sarah, Annie 1), mothers who disappear (Annie, Matty's), virgin-prostitutes (Annie 2 in the final superimposition, the angelic version of Sandii). Hence it is clear that the figure of the actress allows the liberation of fantasies about the figure of the mother.

The evolution of the triptych is clear on this point. *Dangerous Game* guarantees a classical narrative equilibrium between the question of the actress and that of the wife—the duality organizes itself into a comparative structure, dramatized in an amorous rivalry between Sarah the star and Madlyn (Nancy Ferrara) the wife. *The Blackout* accords primacy to the question of the mother, which unites all the actress figures (Annie 1 and 2, and by extension Susan). Inversely, thanks to its polymorphous heroine (singer/prostitute/actress/spy/angel/demon), *New Rose Hotel* opens up the general question of the origin of life while short-circuiting the mother's existence. In contrast to *Body Snatchers'* mother as "too much," mothers (real or virtual) in the actor triptych are "too little," while fathers kill themselves rather than come to terms with the idea of having a child (Matty develops a death-fiction starting from Annie's abortion and aggravates it upon learning of Susan's pregnancy).

In this trilogy, the actor-characters authorize an existential investigation into the relationships between the individual and the character, a domestic investigation into the relationships between wife and mother (or husband and father), and consequently, perhaps most profoundly, a psychic investigation into the relationship between death and creation.

### *Mother of Mirrors:* Murdering the Film

*Dangerous Game* belongs to the genre of the exposé movie, in which the making of a film-within-the-film aids the goal of total disclosure. It describes the Los Angeles studio shoot of a film titled *Mother of Mirrors* by a director, Eddie, working with his two main actors, Sarah and Frank (who play the characters Russell and Claire). The crux of *Dangerous Game* can be summed up thus: to concretely and radically upend the demiurgic tradition. To the reflexive, essentialist question, What does it mean to create? the film responds with two clear, systematic propositions: a fundamental aesthetic proposition according to which creation amounts only to a process of continual devastation, and a practical proposition according to which making a film consists solely of directing actors (thus not writing, staging, editing, and so on). Cinema is yoked not to the goal of storytelling but to transforming the actor into a vector of truth. The actor, as the sole subject of cinema, must become the person who reveals the greatest truth about phenomena. It should be noted that the script and an earlier pre-edit of *Dangerous Game* contain a number of preproduction scenes for *Mother of Mirrors:* this material, arranged in linear chronological mode, would have shown Eddie meeting his producers, discussing money, arguing with himself over his choice of actress, and so on. The final version prunes these preparatory incidents and integrates everything that is "off stage" into the shoot itself. The shoot, moreover, does not cover an entire story but only one long domestic sequence between husband and wife (a thematic monomania that recurs in Ferrara's 2003 video for "You Don't Look So Good," by Dead Combo).

The cinematic adventure thus does not involve the epic production of a film, as Dennis Hopper (the video artist in *The Blackout*) presented it in *The Last Movie* (1971). Rather, it is woven from several kinds of direction scenes shown in alternation: public direction on the set (shot on film), private direction away from the set (filmed on video), and intimate power-relations in hotel rooms (shot on film). However, despite this intensified reflexivity, *Dangerous Game* postulates that the sensational adventure of a Hollywood shoot and the affective adventure of a claustrophilic psychic trajectory are, in the depths of their singularity, indeed equivalent. When, near the end, Eddie watches a tape of Werner Herzog (in Les Blank's documentary *Burden of Dreams* [1982]) commenting on the infamous shoot of *Fitzcarraldo* (1982), it is clear that the person who works with daunting logistics in a foreign country (Herzog in the Peruvian jungle) and the person who descends into the hell of the most confined intimacy (Eddie in his Californian studio) effectively experience the same thing: a disastrous dispossession.

*Dangerous Game* fully justifies its status as a "mirroring film" by producing the inverted reflection of a received opinion. Creation does not consist of building but destroying, and shooting amounts to a general carnage (this term appears twice in the script), while acting (this epicenter of creation) does not consist of simulating and making things clearer but overexposing, going down into the depths. In this sense, the film belongs to that great romantic tradition inaugurated by Milton's *Paradise Lost:* the Bible told from Satan's viewpoint, the rebel angel struggling

Madonna, Mother of Mirrors in *Dangerous Game.*

Mother of Mirrors in *Dangerous Game.*

against the "tyranny of Heaven,"[63] an agent of knowledge and revolt, the ill-fated version of the demiurge. "The devil . . . is the pure essence of poetry. Even if it wanted to, poetry could not construct: it destroys; it is only true when in revolt."[64] *Dangerous Game* re-creates this romantic tradition in cinema, treating creation as a negative passion, the filmmaker as an antichrist, and all participants in the process as burdened and condemned to propagate evil—starting with the spectator. As Eddie returns to Los Angeles, a flight attendant confides to him, "I love your work." Several scenes later, we see her in the filmmaker's bed where, de facto, she replaces Sarah, whom they watch on a television screen being raped. To approach the process of creation, merely to brush up against it, means being swept up in an irresistible, deathly tornado. *Dangerous Game* systematizes this conception. Instead of evoking creation in terms of emergency or becoming, it is treated as an engulfment; instead of construction, confusion; instead of production (according to a classical movement of exteriorization and objectification), something hitherto unheard of: a devouring. Against the organic imaginary of creation as the conjuring of a world, the film exposes creation as a putting-to-death.

*Engulfment Dangerous Game* engulfs its motifs on two levels. On a plastic register, the studio is all shadows, silhouettes, fragments, and smoke. Everything is backlit without the slightest trace of daylight; the blue-tinged shoot is entirely treated according to an iconography of Limbo, a plasticity of the interregnum between darkness and artificial light. If, from this viewpoint, there is an explicit trajectory, it consists of plunging into an ever-deeper darkness, until the final image of the wife's murder fades to black. The film thematizes this reference to Limbo: when Eddie reads a story to little Tommy, who has arrived from New York, it is not *Peter Pan* or *Tom Sawyer* but a tale of how the dead must pass through Hades in order to leave hell. He teaches his son that, according to Greek mythology, the worst fate is to lack the obolus to pay Charon and thus be condemned to wander eternally. Among the tormented shadows who move about on-set, only Frank, who pays his obolus in the form of a gunshot rendered in a white flash, reaches the point of infernal salvation. This iconography also allows us to grasp the narcissistic dimension of an actor's work: in Milton, Limbo represents the place of all vanities, also called the "Paradise of Fools."[65]

More radically, *Dangerous Game* organizes an engulfment of the film in its very structure. As a scenario, *Mother of Mirrors* seemingly possesses neither start nor end; as a work, it is without genesis or aftermath (in contrast to St. John's script, which lays out a troubled preparation, a conflicted shoot based on amorous rivalries, then huge public success for the main actors, parallel with emotional disaster for the filmmaker left in his solitude). As a film, it is shorn of material objectification (there is no celluloid, reels, or screenings). *Mother of Mirrors* amounts to a long, painful shoot involving fragments of the same sequence endlessly reworked—augmented by rushes that play on monitors virtually everywhere, on the set, in hotel rooms, and even on planes. Only the final murder scene does not employ this plasticity of the sketch; instead it is organized around an elision of the reverse-shot.

On the register of fiction, Ferrara's work obeys the same principles that Godard followed in his most genetic essays (*Letter to Freddy Buache* [1982], *Grandeur and Decadence of a Small-Time Filmmaker* [1985], and *The Darty Report* [1989])—genetic in the sense that the film, placed into a *mise en abyme,* vanishes in the course of its fabrication and becomes a question or hypothesis, remaining only in the form of traces, fragments, or desires. But if this aesthetic of the eternal sketch allows Godard to work on the theoretical status of creation (what is an image, where does it come from, what can it do?), in Ferrara it is a question of the nature of creation, its empire, and its existential dimension. And the response is simple, to quote the original script: "Fuck everything for the picture!" Reflection thus consists of identifying the death-drive; ascertaining the extent of the damage; observing the degree to which the Passion invades being; and, above all, admitting to the element of cruelty that underwrites self-sacrifice.

*Confusion* Ferrara, like Godard, harnesses the powers of confusion, rather than the traditional powers of discernment, to elucidate the problems of creation. *Dangerous Game* cultivates trouble in two privileged areas: the status of the shots, and the production of emotion as it is linked to the work of the actor. The shots in *Dangerous Game* turn out to be entirely intermediary:

• The images of *Mother of Mirrors* are staged as moments in a shoot, but we see them as already edited elements in a sequence. Within the period of time traced by *Dangerous Game,* this overlap between the frame (the actors) and its reverse-shot (the director) is insisted upon to the point of turning the shots obtained on set into pure mental emanations of the filmmaker.

• The video footage of discussions and explanations obviously belongs to a preparatory period, but its temporal status is rendered ambiguous by its placement: it becomes hard to tell if these fragments are anterior to the shoot or occurring at the same time.

• Despite their realistic treatment, the domestic scenes between Eddie and Madlyn also evoke a discreetly phantasmic mechanism. This explains the nature of the final scenes of this kind, which are rendered in a guilt-ridden delirium. The film's most violent scene takes place when Eddie returns to his New York home at Madlyn's request, after her father dies. Instead of supporting and consoling her through this ordeal, Eddie, without offering a single compassionate word, completely absorbed in his own emotional interests, announces to Madlyn that he has frequently cheated on her. The nature of this scene is problematized by the way it is framed by the scenes on either side of it. On the flight to New York, a flight attendant asks, "Would you care for some more wine?" On the return flight, another similarly says, "Can I get you another glass of wine?" prompting him to lift his head as if he has just downed the chalice of cruelty to its dregs by dreaming the intervening scene.

• *Dangerous Game* attains its greatest complexity in the presentation of the relationship between these three levels of the fiction. The director's family life seems to be a consequence of what happens on set (conjugal love imperilled by the filmmaker's total investment in his work); but at the same time, it also seems to serve as a referent for the film being shot—*Mother of Mirrors* is the dramatic depiction of that conjugal dereliction. *Dangerous Game* treats the creation of a film as, in the first place, the destruction of love.

Whatever their plastic form (Limbo, "behind the scenes," or domestic realism), all the shots evoke a general regime of the intermediate, which is no longer a dynamic, modern interval but rather a problematic intersection. Each shot presents itself as simultaneously shooting and editing; lived experience and fantasy; preparatory explanation and statutory incompletion. Nothing registers as more real than anything else; their reality is that of the overlap by which a mental vision seeks not to objectify itself in a shot of the film that would furnish its smooth translation but to intensify itself until it reaches the level of a principle. What is this principle? To look right in the face that which one absolutely wishes not to know, to the point of the most unbearable revelation, to discover what in vision gives rise to the true, a truthful emotion that, according to *Dangerous Game,* is snatched after a brave struggle from the jaws of indifference, blind certainty, and affective security.

But this is never a simple matter of an aesthetic fetishization of affects, as can be seen in degraded versions of the Stanislavski/Strasberg Method. In *Dangerous Game*—a salubrious, violent, and haughty work in the risk it takes, opposing its own context to give new meaning to a question that is today profoundly debased by its instrumental, market usage—emotion represents the beginning of ethics. In one of his speeches to the actors, Eddie declares, "The ultimate is to feel the pain and the suffering. Then we have a chance to survive. Because some rat-fucking bastard who's leading a little girl—a little seven-year-old girl with a Star of David on her chest—to a concentration camp, that rat-fucking cocksucker isn't feeling anything. If he was, he couldn't take her to the gas chamber."

On this second major level of confusion, *Dangerous Game* reworks the trajectory of *Body Snatchers,* but in reverse. Where the latter establishes a working definition of the feeling for humanity as an abstract postulate by conjuring the story of its erasure, *Dangerous Game* maintains the opposite notion—delving into the genesis of emotion. Emotion is not a given; it requires ascesis, basing itself—in a profane way that nonetheless retains the memory of its sacred model—on a spiritual exercise. This is exactly what the actor's labor consists of: observing concretely what he must put into the work to reach an emotional necessity without which the relation to every other creature would remain smothered in a thick net of negligence, the state that allows people to neither know nor consider emotion, to deny and hence kill it. The principle of confusion reaches its densest concentration in the character of Sarah. When Eddie tries to obtain a true emotional grandeur from her, and when he gets it, it is because she superimposes, in plain view, the different strata of her persona. When she recites her text, she is Claire (the wife); when in a rage she "channels" her anger against Eddie who is provoking her, she is Sarah (the actress); when she is shown still worked up because of personal attacks made on her, she is Madonna (Eddie accuses her of acting like a "commercial piece of shit"). Like the creation of the film, this creation of an actress, born thanks to an aggression, does not consist of a harmonious putting-in-order but implements the complex fusion of identities that are conceived as simply material for the affective combustion that will eventually reduce them all to ashes.

*Devouring Dangerous Game* proceeds according to a system of multiple transferences—a symbolic vampirization. First, *private life is devoured by professional life.* In practical terms, from the angle of family life, the director works seventy hours a week at the other end of the United States. But a double relationship is established between New York domestic life and Los Angeles professional life. As a referent, the private marital life is translated into the emotional hell of *Mother of Mirrors.* By a simple short-circuit, the wife's name, Madlyn, has as its diminutive Maddy, which refers directly to Madonna and also perhaps to Lady Madeline in Edgar Allen Poe's "The Fall of the House of Usher," the figure of the victim-bride par excellence, one of the "evil things, in robes of sorrow,"[66] who begins to be a subject only when she is dead and persists in not disappearing. By the same token, the domestic ruin is also a model or explanatory schema, since the private dimension of professional life is profaned in the same manner. Claire the character submits to a marital rape; Sarah the actress submits to the assault by her acting partner, who is incapable of faking it—leading to the subsequent scene in which she confides to Eddie that she had previously submitted to rape while menaced at knifepoint, thereby giving him the idea for the final scene between Claire and Russell. So, immediately, the most intimate and traumatic material resurfaces for the actor-creature, and it is this which rightly necessitates excessive exhibition: *Dangerous Game* elaborates a definition of mise en scène as the predation of intimacy. The enraged, jealous rape of the actress by the actor represents the physical manifestation of a mental rape—more secret and thus perhaps even more violent—of the actress by her director.

*Dangerous Game* arranges such a pervasive destruction of private life that cause can no longer be distinguished from effect. We hear as voice-off, from the rushes, under a close-up of Eddie: "Do you like to take a family and rip it apart in your fuckin' search for who you are?" Is it a matter of destroying everything to be able to make a film, or rather filming to authorize awakening the death-drive? The original script responds in classical fashion: the director annihilates his family, but the film is released in cinemas and bowls audiences over. The final version no longer has anything affirmative. Nothing can legitimate this carnage: Madlyn's suffering is transposed into Sarah's murder, all the protagonists wind up crucified, and *Mother of Mirrors* is lost in Limbo. Only the death-drive triumphs. Bataille wrote that poetry "denies and it destroys immediate reality because it sees in it the screen which conceals the true face of the world from us."[67] *Dangerous Game* describes creation as an activity without accomplishment, without remission, and without excuse.

In the second transference, we witness a *mutual devouring of actor and director.* The film proposes a searching study on the technical difference between good and bad actors. Frank incarnates the bad actor because he obeys a logic of contagion and bad transference. He "takes in" everything, to an onomastic degree (Russo echoes Russell, his character's surname). To give him performance instructions, Eddie gets down on his knees before the actor, because the search for the right gesture requires such an attitude; Frank plays his scene but suddenly, unduly reproduces the same exigency towards his leading lady, treating her exactly as Eddie treated him. This abuse of power engenders a conflict that obliges Eddie to enter Frank's trailer and again beseech him, this time not technically but existentially. A commerce of identification, empathy, and hysteria is thus generated around Frank. His acting derives from an anaclitic logic, that is, lacking the least psychic autonomy, forever welded to the Other. By contrast, Sarah, the good actress, is welded only to her own professional image. She accepts the diversity of her position: Madonna's mythic traits (sex, drugs, Catholic imagery, popularity), the traits of a professional who is careful about her work, and the religious crisis undergone by the character of Claire—are all interwoven within her figure. It should be noted here that Madonna the actress—who disowned *Dangerous Game*—is nowhere to be seen in the film, probably due to Ferrara's modern approach to narrative that abolishes all conventions still present in the original script: there, Sarah is the object of constant praise, described as brilliant, funny, strong, beautiful, engaged in her work, inventive, and rigorous. Sarah certainly represents the strongest female character in Ferrara's body of work to date. As an actress, she recognizes her own psychic levels and accepts the superimposition of diverse selves. She materializes this "mother of mirrors," thus affirming the actor's work as a laboratory of personhood. And, contrary to the director, whom the film leaves at the rock bottom of his guilty delirium in a chaotic, hallucinatory vertigo—which, in an earlier edit, takes him to the brink of suicide, almost throwing himself off the Château Marmont balcony—the actress, even in the most difficult moment of her experience, always rationally invests her interior diversity into the production of a character.

Third, the film asks, *What do the actors play?* They play the western archetype of the normal couple, Adam and Eve, but just after the Fall and in inverted negative. Russell, who represents the law, regrets the loss of Paradise and wishes to return to a former state, the frenetic world of sex and drugs that he opposes to the American Dream of consumerism. (Herein lies the film's political limit: today it is obvious that these are complementary faces of the same process of the market's confiscation of fantasy). Claire, who represents evil, is guilty because she has converted and wishes to reach a state of virtue. Their interminable metaphysical domestic scene takes what Milton described and remakes it for cinema: "Thus they in mutual accusation spent / The fruitless hours, but neither self-condemning, / And of their vain contést appeared no end."[68] Even if it is initially a term relating to a configuration of dice, these "snake eyes" completely mirror their biblical origin. *Dangerous Game* respects the Gospel lesson to the letter: evil's origin always lies in the desire for knowledge, here specified as self-knowledge (or "spiritual being," as Eddie calls it) and staged as self-devouring, the most tearing psychic truth possible, on the horizon of which is posed no dialectic and no reparation—only repetition.

*Dangerous Game* paints a portrait of the director as assassin. To legitimately film a murder, he must kill his own wife slowly but surely, and "legitimacy" here signifies that the mise en scène finds itself level with the sacrifice required. This means torturing the actor so that affective carnage translates itself into physical murder, conjugal indifference translates itself into metaphysical cruelty, and familial devastation translates itself into formal dissolution (since the film itself instantly disappears). To perfect this fraud, an impeccable professional morality answers the domestic immorality. In a scene cut from the finished film, but of which many traces remain, Eddie replies to the agents wanting to replace the bad actor, "I'm not gonna fire the guy. I might kill him, but I'm not gonna fire him." Similarly, if he has to stage a wife's rape and, for that, "spiritually kill" his own wife, that will help young women who see the film learn to defend themselves against the conjugal violence to which they will almost certainly be subjected—as Eddie explains to Sarah to improve her performance.

So where does this endless abjection end? Nowhere; one can only sink down into the inferno of the Same. The two final scenes—a pure mirroring shadow-game—establish a relationship not between negative and positive but between two forms of negativity. First, Eddie's backlit stagger, in black against a white background, haunted by the wife he has affectively crucified; and second, the exit of Frank who, in white, moves away into the shadows, leaving the corpse of his rejected wife behind. A hallucinatory image with Christian resonances, and then a descent into hell alluding to Greek mythology: the real is the relationship established between the two, now that the film has determined and admitted that, henceforth, only negativity works. In the course of *Dangerous Game*, between the a capella version of "Blue Moon" heard during the opening credits and Bob Dylan's version (from his 1970 album *Self Portrait*) played during the closing credits, we never see a film being made—only its participants unmaking it. But destruction has become an irremediable plenitude.

## How to Transgress the Negative?

*The Blackout* further intensifies this process of destruction while advancing new propositions about the image. Matty's oceanic suicide owes a narrative schema and a number of figures to a sequence (gathering several scenes in an ensemble) that closes George Cukor's *A Star Is Born* (1954). In both films, an alcoholic star kills himself because of love by walking into the ocean. But, from Hollywood melodrama to Ferraran treatise, we pass from a functional romanticism to a critical essay on the functioning of the psyche. How and why? *Mutatis mutandis*, since it does not constitute a complete remake but is content to borrow some important traits, *The Blackout* is in the same position in relation to its source as *Body Snatchers* is in relation to the earlier versions of *Invasion of the Body Snatchers* by Don Siegel (1956) and Philip Kaufman (1978). Both Ferraran reprises address the treatment of a psychic state. The paranoia at work in earlier versions of *Invasion of the Body Snatchers* becomes in Ferrara an investigation into bodily metamorphosis. Alcoholism, the subject of all four versions of *A Star Is Born* (1932, 1937, 1954, and 1976), becomes an inquiry into the abandonment complex. Ferrara's "remakes" obey the same formal logic. It can be called the *logic of the major image,* which consists of displaying figuratively, and taking all the way to the end, what in the preceding versions is treated only elliptically.

## *A Star Is Born/The Blackout:* Comparative Iconographic Treatment

*The Blackout* and *A Star Is Born* present the same triad of characters: Matty/Norman Maine (James Mason), the film star who is alcoholic or more generally addicted; Annie 1/Vicki Lester (Judy Garland), the future star; and Mickey/Oliver Niles (Charles Bickford), the independent producer-director/Hollywood producer. Both films share the same narrative stake, to liquidate a "deviant" male character, and the same ocean-space: a villa on the beach, with white curtains in Norman's room (Cukor); a hotel on the beach with grand views onto the sea, and a room with white curtains in which the dead-drunk Matty rolls (Ferrara). At the end of their trajectories, both films elaborate a similar *dispositif* of revelation, according to which the truth comes from "elsewhere." In Cukor, this revelation occurs aurally, following an inner/outer division. Norman, waking up in bed, hears the conversation condemning him as an actor that occurs between Vicki and Niles out on the terrace. The revelation, carried by the wind to a man who is feverishly ill, is depicted in the manner of a hallucination or nightmare. In Ferrara, the revelation occurs visually, following a cinema/video division. Matty discovers the truth on an editing-room monitor; the revelation, magically granted (why does Mickey suddenly show Matty the murder images?), proves worse than Matty's worst nightmares. In both cases, the producer-director serves as the pitiless verbal agent of truth.

Also in both cases, the shock is conveyed by a major gestural invention. Mason dissolves in tears, mouth wide open as if to swallow and ingest the truth, his face twisted in sorrow, then he is silent and prostrate in bed: truth is made the object of a process of incorporation. Modine, faced with the images of his crime, shoots out his arms half folded, as if to ward off a blow, the movement standing in for a cry. He then pulls and twists his sweater, tracing with it the gesture of cloaking his face, a movement that possesses at least three dimensions: to show the impossibility of dealing with the thing he sought to see at any cost; to indicate that the intolerable image he discovers objectified on video also wells up from the rock-bottom of his psyche (when pulling his sweater, he seems to be tearing it off himself); and to confer an archaic, sacred dimension upon his gesture, since it is an ancient ritual to painfully rend one's garment in the face of grief and death.

From Cukor to Ferrara, however, the treatment of the relation to truth becomes more complex. *A Star Is Born* proceeds via a split between outer and inner. This split will be overcompensated for by the plastic confusion between figure and ground when, in the morning, Norman appears on the terrace, then as a reflection in the picture window, superimposed on the water and thus already virtually drowned. *The Blackout* elaborates a three-way dialectic, and here the similarity between the two films proves to be strong. The same revelatory *dispositif* is evident, which depends partly on the actor's work: according to Hollywood's criteria, Norman no longer knows how to act; according to Mickey, the independent video artist, Matty the commercial actor was not present at his best performance because he was drunk at the time. The result is the same: identification with evil by somatization, leading in both cases to suicide. The work on the body too is the same (more complex in Ferrara, where truth comes also from within), in a climate of oceanic hallucination, with a common figure, the Siren: Norman drowns to the sound of Vicki's song; Matty, after drowning, re-finds Annie 2's naked body. But to testify to the process of incorporation, the work of expressivity in Cukor is entirely confided to the actor and contained within a single shot; in Ferrara, one is present at a display of the complexity of psychic processes, thanks to the gestural work of the actor but also to montages of internal images (the incrustation and descaling of video within cinema).

*Narrative and Symbolic Deregulation*  Norman's sublime sacrifice in *A Star Is Born* was worthy of a redemption. *The Blackout*, on the contrary, affirms the irrecuperable nature of death, with nothing sacrificial about it. *The Blackout* undertakes a triple deregulation in relation to the harmony that reigns in Cukor's film (the twilight of a man's career and the apogee of a woman's—the career of these "stars" is calculated on a cosmogonic model). The suicide in *The Blackout* is inscribed in no dialectic and sketches no promise: Susan remains pregnant and abandoned; self-annihilation constitutes a flight rather than a solution; the crime itself is not liquidated, since its images never cease returning, persisting well beyond the disappearance of the individual subjects involved. The final superimposition proves that what is at stake truly involves a psychic process, not one character's destiny.

A *Star Is Born* depicts Norman's suicide in an ellipse—it is announced, and then commented on (by the press, the profession, and the public), and finally "restaged" (by Vicki), but never seen. *The Blackout,* inversely, gives itself over to an exhaustive plastic display, according to the same aesthetic operation adopted for the body snatchers. Whereas in Siegel and Kaufman there is an eclipse of the characters who later return in snatched form, the Ferraran version fully describes the metamorphosis in a way that is simultaneously ontogenetic and phylogenetic. *Body Snatchers* asks, What is a body? *The Blackout* explores, What is a mental image?—put into story form and dramatized as, What is a psychic event? Truth is treated not as a radiant illumination but as an irremediable plunging of the world into darkness—the ocean becomes an opaque material in which consciousness struggles, the real an engulfment in an intolerable anxiety. Ferrara's *plastique* of the negative is opposed, term for term, to the flamboyant chromatism of the last light of sunset in Cukor; and if Cukor's shots evoke a romantic monumentality, Ferrara's black-on-black layers echo instead Ad Reinhardt's slogan, "Black is Art, Art is Black."

Ferrara's art explores the frontier-forms of disappearance; on this level, the end of *The Blackout* can be seen as a recapitulation of the forms that allow a transgression of the negative. The first of these forms is remanence. One image has always been there: Matty's behavior is oriented in relation to this fundamental intuition, which makes him prefer the mnemonic trace to external information (the presence of Annie 1 alive, brought back from Acapulco by Mickey, would be enough to end his torment if it were only a matter of a domestic incident). What he swims towards is the full, beautiful version of his intuition, reconstructed on the basis of his psychic scraps and the unbearable video recording. The second form is persistence. The heroic return of the tiny body of the swimmer who drags himself out of the darkness, from one frame to the next, from shot to shot, from wave to wave—but only because he persists in his quest to disappear—gives us the images that *A Star Is Born* could not include. Persistence must thus be understood as insistence but also as obstinacy—an obsessive research into crucial images, images of life and death (Norman's death by drowning, Nana Miami's strangulation for Mickey, Annie 2's strangulation for Matty, organic metamorphosis for Marti in *Body Snatchers*). These images are so easy to economize on and therefore must be interrogated not only for their content but also the deep causes governing their elision. The third form is anamnesis. Thanks to video recording, the forgotten image indeed returns. But the traversal of the negative allows it to be truly understood and declared for what it is. What is looked for in the image is the woman; in the woman, the mother; and in the mother, the vanished child. Matty's adoring posture transforms Annie into the Virgin Mary—a Virgin whose miraculous gift would consist not of bearing a child but in establishing and celebrating lack as man's natural state. The sole reparation possible for the abandonment complex described by Matty to the unseen psycho-analyst—his mother "doesn't write me back, she doesn't call me, she's not willing to"—is Annie 2's final, affectionate question, "Did you miss me?" It is clear that reparation does not consist of filling the lack, only in managing to formulate the identity of the person who is forever lost to you. The figurative trajectory is admirable. Annie 2 represents the most fragile, degraded version of woman: little girl, copycat, occasional and instrumental extra, sacrificial victim. It is only in the spectre of the shadow-woman that she can accede to the prototype, to the original image, to the mother.

Thus there is a fundamental difference between the stakes of the two scenes of oceanic suicide in Cukor and Ferrara: a sentimental sacrifice in the former, the traversal of the negative in the latter. But in relation to their figurative workings, *A Star Is Born* serves essentially as a "rough draft" for *The Blackout* to the extent that the common motif of disappearance determines an exigency of figurative invention. Both films feed their figurative system of acting by starting from the public image of their cast members. This takes place according to a celebrated inversion: the sober Mason plays the role of an alcoholic, while the alcoholic Garland plays the sober wife; likewise, the healthy, sporty Modine plays an addict in the presence of Béatrice Dalle, a star widely associated with diverse dependencies (booze, drugs, sex, and kleptomania), playing a lover revolted by her boyfriend's addiction ("I don't want my baby to have a father who was a junkie"). In both cases, the imaginary fusional couple thus initially establishes its fusion on the fact of each partner playing the other's image, and thereafter because the event of suicide engenders the visual principle of figurative propagation. *A Star Is Born* metaphorizes disappearance before and after the elided suicide. Before, by the transformation of Norman into a reflection: we see him already dissolved in the oceanic image, glazed in the glass window. It is thus an anticipation, a figurative prolepsis. After, we witness the return of the deceased on a new stage, that of the music hall where Vicki, before an immense blue background that transposes the Pacific Ocean into an almost fluorescent monochrome, begins her number with the famous words, "This is Mrs. Norman Maine," thus immortalizing Norman in the form of his alter ego. This time it is a case of figurative analepsis. *The Blackout* obeys a dynamic of generalized disappearance and thus of permanent return. The totality of the film is structured on a logic of transference.

Finally, from the vantage point of absence, *The Blackout* constructs another couple: Mickey and the psychoanalyst. Mickey, the director, makes all images and all bodies return: the film *Nana* as *Nana Miami*, Annie 1 as Annie 2, Annie 1 as herself, and Matty's "performance" as recorded testimony. The psychoanalyst notes the shadow-zones in Matty's discourse, hunts the phenomena of the unsaid, the approximate, and the lacking. Mickey and the analyst both deal in montage, linking present bodies with absent figures; both record, preserve, and protect images rather than beings. *The Blackout* treats the images of *A Star Is Born* in exactly the same way that Mickey searches for the images of his *Nana Miami:* his remake lacks a key image, and he would rather kill, or kill himself, than renounce this search. And when that image is lacking in the original itself (physical suicide in Cukor, organic metamorphosis in Siegel), the film is remade expressly for the sake of this "missing shot"—to bring it to light, repeat it, vary it, analyze the motifs of its previous absence, leaving off only when it is possible to propagate the lack around it. Thus Ferrara's cinema, far beyond its current reputation for arbitrary, violent, vaguely psychedelic provocation, reveals itself, once it is fully understood, as the exigency of critical analysis.

## They Don't Want Health, They Want Truth

"Going to the end of being" in Ferrara's work signifies the laying out of a figure, an affect, or a complex—it is not a matter of characters going to the end of themselves (which would evoke a banal method of self-confirmation) but going beyond their limits. This occurs according to a negative logic of unveiling, disillusionment, loss, and laying bare. The stake of this logic consists of encountering what one does not wish to know, showing what one does not want to see, becoming what one refuses to be. Let us recapitulate the formal invention that Ferrara's œuvre demonstrates in this regard. A lateral structure places a character, via figurative dissociation and division of agency, before his own truth: Reno the painter faces Reno the killer in *The Driller Killer,* Matt faces Pazzo in *Fear City,* Laurie faces Thana in *Ms .45,* the wife faces the prostitute-victim in "California." The second structure, which can be called longitudinal, creates figurative friezes that progressively—by reprises, variations, overlappings, and transferences—lead an ordinary image to its scandalous truth. This anamorphic elaboration is particularly characteristic of Ferrara; it organizes almost all his films. It is obvious that this structure utilizes powers proper to cinema, since it proceeds via visual transference. Thus the cinema can create a work of truth, at least in an endogenous way, in the sense of originating from within.

The passion for truth informs the narrative and figurative economy of the films; equally, it informs the trajectory of the protagonists, caught between denial and revelation. They would rather die than not know: this is the position of Reno (*The Driller Killer*), Kathy (*The Addiction*), Frank (*King of New York*), Matty (*The Blackout*), Eddie (*Dangerous Game*), and L. T. (*Bad Lieutenant*), whether death has already arrived before the film (literally for Johnny in *The Funeral,* metaphorically for Frank), whether it ultimately comes (L. T., Chez in *The Funeral,* Matty), or whether it is consubstantial with their very being (Reno, Kathy, Eddie). For all that, there is nothing dolorous about this position. At this level it refs to an exogenous or external state of the world. Ferrara's protagonists struggle with the burden of the imperative desire to see the real for what it is, in its tearing cruelty, and from there to act as they must, in paroxysmic rebelliousness. The best description of this principle of revolt, insofar as it animates Kathy's character in *The Addiction,* is to be found in the writings of the activist Emma Goldman, in her essay "The Psychology of Political Violence" about anarchist terrorists:

> One's very being must throb with the pain, the sorrow, the despair millions of people are daily made to endure. Indeed, unless we have become a part of humanity, we cannot even faintly understand the just indignation that accumulates in a human soul, the burning, surging passion that makes the storm inevitable. . . . As a matter of fact, those who have studied the character and personality of these men are agreed that it is their super-sensitiveness to the wrong and injustice surrounding them that compels them to pay the toll of our social crimes.[69]

At the end of their respective studies in film, Ferrara in New York and Holger Meins in West Berlin had, ten years apart, exactly the same reflex: to go and film tramps, men who are so difficult to look at because they concentrate in their being all the distress of the western economic world. As Walter Benjamin wrote, the "ragpicker," a key figure of modernity, poses "the mute question: Where does the limit of human misery lie?"[70] This ragpicker was emblematic for the avant-gardes, especially the cinematic avant-gardes: Alberto Cavalcanti's *Rien que les heures* (1926), George Lacombe's *La Zone* (1928), and Robert Siodmak's *Menschen am Sonntag* (1929). Scrupulously, Meins named his final film-school work *Oskar Langenfeld* (1967) after the tramp whose existence it describes. As part of the protest movements against the Vietnam War, Meins made agitprop films, such as one on the fabrication of Molotov cocktails. After the death of a student shot by the German police at close range during a demonstration, Meins became a militant. In 1970 he went into hiding with the Red Army Faction.

For his final film-school work, Ferrara filmed documentary shots of New York tramps; two years later, on the basis of these, he would construct *The Driller Killer.* By this period, activist terrorism had revealed its counterproductive nature; revolutionary movements were completely manipulated by intelligence agencies.[71] Ferrara's films are symbolic bombs. They are not devices that, in an unjust, false world, respond to death by adding further death; they are surreptitious machines that dynamite the shadows in an effort to hollow out a space for love.

## Self-Consciousness: The Visionaries

### The Political Necessity of Inebriation

*Immersed Cinema and Ferraran Prototypes* Can Ferrara's approach be called "American" in the sense that the individual—precarious and problematic as that category is—nonetheless remains the classical depositary of consciousness? Or is his approach an inevitable displacement in relation to the 1960s and 1970s in the sense that our current historical horizon no longer offers any possibility of collective hope? Or does his approach signal a cultural evolution in the sense that the popularization of psychoanalytic knowledge leads us to automatically relate every thought and action back to its drive-origins? Probably all three factors are at work simultaneously.

Ferrara's cinema arouses critical passion, articulating at once polemical analysis and sensory joy, formal exaltation and concrete protest. Its ethical exigency does not, in fact, open up the material possibility of another world; such a world is designated only indirectly. Ferrara's cinema requires a reversal of the psychic resources available to the human creature in order to grasp this world that is intolerable. Typically, *King of New York* transforms a story of greed into an investigation of the ideal. Ferrara's passionate films offer an inexhaustible repertory of torments (obsession, trauma, guilt, anguish, disgust, abandonment neuroses, and melancholy) that are depicted through states of trance, inebriation, and exaltation, whether cold (Frank in *King of New York*) or hot (Mickey in *The Blackout*). The event here is psychic (L. T.'s forgiveness in *Bad Lieutenant*, Kathy's discovery of images in *The Addiction*), the drama consists of having ideas ("I have ideas!" cries Jean in *The Funeral*), and the characters are moved by intuitions, visions, and hallucinations. Thus, to understand what has happened to him, Matty in *The Blackout* needs every kind of dream-specialist: Mickey the video artist, a psychoanalyst, a drug dealer, and, in the original script, he even seeks out a psychic.

If the connection established by Ferrara between psychic investigation and a critical relation to the world were in doubt, it would suffice to consult the script of *The Blackout*. This film, which is ostensibly strictly intimate and beyond history, expresses in narrative terms the banal, ordinary nature of crimes by individuals against other individuals. In front of an automated bank teller, a crook explains to Matty: "Every hour a person is murdered, every minute a woman is raped, there are six million victims of crime a year."[72] It is clear that *The Blackout* represents, in relation to such everyday crimes on the daily television news, what *The Addiction* represents in relation to collective crime and historical fact: a reactivation of the suffering that is ingested, retained, and normalized by our imaginary. It is equally clear that the suppression of an explanatory scene like this testifies to Ferrara's absolute refusal to offer a sociological account of reality. Why? Perhaps because his cinema refuses to take any distance from the real. It wants to be a symptom, entirely dependent on the world, like L. T. at the nightclub, immersed in it to the point of asphyxia.

In contrast to the other filmmakers who filmed episodes in *Subway Stories* (1997) set at night, thus allowing a handy emptying of public space, Ferrara jumps on the train in the daytime and builds his fable completely on flesh and its movements. Likewise, in contrast to those readers who chose the silence of the recording studio to recite a text for the 1998 performance and CD project *Closed on Account of Rabies: Poems and Tales of Edgar Allan Poe,* Ferrara was recorded inside a church and performing in public. Ferrara needs the crowd, the street, and human commerce. His critique does not use the weapons of objectivity; it responds to the real like a sigh responds to a kiss, or a cry answers a blow: in absolute proximity and in an organically proportionate way.

Faced with concrete violence, Ferrara's cinema invents two prototypes: figures who possess no defenses and identify totally with evil (Thana in *Ms .45,* Matt in *Fear City,* Frank in *King of New York,* Kathy in *The Addiction,* Fox in *New Rose Hotel,* and the heroine of *Mary,* all invaded and metamorphosed by the intolerable), and those who are all defenses (L. T.'s denial in *Bad Lieutenant,* Matty's repression in *The Blackout*). In this regard, *'R Xmas* once again takes the opposite tack to the rest of his career. Here, the wife endures, adapts herself, hurls herself materially into reality second by second in a fastidiously traced temporality—a real that she tackles full-on, as symbolized by the dolls she obtains after fierce struggle.

But apart from the wife in 'R Xmas—and everyone in *Cat Chaser*, a project abandoned (perhaps wisely) by Ferrara before editing in which the characters represent the grotesque cynicism of a reality-principle unopposed by any force—Ferrara's characters are usually marked by their ecstatic state. They live in a statutory intoxication that abolishes exteriority (L. T.'s solution) or the difference between exterior and interior (maximum porosity to the suffering of other protagonists).

## The Consciousness Trilogy and the Artist Trilogy

*"How Can We Bear It?"* In the private sphere as depicted by Ferrara, all ordinary human activities are related in ecstatic terms. People do not embrace, they rape (from 9 *Lives of a Wet Pussy* and *Ms .45* to *Dangerous Game* and *The Funeral*); they do not sleep, they black out (Reno in *The Driller Killer,* L. T. in *Bad Lieutenant,* Matty in *The Blackout*); they do not dream, they murder (Matt in *Fear City,* L. T., Matty); they do not work, they kill (Reno, the families in *China Girl* and *The Funeral,* Matty), or they deal drugs (the family in *'R Xmas*), or both (Jimmy Jump in *King of New York*). Take, for example, the act of eating. Generally, Ferrara's characters prefer to drink, but when they do eat, it is in the mode of demented piggery (the pizza scene in *The Driller Killer*), cannibal orgy (*The Addiction*), or hallucinogenic pill popping (*The Blackout*). There are a few scenes of domestic meals, but in the breakfasts of *Bad Lieutenant* and *Body Snatchers* no one really eats, and these family reunions serve only to nourish conflicts. When the dinner scene is calm, as in *'R Xmas,* it focuses on a sweet little girl and her nice grandmother; but right behind them is the sight of the girl's parents calmly preparing to go to work drug dealing in a parking lot. The only legitimate, smooth, functional meals are those enjoyed by lawmakers—except that crime is the law, and so the meal is always a means of settling accounts (the Mafia-Triad dinner in *China Girl,* Matt and the Mafia godfather in *Fear City,* Eddie and Sarah's adulterous dinner in *Dangerous Game*). When normality asserts itself, it is the object of a systematic enterprise of execration: the affectionate meal that opens *Dangerous Game* represents the image of peace that the entire film sets out to destroy.

In the sphere of inner life, psychic processes are treated as a vertigo, manifested in the characters' permanent inebriation. But this drunkenness does not signify negative behavior. It is the sign of a privileged relation to truth—not self-destruction but a euphoric homage to life's vitality. The moment in *The Blackout* when Matty deliberately falls off the wagon is first a rational act (booze serves as the analytical instrument to help re-find an image), then an act of joy (Matty dances and exalts, a party for his spirit).

All this torment—the tortured souls, the twisted-up bodies in agony on the floor—comes from the dolorous distinction between knowledge and acknowledgment, which completely determines Ferrara's image-economy. Knowledge involves a vital, immediate relation to the real (and thus to evil); acknowledgment involves the way in which consciousness admits this relation or not. It is exactly the question posed by the artist Christian Boltanski in the title of a thirty-second film he made in 1970, *How Can We Bear It?* Ferrara's protagonists each serve to demonstrate a particular conflict between knowledge and acknowledgment.

*Trauma and Acknowledgment* A particularly clear trilogy on figures of consciousness threads its way through Ferrara's career: *Bad Lieutenant, The Addiction,* and *The Blackout.* The central characters of these films incarnate three complementary relations to reality, and thus to psychic activity. For each of them, reality amounts to anguish, and agreeing to encounter reality means trauma. The way in which each character lives this trauma determines which figure of consciousness they embody.

L. T. in *Bad Lieutenant* is (as we have seen) the figure of denial: the world does not exist, nothing can touch him. When the news is bad he shoots the radio; there is nothing to see or comprehend. He denies exteriority, otherness, and death, de-realizing everything he encounters (even a corpse is an erotic object to him). Kathy in *The Addiction* is the exact opposite, a figure of introjection: not only does she encounter the exterior, she invites it, absorbs it, and lets herself be devoured by it. She is completely permeated and destroyed by the real, somatizing torment to the point of death. Matty in *The Blackout* represents the figure of loss: he does not know what he has experienced, yet he lives in a state of continual trauma that prolongs itself in multiple replays. This third mode of response, apparently local—it no longer concerns evil in general, only the specific event of a murder—nonetheless constitutes the psychic synthesis of the two preceding modes. Like L. T., Matty is blind (blacked out); like Kathy, he relives the agony in a sharp, repetitive way. In all three cases, the foreclosed real returns in the form of an image. From this angle, the films offer a rigorous survey on the diverse natures and forms of the image.

L. T.'s images are mental, de-realizing concrete phenomena. Images return in their most incontestable form: the ultra-realist, hallucinatory apparition of Christ in the church, which leads to immediate, concrete consequences (L. T. learns the identity of the rapists). For Kathy, the real presents itself in the form of documentary images (Vietnam slides, Holocaust photographs, a television report on a Serbian massacre), prompting a process of appropriation that becomes progressively clearer. Kathy looks passively at the Vietnam slides, receiving the shock as any average spectator would. Then, in the context of the photographic exhibition on the Nazi camps, she strolls among the images as if in a world apart, inside her own consciousness as expressed in her voiceover comments. Finally, at home, Kathy gazes at the television item about a contemporary massacre, and the images form the shot whose reverse-shot is her sudden appearance as its allegorical cause—as indicated by the trail of blood that flows from her dark mouth. In a sequence-shot, Kathy then goes into the bathroom where her victim, doubly framed by door and mirror, is depicted, within the vampiric fable, as the incarnation of the television images. Here, too, Matty in *The Blackout* represents a synthesis. The memory of the buried event returns first as multiple mental images (which prove only approximate), and then as video images whose indisputable status hardly halts the delirium.

Faced with the obligation to stare at the intolerable, how does consciousness function? On this point the trilogy presents three eminently classical forms of the return to oneself, a crucial process in the constitution of subjectivity. L. T. undergoes a conversion. In the scene of Christian hallucination, he finally sees the God who has always been there but he did not want to see. He reproaches Christ, "Where the fuck were you?" or as Lund wrote in the script in relation to this divine apparition, "L. T. is not shocked or even surprised. He speaks to Jesus as to someone he's known all his life."[73] *Bad Lieutenant* develops the profane version of the Augustinian formula—that God is more intimate to me than myself ("deeper than my inmost understanding")—which inaugurated western subjective intimacy under the sign of inner confusion.[74] Traces of divine presence are evident everywhere in the film. They are even more convincing when they are daily and widespread: the religious embroidery on the sofa and the money box in the home of Mamacita (Iraida Polanco); the cruciform arms of L. T. drunk or poised between two hoods; and also L. T.'s paranoia, which obliges him to verify if anyone is nearby, at Zoë's pad or even in the most anonymous stairwell.

It should be noted that L. T.'s sacrificial trajectory has no aura of otherworldiness; on the contrary, it is shown to be anchored in the everyday life of a moving, populist, Latin American faith. This recurs as a motif in 'R Xmas in the beaded curtain representing the Virgin in the family home. Lund's original script for *Bad Lieutenant* violently differentiates faith (sacrificial devotion) from institutionalized religion, which exploits kindness and love as commerce. The Pascalian principle of the wager suddenly takes on an extremely anticlerical dimension: "The fucking Church is the biggest scam going. You know what's the real killer? It costs $8,000 *per kid* for them to go to parochial school. I've got three kids in there already, with two on the way! Christ. That fucking reward is *my* money, man! But that's Church policy. The Pope is the world's biggest bookie. Makes people bet on their own salvation! Double or nothing on Heaven."[75]

Kathy in *The Addiction* represents a figure of repentance. Her spiritual experience consists not of conversion but atonement. Without hope, she swallows everything that is irreparable and expiates the collective evil. Like L. T., Kathy longs to be touched by grace; however, after Casanova's final discourse and her own posthumous discourse, all trust in human faculties disappears; only hardship persists. Matty in *The Blackout* is a figure of reflexivity. The return to the self does not constitute the person who initiates it; in this case, it destitutes and destroys him, all the way to suicide. In this film, which is full of modern iconography, there suddenly emerges a biblical topos: the desert crossing. At the end of the research-by-hallucination scenes, a superimposition appears: we see Matty walking, mobile phone in hand, completely lost on a pale, white beach in Miami—wandering in the desert of abandonment and fear.

*To Suffer and Delight from Knowledge* After the aspects of trauma and psychic work, a third element participates in this mental apparatus: the interlocutor. Distinct from the traditional division between opponent and adjuvant, the interlocutor always proves to be, for the protagonist, at once antagonist, master, and accomplice. For L. T. in *Bad Lieutenant*, Large (the chief bookmaker who is never seen in the film) proves to be an accomplice, since he places the bets, and an antagonist because he ends up killing the gambler. But, above all, Large constitutes one of the most fascinating instances of the divine offered in contemporary cinema. His name recalls the theological attributes of God: Large is uncircumscribable, unrepresentable, invisible, ceaselessly sending his representatives (the bookie friend who warns of danger, the nun, Christ) to L. T. God is an inflexible old black bookie; L. T. forgives, but Large takes his revenge. We can glean a trace of Large's passage in the close-up of the black face that bends down to L. T. in the church. The massiveness of this figure, in the way it is rendered, does not match the body of the old woman who departs in the following shot. The editing constructs a Trinity: the Sulpician Christ (the Son), the improbable Large (the Father), and the old woman (the Holy Spirit) who holds a chalice, dresses in virginal blue, and denounces her neighbors.

Kathy in *The Addiction* has a confidante, Jean (Edie Falco), but she meets her true interlocutor in Peina, the vampire king. He is also an accomplice, since they belong to the same species of predator and hunt together; a master, because Kathy is his descendant; and an antagonist, since he devours her physically and annihilates her intellectually. Like Augustine's God, Peina has always been there; he has existed forever and read everything (Baudelaire, Burroughs, Nietzsche). The allegory is clear: knowledge kills.

In *The Blackout,* the interlocutor for Matty is Mickey, the king of "vidiots." Matty and Mickey are accomplices because they have fun together and indulge in every kind of drunkenness: they take drugs, drink, fuck, kill, and make films together. But, in contrast to Matty, Mickey masters bodies and images. In staging Annie 2's murder, he provokes his involuntary actor's suicide. Mickey behaves like a prophet, rarely departing from a register of declamation, shouting, and cursing. Like Large or Peina, he is the one who knows. He knows, for instance, how to live with death and guilt, as in his final commandment for Matty's consideration: "Learn to live with it!" Mickey masters knowledge locally (he knows what happened, where to find Annie 1 alive and Annie 2 dead,

Dennis Hopper and Matthew Modine in
*The Blackout.*

where to find the right image) and universally, since he announces to all
that the Age of the Image has come.

A long way from the traditional narrative motor, which opposes
knowing to not knowing, the functional division of Ferraran couples plays
on the relation to knowledge itself. The protagonist feels and suffers
(he is crucified for what he knows); the interlocutor acknowledges and
delights (he is jubilant in what he knows). The interlocutor represents
not so much the one who causes pain, or even the one who recognizes
its cause, as the one who has learned to live with suffering as if it were
the very stuff of nature. Thus, despite all the evils they spread, despite all
their stings and insults, Peina and Mickey do not appear as executioner
figures. Their demented exaltation constitutes the refusal and energetic
reversal of resignation within an ethical system where the true evil would
be indifference.

*The Two Destinies of Self-Consciousness: Dissolution and Devastation* If,
beyond this trilogy of *Bad Lieutenant, The Addiction,* and *The Blackout,*
we reconsider Ferrara's œuvre in its entirety, it becomes clear that self-

consciousness has two possible destinies: a happy destiny (dissolution), and a catastrophic destiny (devastation). The happy trajectory occurs when consciousness reaches the level of the universal. It dies but, in a sense, goes on. L. T. in *Bad Lieutenant*, Frank in *King of New York*, and Kathy in *The Addiction* die in their effort to reclaim the world—they disappear into a universality that, on all three occasions, is signaled by being intermingled with the life of a Manhattan street.

In the original script of *Bad Lieutenant*, death occurs as an apogee, the perfect synchronization of two "hits": the final hit of Darryl Strawberry's bat in the decisive game of the baseball championship series, and the bullet fired by the unseen Large at L. T. The script ends on the doubled enigma of the wager: did L. T. bet judiciously, on Strawberry and on life? In the film, the eventual failure of Strawberry is no longer an issue, for victory has become solely a matter of morality: the nun's forgiveness, L. T.'s confession, the revelation in the church, and finally the redemption of the rapists all establish a logic of the propagation of good that the protagonist's dissolution in the crowd diffuses limitlessly.

Catastrophic destiny occurs when death does not signify a release from singularity, when self-consciousness turns in on itself and merges with a bad infinity—where lack spreads without limits. This destiny is treated in Ferrara's three films about image-making protagonists: *The Driller Killer*, *Dangerous Game*, and *The Blackout*. These films constitute what I call the Artist Trilogy.

*To Kill/To Create Images*   Ferrara's films explore all possible variations on the relation between the acts of killing and creating images: comparison, metaphoric relation, cause-and-effect relation, homology—everything except simple opposition. *The Driller Killer*, *Dangerous Game*, and *The Blackout* invent, each in their own way, an apparatus that responds to the question, Can a film kill?[76] These three films raise the image to a crucial intensity. They explore the powers of the image, as well as the links between mental images and concrete images (the image as a psychic complex or as a plastic object). This trilogy is about the links between singularity and destruction. To better grasp the way in which they articulate themselves, let us review a few basic points.

The three films feature four male protagonists: Reno the painter in *The Driller Killer*, Eddie the director in *Dangerous Game*, Matty the actor who creates mental images in *The Blackout,* and Mickey the video artist who creates plastic images in the same film. These four image-creators are all killers, whether open (Reno and Matty, murderers depicted by the films as victims) or secret (Mickey and Eddie, who do not themselves kill but are truly responsible, respectively staging the criminal gestures of Matty and Frank within *Mother of Mirrors*). Note that Ferrara's female killers—Thana (*Ms .45*), Kathy (*The Addiction*), and Sandii (*New Rose Hotel*)—are not image-creators.

The three films are organized, in narrative terms, on the basis of sexual triangles: in *The Driller Killer*'s loft, a man and two women (Reno, Carol, and Pamela [Baybi Day]) together live out creative experiences (pictorial and musical) and sexual experiences (complete freedom, with no fixed couple), testing the limits of money and life itself (Reno prepares to disembowel Carol: end of film). *Dangerous Game* interweaves two triangles: a man (Eddie) goes back and forth between two women (his wife and his actress); a woman (Sarah) goes back and forth between two men (her director and her leading man). *The Blackout* complicates the situation: a man encounters three women (Annie 1, Susan, and Annie 2), but Annie 2 incarnates the degraded double of Annie 1—and even initially appears dubbed with Annie 1's voice.

In all three films the image-creator lives out a solitary, unshareable experience in the midst of a close-knit group: Reno's apartment is a little Warholian Factory housing two artist colonies, neither of which distinguishes work from life or private from public; the painter tribe and the muso tribe intermingle, create with or despite each other. In *Dangerous Game* the underground tribe is transformed into a professional team; the affective relations are much more intense there than in the family unit, the model that is being slowly vampirized. In *The Blackout,* the apparatus of confusion between creation and ordinary existence is stretched to its utmost, as anyone who enters Mickey's studio instantly becomes an actor.

The three films proceed via conflicts between rival artists: opposition between Reno the painter and Tony Coca-Cola (Rhodney Montreal, a.k.a. the producer Douglas Metrov) the musician, which resolves itself when Tony shows up to be transformed into an image by Reno (he asks for a portrait to be painted on the spot). In *Dangerous Game,* as with its sexual triangles, the opposition is doubled, occurring between the director and his actors as well as between the actors themselves—but all this competition serves to create an emotional atmosphere that will enhance the project.

In *The Blackout*, the superficial opposition between actor and video artist (one stages the other: that is their professional relation and their "contract," even once the manipulation has been transposed to the stage of real life) is doubled by a deeper rivalry between video artist and psychiatrist. The video artist Mickey directs Matty within a logic that confuses and hides images, whereas the psychiatrist, who also literally directs Matty, since he records all his statements, seeks to discern and re-find images. But this rivalry is not a strict, territorial division (a bad-versus-good image-economy). It intensifies itself in a spiral of exchanges and transferences signalled by a particular phenomenon: the film's co-scriptwriter, Christ Zois, plays the psychiatrist (we see him only from the back in close-up, just as Moses on Mount Sinai saw God only from the back), while his son Elia plays one of Mickey's cameramen. The psychiatrist's office is in fact decorated with a poster of Fellini's 8 1/2 (1963). As Mickey yells his vibrant celebration of video recording ("truth twenty-five times a second"), he re-creates in his fanciful way the professional accolade that Christ L. Zois and Margaret Scarpa profess with regard to Zois's pioneering use of video within a psychotherapeutic context: "The video camera has done for psychotherapy what the electron microscope has done for biology. It has brought therapy into the modern world."[77]

On the level of structuring conflicts, the three films also vilify (with a certain glee) those who turn art into commerce: the obese, horny, and tasteless art dealer Briggs in *The Driller Killer*, who refuses Reno's masterpiece and mentally crucifies the artist, is himself physically crucified on the studio door. At the antipodes to this we find Susan in *The Blackout*, pretty, blonde, and healthy—not to mention a seller of hyperfigurative paintings—encouraging Matty to sell himself to television (for seventy-five thousand dollars a week), which soothes the bad vibes the protagonist harbors on this point. As for the agents and producers of *Mother of Mirrors* (in *Dangerous Game*), their principal scenes were cut (practical scenes of preproduction and casting), but they appear almost entirely as Judas figures, since they encourage Eddie to betray and abandon his principal actor.

The three films develop the same idea of destruction as the supreme formal creation. All three invent a particular dialectic involving abstraction and figuration. *The Driller Killer* elaborates a convulsive equivalence between painting and killing, to the point of assimilating Reno's murderous gesture with the film itself, thanks to the final red monochrome that (as we have seen) places the figures "underneath" the image. *Dangerous Game* constructs an equivalence between directing and killing, according to which acting consists neither of imitating nor inventing but reactivating a trauma; direction thus consists not of producing images but of destroying people. *Mother of Mirrors* cannot be completed; it ends in a white flash, the gunshot that the husband fires at his wife. We cannot be sure whether the male character liquidates the female character, the actor liquidates the actress, or the director liquidates his wife—but we can be sure that *Dangerous Game* liquidates *Mother of Mirrors*. The creation of images thus ends, once and for all, in this white flash that works to summarize everything in cinema that partakes of projection, in the material sense of a film projector with its flicker and lit-up screen, as well as the psychic sense of self-projection, narcissism, and blindness.

*The Blackout* constructs a triple equivalence between delight, the production of images (whether hallucinated or on video), and killing. The film ends on the pictorial superimposition of water and the phantom Matty/Annie 2 couple, rising up from blackness—evoking the sense that it is seeking something "beyond" the image, just as artists in the 1920s sought to paint the "last painting." This is an image that would be narratively beyond death, symbolically beyond disappearance, and formally beyond the shot, placeless, without a subjective tie—the logical emanation of a lengthy elaboration of images that end up becoming autonomous. Ultimately, *The Blackout* can only find its ending in another dimension: sound (the song "One Fateful Day"). This "post-ultimate" image formally concludes a narrative trajectory during which nothing has been successfully created and where actions only verify failures: the child has been aborted, *Nana Miami* remains in the Limbo of perpetual recommencement, and the therapy, "looped" at the film's start and end, concludes only with the patient's suicide.

*Œuvre and Infinity* According to the Artist Trilogy, the work of art (the activity of images) involves simultaneously the production of objects (such as paintings) and a hallucinogenic flowering. Ferrara invents forms of visual translation between these two image-dimensions. *The Driller Killer* and *Dangerous Game* proceed essentially via a montage alternating between private and public spheres. The first part of *The Blackout* is devoted to the elaboration of superimpositions of the real and imaginary; its second part is organized as the vast analysis of a tragic superimposition staged by the video artist, that of Annie 2 upon Annie 1, where Matty must disentangle the two figures and re-find the real that has been covered over by fantasy. The work of art, thus thematized, is never merely a surplus, something that comes to be added to the real in order to embellish, illuminate, contradict, or contravene it. On the contrary, the work of art aspires to life's vitality, destroys all that approaches it, and eventually destroys itself. The work of art proves to be a general devastation—not by deathly predilection but because the true work consists in letting infinity's forms emerge.

According to ethical infinity, *amour fou* and the total communion of two subjects must never be renounced, even if one must die to avoid this mourning. Plastic infinity refers to the forms of the incomplete, which are organized into three principal modes: incompletion *en abyme* (films left as a collection of shots, like *Mother of Mirrors* and *Nana Miami*); sequences that are punctured, broken, in pieces (the suspended sequences in *Dangerous Game,* like that of the party suffused in red light where a drunken Sarah invents the "Privilege" tampon commercial; blacked-out shots; sharp caesuras, like the title "18 months later" in *The Blackout;* snatches of approximate images from Matty's memory in the same film); and motifs swarming in broken multiplicities that dissolve their origin, appearing as nagging repetitions (for example, ceaselessly remaking the same scene in *Nana Miami* and *Mother of Mirrors*), proliferations of images incrusted in the frame, and confusions of figures. The organization of motifs evokes what is unstoppable and thus can only come to rest in an infinity of vibration. The exigency of infinity makes the work of art loop in nothingness, and this work annuls what it produces. What defines consciousness in these terms can be found at the heart of Hegelian negativity: "If we thought of consciousness as going beyond that [individuality as '*special* capacity, talent, character and so on'], and as wanting to give reality to a different content, then we should be thinking of it as a Nothing working towards Nothing."[78]

However, the opposition between happy disappearance (the Consciousness Trilogy, which intensifies the relation to the intolerable and ends with the dissolution of consciousness in the universal) and dysphoric devastation (the Artist Trilogy, which explores the devastation of consciousness closed in on itself by its own "work") remains a narrative opposition. Something more profound unites the totality of Ferrara's descriptions of the psyche: a *passage through delirium.* How does delirium enter into a relation with infinity?

### From Local to Total Delirium: Unleashing Images

All of Ferrara's films since 9 *Lives of a Wet Pussy* use psychic images as their primordial material. Most of the films contain fantasy sequences or treat real sequences as fantasies—such as the nun's rape in *Bad Lieutenant,* simultaneously established within the fictional world and dreamt by L. T. Certain films are entirely constructed as phantasmatic translations of ordinary experiences (*Bad Lieutenant, Body Snatchers, The Addiction*); others explore the properties and nuances of different states of altered consciousness: recollection, premonition, the "flash," dream, vision, trance, and impressions of déjà-vu. *King of New York* contains no images marked as unreal in this way, but its protagonist is the greatest visionary in Ferrara's œuvre. His moral mission transforms the city into a fantastic universe where things glide in silence, such as his limousine cruising through the cemetery.

*Local Delirium (Minor Mode)*  The direct treatment of psychic images in Ferrara's films occurs in two regimes: local and total. During the 1980s Ferrara made three films founded on the same script principle of a hero completely transformed by a memory of death: *Fear City, The Gladiator,* and *Cat Chaser.* Detective Michael Torello (Dennis Farina) in *Crime Story* can also be cited: he instantly converts events experienced in the course of his investigation into nightmares or visions (such as the oneiric return of his murdered assistant in his office, which prompts a grief-stricken monologue that anticipates similar speeches in *The Funeral*).

In *Fear City* the division of the principal figure into two characters determines a strict distribution of interiority. Pazzo possesses no interiority. He is all athletic training, a murderous, glacial resolution, and implacable efficacy. His mind seems as empty as his loft, which lacks any furnishing beyond a mirror, whereas Matt is all troubles, memories, reminiscences, nostalgic returns to old loves (he falls in love again with his ex-lover Loretta), photographs pinned to the walls, haunting, and repetition. It is clear that what vanishes in this economy—the confrontation of an absence of interiority (Pazzo) with an overfull soul (Matt)—is the possibility of an equilibrious relation within the self. The film suffers from a structural problem in the sense that it manages to create only false conflicts: between the boxer and his ex-fiancée, who left him because she "loved him too much"; between the boxer and the law, since Detective Wheeler (Billy Dee Williams) only ever wants to help him; and between the boxer and the underworld, since the Mafia also wants to participate in the hunt for the serial killer who imperils their source of criminal revenue (the girls). The only real conflict resides within Matt himself: his guilt anxiety, even when carefully detached from its source (the death-drive is taken over by Pazzo), and the torment that takes him all the way to delirium.

Consider this sequential linkage. Pazzo decapitates yet another dancer with a sword, and the murder is announced to Matt. Instead of seeing flashes of the (elided) murder, Matt re-sees flashes of the boxing match years ago in which he killed an opponent. This transference-montage produces three symbolic results. First, Matt is effectively guilty of the murder (he detained Loretta, who had wanted to accompany her lesbian girlfriend, thus leading to the latter's death and eliminating his female rival). Second, the only true opposition in the film is between he who controls his violence (the implacable functioning of the serial killer: an idea leads to a gesture leads to a death) and he who cannot control it (Matt's complex, which propagates and transfers itself, connects and disconnects events). Third, there is no real solution offered by the film. Under the cover of an almost caricatural iconography of the happy ending (death of the serial killer, the lovers' kiss dissolving into an aerial panorama of New York by night), it affirms the reign of madness and despair. The final street fight between Matt and Pazzo should logically constitute redemption for the professional fight: Matt should vanquish his own demons, and the heroic fight (against Pazzo) should compensate for the accidental murder (in the ring), thus halting the torment. Once he has technically won the fight against Pazzo, Matt hesitates for a moment and then decides to deliver the fatal blow, killing him. The appropriate mental and legal solution would have been to *not* kill his adversary this time, to halt the process of death; however Matt, after vacillating at the threshold of this logic, chooses to cut down Pazzo with one last blow, thus failing to resist the lure of violence. The film ends up saying two things at once: in killing Pazzo, Matt rids himself of the death-drive, but in deliberately reproducing the gesture of killing, the second murder remains a phantasmatic translation of the first—not an act of healing, but an aggravated heroic fantasy. Madness prevails, and the death-drive gains legitimate appearances (the cop hardly protests, the dancer succumbs to love). For the hero, access to normality in this world consists of killing his neighbor, who is himself.

Two years later, the telefilm *The Gladiator* takes up the same structure, changing only the lineup of heroes. Again, a protagonist is haunted by a traumatic event, and the principal figure is again split into two characters. Far from being a lazy reprise, however, this project offers an opportunity to interrogate the ending of *Fear City* by clarifying the question of violence. The stake of *Fear City* consisted of noting the irrepressible aggressivity of the individual; *The Gladiator* asks whether there is a difference between aggressive and defensive violence.

Here is how that question is dramatized: A serial killer murders his victims with a car (*The Gladiator* takes up the figurative principle of Steven Spielberg's telefilm *Duel* [1971], in which the driver is seen only at the very end of the film and the true protagonist is his black car). Similarly, the true hero of *The Gladiator* is the morbid character of "car culture," in opposition to the traditional American glorification of cars, motorcycles, and other individualistic machines. The serial killer murders the protagonist's young brother. Crazy from sorrow and guilt, this hero, Rick Benton (Ken Wahl), decides to equip his van to hunt down the killer himself and, beyond that, to eliminate all hit-and-run drivers. Transformed into a highway lawman, he finds himself tagged by the media with a name: the Gladiator. For the public, however, this Gladiator is a confusing figure who represents at one moment an executioner and the next a lawman. Rick ends up behaving the same way as his antagonist, putting another person's life in danger. He harpoons a car that is traveling too fast; in fact, the driver is taking his pregnant wife to the hospital. Rick also begins to realize that teenagers are acting up while claiming to be the Gladiator. Matt's final gesture in *Fear City* is thus spread across the whole of *The Gladiator*: for someone to deliver justice, he or she must become confused with an executioner. The film constructs, step by step, an equivalence between attack violence and self-defense violence. The character of Rick allows us to reconsider the myth of the virile, highly equipped lawman: he is in fact a traumatized, depressive, uneducated man, incapable of sane reasoning. Like Matt and his boxing-ring memories, Rick is haunted by images of his brother's murder. In both films, hallucination is rendered by very conventional means: slow-motion sound and visuals for the boxing-match death in *Fear City;* fragmentation, distorted image, and sonic echo for the brother's murder in *The Gladiator.* In both cases the characters act in the grip of mental images that express the same logic of guilt and the same desire to take action. What marks the minor status of *Fear City* and *The Gladiator* in Ferrara's output is less their simplistic structure than the purely functional role of these mental images.

*Cat Chaser* further simplifies the situation, since the traumatic memory explicitly serves as the film's preamble. (This sequence does not appear in the director's extended workprint.) We see a Marine, George Moran (Peter Weller), in the middle of an American invasion of the Dominican Republic. He is captured by a group of resistance fighters, one of whom, Luci Palma (Maria M. Ruperto), he shoots on a roof in the midst of an exchange of fire and faces likely death. This black-and-white, slow-motion preamble comes back much later in the film, when Moran returns to Santo Domingo to look for Luci, who spared his life. This time, the morbid memory no longer concerns the individual (*Fear City*) or the collectivity (*The Gladiator*) but history itself. *Cat Chaser* should have been a great film. Based on an Elmore Leonard novel, it dramatizes a question repressed by the entire American cinema: what happens in a country after an imperialist American war? Something of an equivalent to Cuba before Castro's revolution, Santo Domingo has been invaded on every occasion since 1916 when a non-pro-American power had the possibility of installing itself there. The case here is the 1965 invasion of Santo Domingo—a sort of hideous "wrinkle" forgotten by history in the shadow of the Vietnam War. This event served to maintain the island in its colony status, home to every criminal traffic (weapons, drugs, and human flesh) that the Mafia—here represented by Andres De Boya (Tomas Milian), simultaneously a general, businessman, gang leader, domestic tyrant, torturer, and polymorphous pervert—enjoys under the American sun.

Haunted by his memory, Moran returns to Santo Domingo (peaceful at present, "not like Salvador or Nicaragua"), but instead of finding Luci, he once again encounters Mary (Kelly McGillis). She comes from the same city (Detroit) and the same milieu and furthermore is linked to him by a "guilty secret"—a rather obscure aspect of the story about which we learn nothing. Mary is married to De Boya, and their union clearly represents the criminal links that unite imperial America (Mary: rich, blonde, and white) and the central and South American dictators (De Boya: Mafioso, ugly, and sadistic). The polemical potential is strong and clear from the first occurrence of the traumatic memory. During the initial invasion of Santo Domingo—"making democracy safe for Gulf and Western," as the voiceover ironically affirms—George is hit by a grenade. But as the film unfolds, the violence completely swerves away from the De Boya side, and Mary remains a victim-figure cleared of wrongdoing. The film superimposes diverse crimes in a rather suspect fashion. They are all worth roughly the same price, a "couple of million": two million dollars is at once the price of the prenuptial agreement between Mary and De Boya, the price at which De Boya wishes to buy George's Miami hotel, and the sum that De Boya keeps under his bed because it amounts to a year's worth of living, or what he must keep in cash in case he needs to flee. The film's only problem thus becomes how to free Mary without having her lose the proceedings from her marital contract—like an American enterprise implanted into a Third World country trying to recover the benefits of its exploitation while retaining its respectability.

This dubious conflict veers towards the parodic. To recover the money, George's associates simulate a revolutionary assassination attempt against De Boya—liberation struggles serve only to mask conflicts between private interests. At the film's end, the voiceover assures us that George is now fine because he has "just made the dream come true: he's killed someone he didn't know who was trying to kill him." This healing remembrance declares its intimate character: Luci yells from a Santo Domingo balcony, "Cat chaser, cat chaser, I'll show you some real bad pussy"—a sexual invitation that really means, "I'm going to kill you." The elimination of this nightmare signifies that George, the white Detroit guy, can now sleep peacefully with Mary, the white Detroit girl. He is no longer afraid of her; the imperial war has served only as a metaphor for sexual anxiety. This is the true "guilty secret" that the film finds it impossible to admit: at no moment do the Dominican characters exist as anything other than repulsive figures, and the two white Americans cannot imagine their relations with colonial citizens as anything but exploitative, whether that means marrying them, killing them, or letting them die in their place (as occurs with Moran's local adjuvants). In short, even before becoming lovers, the American heroes are complicit on every level. Returning to the colony consists of verifying "on the ground" what can still be plundered, recovered, or redirected. It would be hard to reduce the script's possibilities in any more pitiful way; the polemical fiction promised by the nightmare prologue comes to be transformed into a sordid genre film, as if it were scared by its own critical potential. After *Cat Chaser*, Ferrara stopped using such simplistic tales about the liquidation of traumatic memories.

*Total Delirium (Major Modes)* What qualitative changes are evident between the three films founded on recollection (*Fear City, The Gladiator*, and *Cat Chaser*) and the work devoted to delirium? We pass from a conventional representation to a critical treatment of hallucination. In place of localized and cinematically overidentified memory-traces, hallucination becomes the object of a complete and integrated treatment. Reality and hallucination are presented in the same plastic and sonic terms; it is no longer the protagonist who becomes delirious but the film itself. Trauma no longer functions merely as a narrative cause or motor; it becomes a structuring principle.

In the memory films, the protagonist suffers; he seeks to reduce his suffering and reach the stage of healing (obvious, at least, in the case of *Fear City*). In the delirium films (*The Driller Killer, Ms .45, Bad Lieutenant, Dangerous Game, The Addiction, The Blackout*, and *New Rose Hotel*), trauma liberates an image-regime, and the point is not to reduce but to cultivate, propagate, refine, and understand it. In such a regime, the disappearance or death of the protagonist does not halt the outpouring of images.

This second logic no longer aims to liquidate itself (the miserable happy endings of *Fear City, The Gladiator*, and *Cat Chaser*, all showing a man in a woman's arms) but, on the contrary, gets carried away: the figurative and plastic inventions transform the endings of the delirium films into codas that are often held in suspense, iterative, as if the film no longer wants to stop. In the memory films, there is a conventional access to a supposed state of normality; in the delirium films, there is a logical, unqualified use of image-pathologies, leading to the limits of understanding (enigmas, paradoxes, speculative spirals upon which the films suddenly "pull up," in the way the sound of a heavenly song might pull up a sleepwalker on a cliff edge).

*The Driller Killer* offers, in visual terms, the passage from local to total delirium. The first murder committed by Reno comes after an outpouring of hallucinogenic images whose syntax and plastic qualities remain conventional: floating sounds, mysterious guests (the motifs painted on his canvases whisper his name), angled painting shots, allegorical hallucinations (Reno in a trance shaking his hair in slow motion before a blood-spattered background), and an allegory of hallucination (Carol with her eyes cut out). This hallucinatory sequence mixes premonition, reinterpretation, magnification of detail, phobic insistence, and displacement (Carol's bloody eye sockets are associated with Reno painting the eyes of a bison), using the iconographic repertoire and syntactical resources most commonly associated with dreams. In this sequence, the link between creative torment (painting a canvas) and murder (drilling a tramp's body) undergoes a lengthy visual elaboration.[79] The rest of the film is devoted to economizing these transitions, directly joining creative act and criminal gesture, neither of which is connoted as more realist than the other. This leads to the formal fusion of both dimensions of experience in the final red monochrome.

*Ms .45* takes off from a similar approach, treating reality and hallucination in the same plastic and sonic terms. Formally, however, we pass from distortion (the metamorphosis of the real is rendered explicitly) to translation (which the spectator must reconstitute). The film adopts this new structure with the greatest care—a compositional apprenticeship that will then authorize the unbelievable architectonic audacity of *The Addiction, Dangerous Game, The Funeral, The Blackout,* and *New Rose Hotel.* Consider the narrative premise of *Ms .45,* which offers a true script oddity: why, against all believability and any rule of narrative economy, is Thana raped twice in a row? Because the film's opening is constructed as a chiasmus (defined in literary parlance as an inversion in the second of two parallel phrases of the order followed in the first). The studio workers undergo two harassments, from their paternalistic boss and then from the guys in the street. After a caesura provided by Thana's journey home, the two ordinary acts of harassment are transposed into two extraordinary acts of aggression. The first rapist, lurking among the trash bins—played by Ferrara himself, still wearing under his mask Reno's red make-up from the end of *The Driller Killer*—corresponds to the guys in the street; the second rapist, in the house, corresponds to the studio boss. In the street rape, the relation of phantasmatic translation is guaranteed by the urban context and by the fact that the rapist vows to return, a permanent menace. In the house rape, the relation of phantasmatic translation is guaranteed by the use of an iron that goes from the studio to the house via the context of the domestic economy (work/private property, underlined by the act of breaking into Thana's window, which also signifies the violation of her hymen). The synthesis, the figurative knot, is tied via the trash-bag motif: the second aggressor, who first belongs to the domestic paradigm, ends up cut into pieces and thrown into random bins on the streets. Human flesh contained in a bag finds its everyday-reality referent when, at the supermarket, Thana gazes fascinated at the endless display of pieces of meat wrapped in plastic, enlarging this young girl's sexual anxiety to the scale of a general body-phobia.

The strongest visual translation is not the connection from harassment to rape (and thus from the murders to a symbolic reparation) but the connection from the preparation for the murderous expeditions (Thana dresses, makes herself up, does her hair, and looks at herself) to the taming of her own body, the source of her self-reconciliation. The rape-revenge film as a genre is also a story of apprenticeship: a young girl learns how to surmount the anxiety of having a body and how to play with it to the point of pleasing herself with her own appearance. The totality of these connected events (ordinary experience and its extraordinary translations) establishes a general emotional translation between the usual irritation tolerated within social life and the strange rapture experienced by Thana (stupor, muteness, passivity, then an abrupt passage to action and a delirium of revenge). No element comes along to de-realize the scenes—apart from the horrific touch of the first rapist's face swollen in a stocking—until the final extravagant return of the entire iconography of the *fantastique* during the Halloween ball (vampire disguises, giant spider webs, bats, zombies, brides), along with its most frequently used cinematic attributes (visual and aural slow-motion).

Ultimately, the structure of *Ms .45* liberates delirious flashes (Thana re-sees the first rapist in her bathroom mirror, and at night she has dreams in which she hears her own voice as a child) that, tacked onto the overall composition in this fashion, escape the confines of the narrative anecdote. But the most violent phantasmatic transposition is also the most discreet: the burlesque treatment of Phil, the "husband" dog that lives with Thana's neighbor, Mrs. Nasone (Editta Sherman). Thana is suspected of having killed this dog on the New York port. The dog represents the ideal companion for the ideal matron: he is always there, obeys all, says nothing, eats everything he is given (including human flesh), has his framed photo atop the piano, and represents no sexual threat. Thana can thus spare him, and that is why Phil returns in the film's final shot, scratching at the door of his home. He justly deserves his second billing in the credits, right after Lund.

In *Bad Lieutenant,* L. T. wishes to see nothing, know nothing, and encounter nothing. As if to attest to their nature as figures of fantasy, his interlocutors always come in pairs. But that does not suffice. L. T. must also transform them into toys—the corpses in the car eroticized as dolls, his sex partners in the studio transformed into puppets, the misbehaving young women turned into porno actresses, and the rapists made into pals with whom he watches television and smokes crack. Everything is a vision to him: the nun's rape is a dream; her pale, nude body in the hospital is a dazzling apparition; his betting decisions are revelations of certainty; and life is an endless blessing.

But how can there be a hallucination in this world that is already entirely hallucinated? By a hyperrealist eruption: the Christ who, as a statue, seems to cry in pain during the rape descends in flesh and blood from the cross (played by the Ferrara regular Paul Hipp) to meet L. T. The hallucinator and his hallucination dwell on the same plane, in an unexpected apparition-effect that will be reprised—in a minor, profane mode—with the sudden appearance of Susan in Miami during her telephone conversation with Matty in *The Blackout*. In L. T.'s de-real-ized universe, the event is characterized by a presence towards which he must crawl, that he must kiss, whose incontestable tactile nature he must verify. This encounter serves a triple function: conversion (the act of forgiveness); revelation (in a profane sense, the solution to the criminal investigation is provided); and denouement (in the psychic sense, he recognizes the existence of an alterity). In *Bad Lieutenant*, hallucination offers a resolution, and delirium explicitly passes to the side of knowledge—a postulate that will feed all of Ferrara's subsequent films.

Led by the old woman (Minnie Gentry) dressed in a blue jacket, L. T. enters the dwelling of the two guilty parties, Paulo (Joseph Micheal Cruz) and Julio (Fernando Véléz). Here begins one of the film's most incredible scenes. Instead of entering with precaution, menacing, arrest-ing, and taking the crooks away as any other cop in any other American film would, L. T. penetrates into the dark lair of the rapists, sits down, and watches the baseball game on television with them on their couch. All the while threatening them with his gun, he shares a smoke from their crack pipe—almost as if it were a peace pipe. How is such a depiction, completely contrary to every convention, made possible?

The Trinity cannot be contemplated without a long preliminary spiri-tual trajectory. According to Augustine, for whom God's trace is found within us like a haunting, we must cultivate "a mind more developed by exercise in these lower things" and work to "ascend as it were by steps."[80] *Bad Lieutenant* is structured upon such a movement (called *anagogy* within theological tradition): it proceeds via sliding, variation, and mutation between one figure and another, by means of copies, analogies, and inversions. This "curling" construction illuminates the film's figurative economy. Two major trajectories are criss-crossed and interwoven. First, the "curl" of the boys:

—the two sons in the car
—the two young female corpses in the car
—the two young hoods in the Korean grocery store
—the two young rapists in the "black church"
—the two sons receiving their first Holy Communion in the "white church"

—the finding of the two rapists (who, according to the script, were
to be dressed in cassocks stolen from the church, to emphasize
the relation to the children's communion scene)
—the two rapists in the car, forgiven and freed

Second, the "curl" of the little girl:

—L. T.'s little daughter
—the junkie Zoë (ex-Magdalene)
—the shattered Virgin Mary
—the raped nun
—the little daughter of the Korean grocer

Three consequences follow from this twin structure. The demented
Trinity that L. T. ends up meeting face to face synthesizes both threads:
two boys and a girl / two men (Son and Father) and a woman (the
Virgin Mary as a compassionate black mother). The film is filled with
transvestite figures: Bowtay the androgyne; Veronica (Lambert Moss)
the informant; and the dancer who opens the scene of Paulo and Julio's
arrest, dressed in a red cassock that the thieves would have stolen and
whose ambiguity the film maintains, desexed like a figure so eaten away
by drugs that she has already returned to the skeleton stage. These three
figures guarantee the connections between the sexes and transform
normal couples into strange trios. They represent link-figures, rather
like the Holy Spirit, a connection principle invented by patristic culture.
Most importantly, tracing back the "curl" allows us to grasp its origin,
its substratum. *Bad Lieutenant* turns out to be a paternal nightmare.
L. T. lives out a nightmare in three ways: the hallucinogenic nightmare of
seeing his two sons turn to evil; a surge of incestuous fantasies regarding
his daughter; and an absolute hatred of his wife, almost entirely expelled
from the frame and replaced, on the one hand, by his mother-in-law
presented as a white-haired old witch (another unidentified woman in
this extended family, Aunt Wendy, is blamed for making the sons late for
school, thus triggering the general nightmare) and, on the other hand,
by the illegitimate couple Ariane and Bowtay. The parallel between the
execrated wife and Ariane (Robin Burrows) appears more clearly in the
script: of the wife, there remains only a pile of bills to be paid, while

Ariane never stops demanding rent money. Even if L. T., in contrast to an ordinary junkie, has no need to perpetually look for money to buy drugs, since he has an inexhaustible "professional" stash (given to him by the dealers, not the other way around), nonetheless the fantasies of the bet and the reward serve as compensatory financial dreams to ease the perpetual conjugal demands for money.

What will become of my children, what can I do for them, and how do I provide for their needs? The film transposes these ordinary agonies of a father into a criminal nightmare. Thus the meaning of the peace-pipe scene becomes clear: it is a fantasy of perfect familial happiness, a Dad looking at a televised baseball game in the company of his two kids. But in Ferrara, to authorize the figurability of such a happy daydream, it must be the case that the father is drugged, the sons are delinquents, the home is a hovel, and the situation is illegal. What is the psychic benefit of this transposition? It allows a dream of forgiveness and freedom: in passing from the bourgeois world of the police to the Spanish Harlem underground, woman becomes a solution and no longer a problem. The future delinquents leave freely with their father's heritage, and this Dad can die peacefully in his car—his only true home. For once, the impoverished world shelters everything that is positive, while the bourgeois world possesses only what is negative. Thus, "the detective finds the secret hidden among men,"[81] the secret of impossible happiness, the promise of which is forbidden us by the violence of the material universe. The film's energy thus arises from the conspicuous nature of its anagogical structure, the clear, simple progression that proceeds by similitude or contrast from one figure to the next. Its elegance is born from what is not explicit in its underpinning (the familial horror), while it concentrates upon the linking and relating of its figures. To put it another way, far from those films that are content to illustrate an explicit situation with more or less original incidents, *Bad Lieutenant* works upon the slow translation of an affect of agony within the form of an image-story. This is why the film is significant: it considers the image not only as a plastic entity but above all as a spiritual exercise. Such a formal proposition largely surpasses the Christian anthropology in which it is anchored.

*The Addiction* uses exactly the same structure as *Ms .45*. The film's opening gives us a reality check: Kathy's discovery of historic horror as she views the slides of the Vietnam War. This intellectual shock is later transposed into a physical shock thanks to a caesura depicted by an extended moment of blackness and a lateral tracking shot—brilliantly comparing the passage between the real and its translation with a slide change on the screen. The film proposes, on the basis of this structure, several developments in relation to the analysis of images. Take, for example, the sequence covering Kathy's visit to an exhibition on the Nazi death camps and her experience of its affective consequences—an ensemble of three scenes physically linked by the same passage of the musical score. In scene 1, the photographic images are already present, huge, attached to transparent glass that covers the border between the museum and the street. Kathy moves from one display to the next in a dreamlike space that is simultaneously interior and exterior. This space opens out further due to the soundtrack, which juxtaposes and links a prayer, a Nazi speech, and Kathy's voiceover meditation; this soundtrack confronts past and present, cause and effect, historic catastrophe and the psychic attempts to understand it. These attempts prove to be of two orders, at antipodes to each other, and both set against the Nazi speech, on either side of it: the ritual prayer pacifies, while Kathy's meditation inflames.

Here we see—or rather, hear—exactly what Ferrara's enterprise consists of. Empathy with suffering does not pretend to console; reflection does not liquidate the traumatic event but, on the contrary, sharpens it and lets it vibrate. The exhibited images do not represent tiny gaps in the world; they *are* the world. Their photographic fixity reinforces this effect of presence *sub specie aeternitatis.* The traumatic image becomes a subject, and the creature who strolls about and receives it constitutes the object. In Nicholas St. John's original script, the walk is purely pedagogical, like the slide sequence. Kathy goes to the Holocaust Museum, her friend Jean takes notes, and both of them, overwhelmed and unable to bear the images, flee: "I can't look at this . . . I'm going."[82]

The film negotiates in a completely different way this reaction to what is intolerable. Kathy not only withstands the vision, she somatizes and propagates it. In scene 2 of the sequence, her terror transcribes itself immediately in vampiric terms: she leaves the exhibition and finds a bum asleep on the street. Using a syringe, she withdraws blood from his arm; the scene reworks the plastic characteristics of Jacques

Tourneur's *Cat People* (1942)—a palette of extreme deep blacks, and a cat shadow on a brick wall. In scene 3, Kathy goes home and injects herself with blood from the syringe. In flashes, we see a memory of Casanova, a home-movie image from Kathy's childhood, and a little girl coming towards us like Kim Phuc, the famous girl of Trang Bang running along a road, seared by napalm. Instead of turning away from such terrifying images, Kathy introjects them and then observes the extent to which they contaminate her innocent memories. Can a child, ignorant of evil, be considered innocent? Or was she already, without realizing it, this vampire who spreads suffering, an all-American kid profiting from the benefits of an imperialist civilization? Evil is literally an epidemic, ignorance constitutes its best vector, and reflection offers absolutely no protection—quite the contrary. *The Addiction* represents the cinematic version of a proposition concerning the Holocaust formulated by Primo Levi:

> [W]e felt that . . . now nothing could ever happen good and pure enough to rub out our past, and that the scars of the outrage would remain with us forever. . . . Because, and this is the awful privilege of our generation and of my people, no one better than us has ever been able to grasp the incurable nature of the offence, that spreads like a contagion. It is foolish to think that human justice can eradicate it. It is an inexhaustible fount of evil; it breaks the body and the spirit of the submerged, it stifles them and renders them abject; it returns as ignominy upon the oppressors, it perpetuates itself as hatred among the survivors, and swarms around in a thousand ways, against the very will of all, as a thirst for revenge, as a moral capitulation, as denial, as weariness, as renunciation.[83]

In *The Addiction* the range of image-apparitions is heteromorphous by nature (covering photography, cinema, visual exhibits, optical flashes, and so on) and wielded, on the formal level, with enormous freedom. But their relations of translation and (even more dynamically) contamination are extremely complex. The film invents a critical circulation of images—tearing those images away from the univocality of memory in an attempt to radically manifest their current, active nature (dramatized in terms of their harmfulness). In this economy the image no longer represents a prop but an agent, no longer a reflection but a cause—and it is impossible to be cured of it. On this level, the film has nothing to do with those overweening memorial spectacles that, in the United States, characterize the mainstream depiction of history's genocides, in the vein of *Holocaust* (1978), *Schindler's List* (1993), or the many Hollywood films about the Vietnam War that are devised to regain symbolically what was lost militarily. Rather, *The Addiction* belongs to the tradition of avant-garde films that work not to embalm the dead but to resuscitate images—by, for instance, inscribing pain and heartbreak onto the celluloid itself, as was practiced in relation to Vietnam by Carolee Schneemann in *Viet-Flakes* (1965), by Michèle Ray in her episode of *Far from Vietnam* (1967), and by Santiago Alvarez in *79 Springs* (1969). Such works are the opposite of those films that reproduce the external signs of a catastrophe, known as "historical re-creation" or, in Nietzsche's terms, antiquarian history. These artists invent films in the form of psychic processes, where it is not a matter of re-creating history (to an obscene point, in the case of the death camps) but looking for speculative logics by which we can grasp its horror. *The Addiction* transforms dread into a critical instrument for the analysis of history: "Only he who is oppressed by a present need, and who wants to throw off this burden at any cost, has need of critical history, that is to say, a history that judges and condemns."[84]

We have already seen how, in *Dangerous Game,* the different images (movie shots, video rushes, the film *en abyme*) partake of a structural confusion that emphasizes their nature as mental phenomena. There exists another instance of delirium in the film, an organic model of aesthetic construction: the delirium of the actor who separates herself from herself in a segment that can be called the "Privilege" scene. During the *Mother of Mirrors* shoot, Sarah is really raped by her acting partner because he is incapable of pretending—and because he wants to humiliate her. A little later, in a red-lit ambiance, Sarah in close-up, surrounded by pals and extras, improvises a theory of the actor's performance in which expressivity (as she says) is a "heavy flow of bullshit" requiring a Privilege tampon (the scene does not exist in the script). While the previous instances of delirium had to abandon their conventional stylistic attributes (chromatism, play on speeds, and so on), here these attributes reappear, transfigured in a sensual apotheosis. While the other forms of delirium are integrated within a structure via visual transference, here the delirium connects to nothing, neither time nor space nor fiction. The

"Privilege" scene offers the reverse side of the total delirium invented by Ferrara: it is a euphoric scene in which verbal delirium dissolves anxiety in laughter, an unexpected parenthesis of healing at the heart of a film where destruction sweeps away everything.

In a pre-edit of *Dangerous Game* there was another scene of delirium, experienced this time by Eddie. Totally wasted from drugs and alcohol, but even more from fatigue and absolute investment in his film, Eddie crosses his bedroom at the Château Marmont, goes out onto the balcony, and, moaning and crying in the manner of L. T., straddles the guardrail and almost throws himself into the void. He sees Madlyn in the midst of this delirium, overexposed and floating in light; she reproaches him for his cruel and irresponsible lifestyle. Why did this scene—which was surely Keitel's finest moment in the film—disappear from the final cut? Doubtless because his tears were too much like L. T.'s in *Bad Lieutenant,* not to mention Mr. White's in Quentin Tarantino's *Reservoir Dogs* (1992). But, more than that, because Ferrara's entire effort consists of not splitting up scenes of experience (the suicide attempt) and scenes of explanation (Madlyn's indictment); these scenes must be superimposed and confused.

Eddie's suicide attempt will reinvest itself differently in *The Blackout,* where Eddie divides into two characters, Matty the actor (somatized inebriation) and Mickey the video artist (controlled inebriation). And the cut Château Marmont scene also divides into two: Matty's methodical trance on his hotel balcony and his final watery suicide to the accompaniment of his deserted wife's tears. *The Blackout* reworks, completes, and intensifies all the figurative inventions hitherto explored by Ferrara by directly tackling inebriation as its subject.

## Toxic Truth, Experimental Situation

*Knowledge from Delirium* *The Blackout* does not tell a story; it explores a psychic complex. The film takes every conceivable risk. As a veritable essay on the image, it adopts the outward signs of the most ostentatious frivolity (commercial stars, iconography of luxury, a banal interpersonal intrigue). As a spiritual odyssey like Ferrara's other films, it abandons the glory of Christian imagery and places itself on a terrain not only profane but trivial. As an ode to affective fusion, it renounces the dark splendors of heroic virtue that preside over Ferrara's preceding work

Béatrice Dalle in *The Blackout*.

and charges its protagonist with an unforgivable crime. On its release, the misunderstanding by critics was total. But *The Blackout* succeeds in its bold attempt to conjugate the genre film with the theoretical essay, inventing an alliance that weakens neither the accessibility of the former nor the exigency of the latter.

The film is about the work of the imaginary upon the real. To place itself at the height of such a subject, the film probes an experimental situation: what happens when there is an "image missing"? The film dramatizes this question on two planes: Mickey's film *Nana Miami* lacks a shot, that of Nana being strangled; and Matty—who has been led to perform the strangulation scene despite himself—lacks a memory. Whether it is achieved or not, the image creates lack in every way; as soon as the filmmaker obtains his image, it instantly becomes a vertiginous absence for the actor. *The Blackout* dramatizes lack thanks to a precise pathology: the alcoholic amnesia (or alcohol amnestic) syndrome. Due no doubt to Christ Zois's input, the film effortlessly displays a thorough medical knowledge of delirium. However, even more crucially, it articulates this understanding in relation to several different clinical, philosophical, and ethnographic forms and traditions.

Alcoholic amnesia is clinically described as a "syndrome of prominent and lasting reduction of memory span, including striking loss of recent memory, disordered time appreciation, and confabulation," sometimes associated with alcoholic jealousy (or alcoholic paranoia), "chronic paranoid psychosis characterized by delusional jealousy." Matty does not want to have a child and forces Annie to have an abortion because he imagines that she has slept with other men—thus triggering the death-fiction. Clinically, alcoholic amnesia "occurs in alcoholics as the sequel to an acute alcohol psychosis (especially *delirium tremens*)."[85] In *The Blackout,* manifestations of delirium tremens suffuse not only the big crisis scenes but also the permanent behavior of the central couple, Matty and Mickey: anxiousness, psychomotor agitation, spatiotemporal disorientation, tactile, visual, and aural hallucinations, and language disorders. This last aspect is particularly revealing: the film's language disorders take several forms, notably inner voices (Matty hears an absent Annie) and the use of foreign languages (the French-American pidgin used by Matty when he searches for Annie on the telephone) but also verbal automatism, mainly from Mickey. This video prophet expresses himself in a coprolalic mode (in systematically basic terms) and in an onomatomanic mode (repeating certain words in an obsessive fashion). The cursing litany with which he exits the film—"Out! Out! Out! Out! Get outta here, fuckin' live with it, motherfucker!" compulsively continuing his rant after Matty has already left—brings all these symptoms to their zenith. In this respect, *The Blackout* fully exploits the verbal resources that are so emblematic of Dennis Hopper's acting.[86]

Erotomania, jealousy, and constant demands, which characterize morbid states of passion, define the behavior of both Mickey and Matty.[87] This affective ambiance, concentrated and intensified on the video artist's set, introduces the specific work of hallucination into the economy of psychic images. Two types of hallucinatory crises in fact exist. Visual agnosia erases all images and corresponds thus to the blackout, which can further be associated to a raptus, a "violent and sudden impulse which can lead a delirious subject to commit a grave act (homicide, suicide, mutilation)."[88] And hallucination, strictly speaking, also occurs in two regimes: positive hallucination, or the birth of an image by alteration of a referent; and negative hallucination, which consists of simultaneously acknowledging and repressing a traumatic perception. Such is the psychic adventure experienced by Matty: he knows that he has committed some act but is unsure exactly what, and this act ceaselessly returns in the form of nightmares of abortion and strangulation.

The emergence of a negative hallucination presupposes four stages. First, *affirmation of the pleasure-principle,* Matty's modus vivendi and Mickey's raison d'être: to ceaselessly enjoy oneself in a space entirely given over to such pleasure, a space that superimposes a work set, a spectacular party, and a permanent orgy. Second, *eruption of an unbearable stimulus* (the loss of Annie). Third, *suspension of perception* thanks to diverse means (in this case, alcohol, cocaine, crack, passing out). Fourth, *scotomization:* the simultaneity of knowledge and repression. Negative hallucination thus allows the intrapsychic representation of an object's absence while it remains present in external reality.[89]

It is clear that, on this level, delirium allows an extremely organic exploration of the process of representation. The delirious person is a performer who grandly "works" images. Contrary to common-sense opinion, delirium constitutes neither a flight from the real nor an arbitrary fantasy. It testifies to an intensive relationship with knowledge.

But it is the body that carries this testament. "A certainty ceaselessly unleashes in actions a massive bodily response, somnambulistic and unmediated."[90] We recognize, in this description of drug-addicted delirium, the figure of the vampire, like Peina and Kathy in *The Addiction*—creatures of the night and of knowledge—but also Frank in *King of New York* and L. T. in *Bad Lieutenant,* the characters of an always traumatic metamorphosis of knowledge within the body. Those who learn of or transmit the equivalence of truth with evil are the creatures of disillusion. The purest instance of this is Peina, the bearer of a cruel truth, and the most complex is Frank, to the extent that he maintains his mission despite disillusionment.

In the same way, Matty's recourse to alcoholic delirium is represented as an analytical relation to knowledge, an instrument with which to reach the truth. He plans out his trip to Miami because his euphoric reunion with alcohol will allow him to find an explanation for his torment. "Delirium is an attempt at self-healing, the reconstruction and restoration of a world lost through object-withdrawal."[91] Such a definition of delirium as the solution to a psychic conflict explains a remarkable oddity of the script: why, in his mental expedition, does Matty not bother to bring along his own provisions of alcohol and drugs? To be efficient, the hallucinogens and associated props (alcohol, cocaine, bedsheets) must be found at the same place as the birth of the torment; if they do not belong to the scene of the crime, they cannot constitute convincing tracks to truth. Because the shots of alcohol that Matty finds in his hotel mini-bar resemble medicine vials, the return to drinking does not represent so much a "falling off the wagon" as an attempt at healing. And finally, the very small (the booze shot) is transformed into the very big (the pitcher), without passing through the normality of the bottle—thereby following the major model of the plunge-into-dream, namely, *Alice's Adventures in Wonderland.*

So if delirium is an instrument, what purpose does it serve? It is not enough to say that the delirious person is in search of a lost or absent object; he unconsciously intends to reconstitute or repair an object that in fantasy he feels he destroyed or damaged by aggressively incorporating it. The delirious person's system represents a re-creation and a resurrection of the object.[92] *The Blackout* puts this dynamic of re-creation into narrative form in various ways: Matty makes images return; Mickey, the "remake" specialist, re-creates Annie 1 from Annie 2; the film makes a living Annie 1 return right in the middle of Matty's delirium; and it also makes Annie 2 and Matty—both dead—return in the final superimposition. Ultimately, the work of delirium stretches far beyond Matty and touches the film itself, which enters into a delirious process far more than its characters do.

There are two regimes of delirium: in acute or semi-acute forms, and in forms organized over a lengthy evolution. Matty incarnates the former regime, according to which "the subject, identified with the world, himself becomes a sort of swarming and unsettled scene, where the processes of introjection and projection succeed each other at a rapid rate."[93] The film organizes itself according to the latter regime, where delirium is no longer a crisis but a way of life. It functions on an alternating dynamic of engulfment and resurrection by means of visual and aural reprises and variations—in clinical terms, palinopsia. Delirium does not arise from alcohol or drugs (which are only accessories) but from the disorganization of functions of the self due to object-loss. On this level, the fantasies of abortion and murder are not meant as credible plot incidents but so many litanic realizations of a relation to the world as a relation of loss.

Certain more discreet traits enrich the trance dimension of delirium, considered within an ethnological perspective. Beginning with the Miami scene of unleashed hallucination, the deliberate, concerted aspect of this project resembles a rite of possession. There are two types of possession: exorcism (refused possession) and adorcism (cultivated, ritualized possession). Matty's case clearly belongs to the latter type. As an actor, he is the "certified" possessed, a vehicle for the transmission of images; and then he truly "becomes" his work when he transforms himself into a medium, a building site for images. His enchanted reunion with alcohol adopts the traditional characteristics of a possession ritual: music, dance, entering into a trance, transformation into a medium, manifestations of the possessing entity (Mickey) with whom the medium can establish an alliance and who can demand that the person in crisis become his servant (a radical mode of the director/actor relation). Thus possession transforms this superficial star (his superficiality is indicated by the tiny, infantile vehicle on which he leaves the airport and a magazine photo showing him in the company of the top stars of the moment) into an actor who rediscovers, in a profane mode, the nobility of his profession by returning to the ritual sources of his work.

*Figurative Logic: Forms of Illusion and Dementia* The Blackout methodically explores the difference between knowledge and acknowledgment. Matty knows that he has committed an error but has no idea what it is; he must convert this immediate intuition into objective knowledge. The film takes on the task of converting the (affective) crime into a (physical) murder. When Mickey visits his studio for the first time, an argument unfolds on one of the video screens between two assistants (Nancy Ferrara and Steve Bauer, the guy who earlier parodied the reunion kiss between husband and wife, a kiss visually transferred throughout the film via Bauer's miming of a hand-cranked "zoom-in" on this gesture). During the later scene in which Matty returns to the studio to search for his vanished wife, we see a similar quarrel only "live," experienced in the moment by Nancy Ferrara and another assistant. The scene goes on forever, just as the lack that joins the allegorical couple in the final image goes on forever. But that also signifies that no anteriority exists between the referent and copy, between the real and its recording. Does "the real" mean to live in the immediacy of things without being able to reflect on them (the blacked-out crime), or to know them without being able to admit them, thus losing the ability to live (the avowed murder, with suicide as its corollary)?

*The Blackout* responds clearly to this question: ordinary psychic experience organizes a permanent desynchronization between the event and its intellection. Ferrara's cinema reproduces the phantomatic latencies, echoes, remanences, transferences, confusions, and illusions (hallucinations, fantasies, and approximations) that disalign us from the real and yet are our own life. Following the Ferraran logic of ecstatic exacerbation, *The Blackout* describes the ordinary mode of affective experience as delirium, an ensemble of silhouettes, contours, and overlappings—what Edmund Husserl calls "phantoms."[94] Only by seizing this ensemble can we get at the real.

The film provides a rigorous inventory of delirium's clinical forms. It articulates three major modes of delirium: gap, fragmentation, and confusion.[95] The gap (where there should be something, there is nothing) is the explicit subject of *The Blackout,* and so it embodies the phenomenon in numerous forms: fades to black, the "shot missing" in Mickey's film, multiple cracks in the fiction, darkness of every kind, and a veritable parade of lacks (disappeared fœtus, vanished wife, absent mother, forgotten victim).

What is normal perception? Following Husserl, Ludwig Binswanger offers this definition: "Reality, generally, is only possible with the continuously prescribed presumption that experience will be pursued continuously in the same way."[96] What, in opposition to this, is delirium? It is fragmentation, the impossibility of assembling and synthesizing the various aspects of experience. This process proliferates in *The Blackout* in the form of the fragmented bodies and juxtaposed images filling Mickey's studio and in the scraps of recollection surfacing in Matty's memory. But the film especially cultivates confusion, in four modes: coalescence, superimposing two figures; misunderstanding, substituting one figure for another; projection, turning an internal image into an external event (such as when Annie 1 returns in the guise of Annie 2); and repetition, where everything is déjà vu, since delirium essentially consists of a blockage, a scratched-out image that places the world under the regime of cliché in such a way that (in Binswanger's terms) in the place of stable continuity, "there arises a simple recording."[97] In fact, Matty's discovery of the truth does not put an end to delirium but brings it to a peak: the horror experienced by the actor in front of the screen as he discovers his crime is followed by Mickey's hate-filled outburst, then Matty's impulsive suicide, and the production in the final image of the real as a generalized desertion. Reciprocally, the "recording" does not represent the opposite of delirium but its very essence: the recorded image arises from a demented desire, the video artist's morbid fantasy. Characters get to that point by taking three successive drugs (alcohol, cocaine, pills); they achieve this state only after the real has returned (Annie 1, who escapes all rules); and they die from looking reality in the face. Thus, chimerical coalescence (cinema) and pure recording (video) do not represent antithetical regimes of images but two sides of the same precise perception—in Ferraran terms, a perception that is delirious from desire.

Three forms of illusion correspond to the forms of dementia (confusion, fragmentation, and gap). The experience of defusing corresponds to confusion. This is the moment of the return of the real: Annie 1, with whom Matty tested the limits of the "given." The dark massiveness of Annie 1 (black sunglasses and clothes) evokes the real as a pure, opaque block. But she also brings phenomena down to their literal reality: "He looking for me?" she asks Mickey as Matty lies on the floor, dead drunk from alcohol and fatigue, declaring: "I'm not drinking." In fact, both interpretations are true: Matty drinks, but it is a work of anamnesis that allows him to re-find the image to which now, stupefyingly, Annie 1's return gives the lie. So Matty has not yet drank enough: he must continue disentangling the images.

The experience of inclusion corresponds to fragmentation. When Matty finds himself faced with the video images of the murder he has committed, he watches them on the same monitor on which he watched Annie 1 dance—so he is already situated within the image that he discovers. We observe a triple embedding: Matty in the image of love where he kisses Annie 1; Matty in the image of death where he watches himself kissing Annie 1 before strangling Annie 2; Matty moving his hand over the screen, as Godard does in *Scénario du film Passion* (1982). In all three cases, the film puts into play physical effects that are obtained by the most violent optical experiences. In this scene, he kneels before an image—just as he had knelt before his wife's empty bed—kisses it, suffers for it, and cannot bear it. Matty's gestures of sacred terror constitute one of the most beautiful homages ever rendered to the power of images.

Finally, trauma corresponds to the experience of gap. The re-found images of the crime are clearly unbearable because they are life itself, and, as Nietzsche said, "It is not doubt, it is *certainty* which makes one mad."[98] Delirium appears, once and for all, as an intensive relation to the truth, all the more irremediable and obsessive because this truth cannot be escaped.

*Virulent Attacks*  The experience of delirium allows the stretching of the exigency of infinity across all cinematic dimensions. It allows a surpassing of the two fundamental principles upon which orthonormal knowledge rests: identity and discrimination. According to the principle of identity, that which is, is. All "strange cinema" contests the validity of this assertion, by substitution (this mother is not a mother but an alien [*Body Snatchers*]), complementarity (this man is also another, younger man [*Lost Highway*]); and superimposition (this woman is and is not the same as some other woman [*The Blackout, Vertigo*]). *The Blackout* is not content to merely destabilize the principle of identity in narrative terms. It takes this disorder all the way to the shot level—for example, when Matty prepares to resume drinking, he turns his head towards the bar in his hotel room; instantly, a close-up shows his hand seizing a small bottle from the mini-bar, preceded by the reflection in the glass door of his approach; then the scene returns to him at the window from where, in fact, he has not yet moved. The close-up thus appears at once as a recollection (Matty remembers a conversation with Annie 1 in the same spot, and we hear the aural flashback of his words over the shot: "I told you about Mickey, right? The moment of 'ahh,' the moment of 'ahh' . . .")[99] and an anticipation, since he will reproduce the same gesture in a moment.

Then there is the huge noise this tiny bottle makes when it breaks, after Matty, having drank the contents, casually lets it fall to the floor—a disproportionate blast, as if suddenly the event involves a giant bottle. We could go on noting every detail of the film—every match, every sound, every reflection in glass all subtly participates in this principle of unalignment that tears phenomena away from themselves to the extent that things seem to flee, leaving only traces or empty outlines, allowing no "grip" for a consciousness that refuses to go into mourning but joyfully prepares to learn why it has lost all this.

The principle of discrimination also undergoes a virulent attack—an attack all the more systematic in that it works on both Matty and Mickey. According to the discrimination principle, which establishes paradigms on the basis of the identity principle, what is here cannot be elsewhere, what is inside cannot be outside, and so on. Matty wreaks havoc with discrimination by proceeding by subtraction, while Mickey proceeds by superimposition.

• *Undifferentiation of one and other.* Matty works through subtraction by resorting to disavowal: when he is shown a photo of himself, he responds: "That's not me, that's my brother"; when Annie forces him to listen to the insults he made to her over the telephone, he contends, "It ain't me"; when she tells him that she does not want her son to have a junkie father, he is astounded: "Who's a junkie?"

Inversely, Mickey works by multiplication: to remake *Nana,* he multiples the cameras, sets, and screens; to help Matty re-find Annie 1, he brings him jAsmiNe and dAphNe and conjures ANNie 2, so that all women relate (at least nominally) to his Nana, including by contagion the saintly susAN.

• *Undifferentiation of here and elsewhere.* Matty subtracts, which is the mode of transference: when he hallucinates Susan while on the phone, there is no longer any difference between New York and Miami, between here and over there, only a mental space working to annul and compress different places into each other. Inversely, Mickey has organized his apparatus precisely to confuse here and elsewhere but by multiplying one using the other: the erotic images, happening elsewhere, are permanently projected on-set so as to recruit new participants for the orgy shoot.

• *Undifferentiation of inside and outside.* In the sequence of his return to booze, Matty ends up collapsing, positioned at an angle to the room, window open onto nothingness, the curtains billowing in the wind, half inside and half outside, a space of pure, comatose vertigo. Another procedure, more discreet but even more destabilizing, occurs just before this vertigo. After Susan's departure, Matty climbs the stairs of his house, opens the door to enter, and then is back on the beach in Miami. The match-cut is almost Buñuelian: to leave, he need only open the door and enter his house, for the world is merely a vast interior space. The doubling of Matty's face in the beveled glass of his front door shows to what extent the purest of identity-tremors is produced on the very threshold of home. For Mickey, spaces (studio interior, beach exterior, room interior, balcony exterior) overlap in the sense that he always makes the same thing with the same bodies, simple copies of each other. To direct people means for him to erotically possess, supplicate, and kill them (as per the sadistic imagery on every video monitor) to the extent that, under his direction, the most violent superimposition is equally the most literal. Drunk Matty in the hotel confuses his bed with an editing bench because he has already transformed, also when drunk, the editing bench into a bed on which he kissed and then strangled Annie 2. This can be considered as a vivid eroticization of editing analogous to what *The Driller Killer* does for painting.

The work of undifferentiation can be detailed in the same way with regard to public/private or before/after, and in every case the logic is the same: Matty annuls, and Mickey multiplies. In one sense they correspond to the concrete dual existence of film celluloid: the black interstice that guarantees the interval between two frames (Matty) and the mental overlapping between those two frames that guarantees the illusion of movement (Mickey). Does this mean that cinema itself is a delirious apparatus? Doubtless—after all, it is the greatest hypnosis machine ever institutionalized. But here the analogy between the two protagonists corresponds more broadly to two psychic procedures: Mickey interlinks, while Matty seeks to unlink.

Delirium in *The Blackout* evokes neither fantasy nor disintegration. It ties together the excessively immediate, numerous, and meaningful relations between images, thus allowing the multiplication of forms of linkage between phenomena. It also allows the description of aspects of bridging and projection in each phenomenon, hence showing how phenomena are not entities but elaborations. When Matty meets Annie 2 he hears Annie 1's voice and attributes his own story to her—he never truly sees her, content only to look, in her, for the traces of what he has lost. This pretty waitress represents the way in which one never truly sees the Other, woven from self-projections: Annie 2 is the emblem of post-psychoanalytic realism. Delirium ends up seeming a model of construction and inventiveness, thanks to which we see the forms of montage function at their optimum level.

But why should delirium be morbid? Why is disappearance its principal material, immediately put into narrative form as abortion, abandonment, neglect, betrayal, murder, and suicide? As far back as it is possible to go, further even than the abandonment complex, the realm of affect is cemented by (as Binswanger calls it) the Terrible, which is "at the foundation of all experience, of what unites all specific experiences, and what functions even for them as the *obligatory connection.*"[100] This Terrible starts seeping out once psychic defenses tremble. It introduces itself into the slightest interstice and, meeting no resistance, sweeps through the entire construction—just as, in the middle of *The Blackout*, a black screen breaks the fiction in two, or, at the end, the dark ocean swallows up Matty's body. And yet the film traces, with this rather alarming material, an almost therapeutic trajectory. It takes us from a passive death (abortion, which is the erasure of someone who never even existed, registered as an indignity) to an active death (suicide, a logical and moral act), to conclude with the final resonant superimposition of love.

Like other great films, including Jean Eustache's *Photos d'Alix* (1981), *The Blackout* entirely reinterprets the cinematic apparatus as a psychic apparatus. But the central stake proves to be less reflexive than existential: to intensify a human experience by following every repercussion and echo provoked by a simple affect—such as the kiss given to a woman by a man who is not really completely "there" in his gesture—and following these traces all the way to their end, if necessary even beyond death. In the absolute exigency of ethical investigation to which it testifies, we could say that the work of this reputedly monstrous, addicted, muddled filmmaker is capable of conserving something of what Durkheim called the "moral patrimony" of humanity.[101]

## Cinema and Symbolic Reparation

*Untimely Remains*  Take a war, such as the first Iraq war of 1991. What does a narrative filmmaker do with it? Jean-Marie Straub and Danièle Huillet, who in that period were staging Sophocles's *Antigone* at the Berlin Schaubühne, decided to dedicate their final performance of the play "to the thousands of Iraqis buried without graves (no name or even number) by the American bulldozers."[102] Ferrara made *Body Snatchers* in 1993, a film populated with the dead who go unburied since they instantly crumble into dust, like bodies disintegrated by bombs. In the early morning this human dust is thrown into garbage trucks that collect the debris of consumer society. The dead do not die; they disappear, secreted from the image in the same way that those sacrificed to the Third World economy are secreted from the collective American imaginary. Hollywood cinema has rarely shown with such violence that to maintain its brutal regime, the American Way of Life—this terrifying economic Moloch—exacts, every morning, a toll of human lives viewed as anonymous and of no value.

In this film of ashes and slag—in which, it is worth remembering, the young soldier Tim (Billy Wirth) has returned from the Gulf War where he admits having killed people—there appears a particularly strange corpse. This corpse completely contravenes the economy of similitude instituted by the principle of snatching (replacement of same by same). It is the father's corpse, appearing from under the marital bed, which hardly resembles its original. While Steve is a young, almost boyish man, his double looks old, with white, ragged hair, all wrinkled and sticky. With its conspicuous, jutting teeth, this face resembles a skull; with its emphasized muscles and tendons, his body becomes a decomposing corpse, not a gestating fœtus, as is the case for Marti's double, which is in the process of being born at the same time. I have argued elsewhere how, via this bizarre figure of the born-dead old person, Marti dreams of aborting her father, thus lodging herself at the heart of the father/daughter incest delirium that organizes the film's figurative logic.[103] But the question remains: Why do these untimely remains indeed ultimately resemble someone whom every cinephile immediately recognizes, namely, Abel Ferrara himself?

Naturally, we can attribute this figurative surprise to a "signature effect," a sort of macabre Hitchcockian touch. But we can also see here a sign that *Body Snatchers* displaces the question of the corpse, refuting its function as the organic, natural model for the image, whether in André Bazin's Egyptian version (the "mummy complex" of "embalming the dead") or Blanchot's modern version ("cadaverous resemblance").[104] This contravening corpse disturbs the economy of resemblance: evil reflections that effect a spiriting-away. His individuated, wizened flesh suddenly imposes a true effect of presence, as incongruous as it is unassimilable within the fiction. His presence is even more striking because his face is turned towards us and because his viscous hand seizes Marti's ankle—an act of prehension that is completely transgressive in relation to the self-matting logic of snatching. The iconography evoked by this corpse in mid-putrefaction returns us to other filthy, panting bodies, occupied with similar masquerades of death: the bodies of the Viennese Actionists such as Hermann Nitsch and Günter Brus, exorcising Nazi crimes; or those of Japanese performers, the Gutaï and Yomini Independent groups, refusing to forget Japanese fascism. More profoundly, such artistic initiatives constitute the modern, polemical version of an ancient practice born in Italy during the thirteenth century, the traces of which can be found in Andrea del Sarto or Lorenzetti: *infamante* painting, which consists of representing, on the wall of some public edifice, the physical result of torture inflicted upon a guilty person.[105]

To transform oneself into a corpse, a martyr, or something formless and repellent is not a matter of expiating a collective evil but recalling its existence. These simulated remains do not aim to be hidden bodies (that would amount to masking them all over again) but instead manifest as best they can the moral infection that propagates itself beginning with the moment of the Nazi death camps. When Kathy in *The Addiction*, after leaving the Holocaust museum, injects herself with blood drawn by syringe from the sleeping body of a tramp, it is impossible not to recall the actions of the Czech artist Peter Stembera after the Prague Spring, drawing his own blood and then reinjecting it, mixed with urine, hair, and fingernail clippings, in front of an altar.[106] Perhaps one might find an anticipatory fulfillment of Ferrara's work in the act of Patrick Geoffrois, the protagonist of Michel Bulteau's film about heroin, *Main Line* (1971): at one screening, Geoffrois drew his own blood with a syringe and sprayed it onto the cinema screen where the film was then projected.

*Fusional Compositions*  From this self-portrait of the filmmaker as a corpse, one can gauge the extent to which Ferrara's work innovates in the area of figurative economy, inventing at once a logic and the prime necessity for disturbing that logic. But is this funereal cinema of crime and torment entirely apocalyptic and sacrificial?

The exact opposite claim could be argued. Ferrara's whole effort is devoted to observing the nature, role, and workings of images within the individual psyche and the collective imaginary. There are plastic images, desirable images for which everyone must be killed (Reno's painting in *The Driller Killer*), images to be revivified all the way to giving them mortal form (*The Addiction*), and shots to make or re-make so that they destroy their protagonists (*Dangerous Game, The Blackout*). There are also psychic images, present and absent, that confront us with what is unwatchable (within vision) and unavowable (within consciousness): *The Driller Killer*'s tramps, Eddie's constitutive cruelty in *Dangerous Game*, the suffering everywhere. To the extent that Ferrara's cinema confers, in an argued-out and passionate way, a crucial importance to images, it is clearly an affirmative enterprise.

From the story angle—whatever the type of story—images always find themselves dramatized in terms of obsession, destructive somatization, and death. But after observing the architecture of these films, it becomes clear that their compositional work elaborates contrary values. Sébastien Clerget has shown how *The Funeral*—a fable of paranoid avidity and the destruction of all by all—is elaborated according to a fusional structure that guarantees a community of consciousnesses. Thanks to a "surplus" shot inscribed within a complex organization of successive flashbacks and repetitions—the shot of Chez passing in a car past the cinema where Johnny gets shot down—"Chez takes over the flashback began by Johnny—the recollection of one becoming the recollection of the other."[107] We have seen how *The Blackout* translates a single gesture—an ordinary embrace—across the entire length of its trajectory to ultimately reach its devout, sacred version. *New Rose Hotel* is the director's most radical film in this regard.

*The Blackout* poses the question, What is a lacking image? *New Rose Hotel* proceeds to a critical extension of incomparable audacity, since it is no longer an image (the murder image) that is lacking but *all* images. And they are truly lacking in that they cannot be recuperated on any other level, whether psychic or plastic. All the key scenes are missing: the meeting of Sandii and Hiroshi, her seduction of him, the betrayal. All action scenes are missing, treated at best as pure sketches: the abduction of Hiroshi to Hosaka headquarters, the theft of the "genetic card," Fox chased by Maas's henchmen (all that remains is an unbelievable suicide after an absent chase), the slaughter in the Marrakech laboratory. All secondary scenes are missing: Hiroshi's renunciation of his wife, scenes of "married life" between Sandii and Hiroshi, the internecine struggles within the Hosaka zaibatsu (without which one can scarcely comprehend events), the explanatory scene between X and the zaibatsu (shot but not included, according to Zois), the scene of Sandii's resale of the "DNA synthesizer" to Maas (without which one cannot grasp that she is a double agent). Characters are missing: the Hosaka rival gang and Maas are virtually unrepresented, and protagonists suddenly vanish (Hiroshi's wife, then Sandii). Certain essential characters appear only as images on screens (Hiroshi and his wife) or as unidentifiable silhouettes (Hosaka's second gang). All characters, in the manner of the limping Fox, prove to be amputated in one way or another: amputated of a past, a history, a name, or an identity, whether an identity they do not possess (X) or one they possess too much, thus remaining nonsynthesizable (Sandii).

The film lacks a resolution on three levels. The first is narrative defection: the final event remains in suspense (X waiting for death, hiding in the little Japanese hotel room—but this is a traditional suspended ending). The second defection is speculative: the symbolic ending remains enigmatic (Sandii's Mona Lisa smile, which at this level refers to the emblematic western enigma, often associated with the smile of maternity). The third defection is demonstrative: the character of Sandii does not make any sense, whereas in William Gibson's 1982 short story on which the film is based, she explicitly incarnates a critique of dematerialization within the globalized economy: "And the funny thing, Sandii, is how sometimes you just don't seem real to me. Fox once said you were ectoplasm, a ghost called up by the extremes of economics. Ghost of the new century, congealing on a thousand beds in the world's Hyatts, the world's Hiltons."[108]

More troubling still, the film lacks two principal questions. A driving narrative question: What can Hiroshi do with his self-styled "hot proteins"? And a practical question: Where do the images that permanently pop up in the film come from? The world of *New Rose Hotel* is organized upon a perpetual projection of images, and we understand less and less, as the film proceeds, where these images come from and where they are projected. For example, images of the devastation of the Marrakech laboratory and of the global spread of the Plague appear already edited, but by whom? The images of Hiroshi's sex life, which is archive footage, can conceivably already have been edited, but we are unable to ascertain where, in space, they are projected. Inversely, when we do witness the production of a shot (Fox and X filming the red geisha orgy), we do not see the result.

The absent, opaque, even impossible nature of the source of these images—symptomatic of a problem of origins—creates several consequences. The images are dematerialized: they are unable to be founded in a practice (in contrast to Mickey's studio in *The Blackout,* or Reno's mind in *The Driller Killer*). Otherwise, we must formulate a hypothesis that no element of *New Rose Hotel* backs up—namely, that there exists a sort of world bank of post-Mabusian images. The images are de-realized: nothing can semantically fix them (in contrast to Matty's fantasies). For example, the film's subtle prologue, describing the kidnapping attempt on Hiroshi, could be a recollection by X, a video recording by Maas, a mental hypothesis formulated by X, or an objective report on the event addressed by X to Fox. Symmetrically, the hallucinated epilogue of the film, which forms a diptych with the epilogue of *The Blackout* (a naked man and woman, close enough to touch each other, one the victim of the other, on a mental stage), clearly belongs to X's reminiscences. But it could not possibly derive from his point of view, which doubles the effect of enigma—ranging from what it signifies (Sandii's smile) to its provenance and its very status. In *New Rose Hotel*'s economy, the source and the support of the images disappear; they exist only in their circulation.

So why this ensemble of lacks, transferences, and aporias? Why this world in pieces, fragments, reflections? Why deprive every phenomenon of its cause? Perhaps because the stake of *New Rose Hotel* concerns the status of woman—the film constitutes, in this respect, the most desperate homage to woman ever made. A question tacitly governs the film's world: at the moment when life is on the verge of becoming pure genetic manipulation, what becomes of the classical status of woman as life's origin? (This classical status itself is already partly usurped and highly ambiguous—but that is another question, dealt with in *Body Snatchers*.) *New Rose Hotel*, which treats Sandii as at once manipulated (marionette, actress) and manipulatrix (double agent, free electron, enigma, femme fatale), stages a reversal: everything disappears, provided that the woman conserves her prerogatives and her powers, and also provided that she remain the origin of all things (biological life, actions, fantasies), even if, in the process, this source must be conceived as bearing evil intent.

The film elaborates a system of general denial on an anthropological scale: I know very well that woman is no longer the sole origin of life, but I maintain her as she is, and the proof is that she can destroy everything. After Peina and Kathy, Sandii represents a new embodiment of the Pandora myth (prefigured in a minor way by the Louise Brooks–style haircut of Madame Rosa [Annabella Sciorra]), with a computer disc instead of a box as her emblem (the ancient Pandora carried an urn until the sixteenth century).[109]

The film certainly studies a psychic complex, but not the one that its fable promises. Reduced to its generic iconography, the film's trajectory would seem to lead us from illusion (puppet Sandii) to disillusion (femme-fatale Sandii). In reality, the path is the opposite. The film's first half lays bare the elaboration of a trap (Sandii's casting and rehearsals—the scam itself not shown), while the latter half (which loops the same images slightly thrown out of alignment and revised) works to credit and reinforce a fantasy: Sandii is indeed the sole cause of all evil, she can do anything and be everywhere, there can be no other origin for actions and events (her disappearance in the labyrinth of the zaibatsu and its obscure quarrels). Each phenomenon must be severed from its cause to be able to relate everything *en bloc* to a sole origin, the accommodating Sandii. Therefore, the pertinent structural couple in *New Rose Hotel* is not Sandii and X—the fantasy and the mind that produced it. The true pair is Hiroshi and Sandii—the combination of a man who only exists in images and can only give birth to images and clones and a woman who holds the secrets of real biological life, since she holds power over life and death. Hiroshi's knowledge is limited to mathematical formulae; only Sandii has the capacity to use them.

*New Rose Hotel* directly tackles an anthropological torment and, to transform it into a poem of *amour fou,* disintegrates the fiction in such a way that the process of denial appears naked. With its cyberpunk iconography, the film evokes the archaic ritual of conjuration. Ferrara thus transforms a film into a profane prayer, tearing the cinema away from its condition of reflection to commit an act, to fashion a gesture of exorcism and adjuration.

*The Great Architectonic Art*  At the end of the 1970s, Ferrara wanted to adapt one of the most brilliantly composed books in the history of modern literature, *The Master and Margarita*, written and rewritten by Mikhail Bulgakov between 1929 and 1940.[110] This is a novel that terminates its narrative in the middle, just like *New Rose Hotel* with its narrative "fold"; surreptitiously changes its narrator, like *The Funeral;* interweaves its stylistics and mirrors its motifs, like *Dangerous Game;* modernizes the Christian Passion, like *Bad Lieutenant, The Addiction,* and *Love on the A Train;* and directs its formal events towards a beyond-writing, like the end of *The Blackout.*

The trace of Bulgakov's architectonic art once again emerges in the initial script for Ferrara's *Mary,* notably because both are organized according to a parallel montage with three terms. *The Master and Margarita*—"the Devil's novel," as Bulgakov called it—traces a parallel polemic involving contemporary Russia and the story of Pontius Pilate.

In *Mary,* the parallel montage (a basic form of Ferraran architecture, particularly by way of the figurative aspects I have stressed, visual transfer and translation) passes between contemporary New York and the story of Mary Magdalene. The cinema appears ever more clearly here as a great apparatus of symbolic reparation. Beginning from a traumatic television image that has passed into universal iconography—a small Palestinian child dying in its father's arms under the guns of the Israeli army—the script of *Mary* experiments with every possible fantasy of reparation: correction of the matrix-image (a nurse, Mary, is discovered off-screen); analytical exegesis (to understand what is truly in this image); transposition (Palestine placed in parallel with the Bronx); and the recreation, multiplication, and transferences, the parallel deliveries of a film and a child.

The cinema of the negative can ultimately aspire to compassion, as long as we understand compassion as having nothing to do with false pacification or aspiring to any fallacious reconciliation. This compassion looks evil in the face and resolves nothing; it cultivates and propagates its rage in the way that rage infects an organism—or as a deathly dream still haunts the mind upon waking.

### Notes

The epigraph is from Georges Bataille, "Esquisse 2—Dossier de Lascaux," *Œuvres Complètes,* vol. 9 (Paris: Gallimard, 1979), 321.

1. Quoted in Nick Johnstone, *Abel Ferrara: The King of New York* (London: Omnibus Press, 1999), 5.

2. Brad Stevens, *Abel Ferrara: The Moral Vision* (London: FAB Press, 2004), 10.

3. Adrian Martin, "Neurosis Hotel: An Introduction to Abel Ferrara," Program, *Twelfth Brisbane International Film Festival* (July 2003), 84.

4. Ferrara interviewed by Alain Garel and François Guérif, "American Boy," *La Revue du cinéma* 436 (March 1988): 51.

5. See Samuel Blumenfeld, "Recherche Carlos désespérément" (Desperately seeking Carlos), *Les Inrockuptibles* 52 (10–16 April 1996): 15–19. See also, in the same register, Claire Legendre's novel *Making Of* (Paris: Éditions Hors Commerce, 1998), and Elizabeth Herrgott, *Abel Ferrara* (Paris: Kfilms editions, 1999).

6. In the documentary-portrait by Rafi Pitts, *Not Guilty: Abel Ferrara* (2003), included in the French DVD of *Bad Lieutenant* (Wild Side, 2004).

7. Abel Ferrara and Scott Pardo, *Mary*, draft, October 2000, 64 (privately accessed).

8. Ferrara on the set of "The Club," Paris Première television, November 1996.

9. Garel and Guérif, "American Boy."

10. See Giona A. Nazzaro, ed., *Abel Ferrara: La tragedia oltre il noir* (Abel Ferrara: Tragedy beyond noir) (Rome: Stefano Sorbini Editore, 1997); Pietro Baj, ed., *Abel Ferrara* (Rome: Dino Audino Editore, 1997); Silvio Danese, *Abel Ferrara: L'anarchico e il cattolico* (Abel Ferrara: The anarchist and the Catholic) (Genova: Le Mani, 1998); and Alberto Pezzotta, *Ferrara* (Milan: Il Castoro, 1998).

11. Gavin Smith, "Moon in the Gutter," *Film Comment* 26.4 (July–August 1990): 40–46; Kent Jones, "Abel Ferrara—The Man: Who Cares?" *Lingo* 4 (1995): 30–40.

12. Quoted in Olivier French and John Strausbaugh, "*Bad Lieutenant's* Director Still Struggles to Find Screens," *New York Press* 15.27 (July 2002): 28.

13. Jonathan Rosenbaum, *Movies as Politics* (Berkeley: University of California Press, 1997), 96.

14. Gilbert Colon, "The Mark of Abel on a Classic: An Interview with Abel Ferrara," in *"They're Here" . . . Invasion of the Body Snatchers: A Tribute*, ed. Kevin McCarthy and Ed Gorman (New York: Berkley Boulevard Books, 1999), 154.

15. Walter Benjamin, "Central Park," in *Selected Writings*, vol. 4, trans. Rodney Livingstone, Edmund Jephcott, and Howard Eiland (Cambridge, Mass.: Harvard University Press, 2003), 183.

16. Zoë Lund, "The Ship with Eight Sails (and Fifty Black Cannons)," *New York Waste*, January 2001, available online in the *Rouge* archive, www.rouge.com.au/stars/02.html.

17. Colon, "Mark of Abel on a Classic," 153.

18. See Michael Baxandall, *Painting and Experience in Fifteenth-Century Italy* (Oxford: Oxford University Press, 1988), 82.

19. Maurice Blanchot, *The Unavowable Community*, trans. Pierre Joris (New York: Station Hill Press, 1988), 18.

20. Georges Bataille, *Literature and Evil*, trans. Alastair Hamilton (New York: Marion Boyars, 1985), viii.

21. Theodor Adorno, *Minima Moralia: Reflections from Damaged Life*, trans. Edmund Jephcott (London: Verso, 1978), 37–38.

22. Emile Durkheim, *On Morality and Society: Selected Writings*, trans. Mark Traugott (Chicago: University of Chicago Press, 1975), 48.

23. Walter Benjamin, "Critique of Violence," in *Selected Writings*, vol. 1, ed. Michael W. Jennings, trans. Edmund Jephcott (Cambridge, Mass.: Harvard University Press, 1999), 251.

24. Siegfried Kracauer, *Le roman policier: Un traité philosophique* (The crime

novel: A philosophical treatise), trans. Geneviève Rochlitz and Rainer Rochlitz (Paris: Payot, 2001), 42.

25. Alexis Philonenko, "Ethique et guerre dans la philosophie de Hegel" (Ethics and war in Hegel's philosophy), in *Essais sur la philosophie de la guerre* (Essays on the philosophy of war) (Paris: Vrin, 1976), 63–64. All subsequent citations from this volume appear parenthetically in the text.

26. Immanuel Kant, *Groundwork of the Metaphysics of Morals*, trans. Mary J. Gregor (Cambridge: Cambridge University Press, 1997), 31.

27. G. W. F. Hegel, *Philosophy of Right*, trans. T. M. Knox (London: Oxford University Press, 1967), 92–93.

28. Ibid., 93.

29. Bataille, *Literature and Evil*, 21.

30. G. W. F. Hegel, *Science of Logic*, trans. A. V. Miller (London: George Allen and Unwin, 1969), 82–83.

31. Bataille, *Literature and Evil*, 120.

32. Georges Bataille, *Inner Experience*, trans. Leslie Anne Boldt (Albany: State University of New York Press, 1988), 43.

33. Ibid., 80.

34. Jean Hyppolite, *Genesis and Structure of Hegel's Phenomenology of Spirit*, trans. Samuel Cherniak and John Heckman (Evanston, Ill.: Northwestern University Press, 2000), 153–54.

35. Zoë Lund, "The Vampire Speech," *Zoë (Tamerlis) Lund*, http://www.lundissimo.info/Zoe/docs/VampireSpeech.html. Lund's own transcription and layout of the text are followed here.

36. Hegel quoted in Hyppolite, *Genesis and Structure*, 151.

37. Ibid., 150.

38. Bataille, *Inner Experience*, 35.

39. Hegel, *Philosophy of Right*, 94.

40. Ibid., 102.

41. See David Pellecuer, Taxi Driver: *Image, Emotion, Affect* (Paris: Mémoire de Maîtrise, Paris I, 1998).

42. For a more detailed analysis of the character of Frank White, see Sébastien Clerget and Nicole Brenez, "White Shadow," *Admiranda* 11.12 (1996): 21–30; and Nicole Brenez, "Frankly White," in *De la figure en général at du corps en particulier: L'invention figurative au cinéma* (On the figure in general and the body in particular: Figurative invention in cinema) (Brussels: De Boeck, 1998), 225–38.

43. Rainer Werner Fassbinder, "'The Kind of Rage I Feel': A Conversation with Joachim von Mengershausen about *Love Is Colder Than Death*," in *The Anarchy of the Imagination: Interviews, Essays, Notes*, trans. Krishna Winston (Baltimore: Johns Hopkins University Press, 1992), 3.

44. Nicole Brenez and Agathe Dreyfus, "Entretien avec Zoë Lund," *Admiranda* 11.12 (1996): 244.

45. All of these appear in Nicole Brenez, ed., *Edouard de Laurot: Collected Writings* (Melbourne: Rouge Press, forthcoming). All subsequent quotations from this edition appear parenthetically in the text.

46. Fernando Solanas and Octavio Getino, "Towards a Third Cinema," in *Twenty-Five Years of the New Latin-American Cinema*, ed. Michael Chanan (London: British Film Institute/Channel 4, 1989), 17–28.

47. Pier Paolo Pasolini, *Saint Paul*, trans. Giovanni Joppolo (Paris: Flammarion, 1980).

48. Nicholas St. John, *The First Forty-Eight Hours of John Temple's Eternity (The Funeral)*, original screenplay, 24 (privately accessed).

49. Franchise Pictures, press release, *Abel Ferrara: Internet Library*, www.miscellanea.de/film/Abel_Ferrara/news.htm.

50. G. W. F. Hegel, *Phenomenology of Spirit*, trans. A. V. Miller (Oxford: Oxford University Press, 1977), 27. Lund's unfinished trilogy has not been published; the author privately accessed the manuscript.

51. Antonio Gramsci, "Politics as an Autonomous Science," in *Selections from the Prison Notebooks*, ed. and trans. Quintin Hoare and Geoffrey Nowell-Smith (New York: International Publishers, 1971), 140.

52. Theodor Adorno and Walter Benjamin, *The Complete Correspondence, 1928–1940*, trans. Nicholas Walker (Cambridge, Mass.: Harvard University Press, 1999), 131.

53. Thomas Hobbes, "Of the Natural Condition of Mankind as Concerning Their Felicity, and Misery," in *Leviathan* (Oxford: Oxford University Press, 1998), 83.

54. St. John, *First Forty-Eight Hours*, 26.

55. Nicholas St. John, *Snake Eyes*, draft, 18 November 1992, 68 (privately accessed).

56. Walter Benjamin, "Capitalism as Religion," in *Selected Writings*, vol. 1, trans. Rodney Livingstone (Cambridge, Mass.: Harvard University Press, 1999), 288–89.

57. Bataille, *Inner Experience*, 42.

58. Stevens, *Abel Ferrara*, 117.

59. Hegel, *Phenomenology of Spirit*, 65.

60. Marc Voinchet, "Des ombres argentées" (Silvery shadows), interview with Abel Ferrara, *Entrelacs* 2 (October 1994): 105.

61. Hesiod and Theognis, *Theogony, Works and Days and Elegies* (Harmondsworth, U.K.: Penguin, 1973), 23–57.

62. For further discussion of the principle of snatching, see Nicole Brenez, "Come into My Sleep," *Rouge* 6 (May 2005), www.rouge.com.au/rougerouge/sleep.html.

63. John Milton, *Paradise Lost* (London: Penguin, 2003), 6 (book 1, l.124).

64. Bataille, *Literature and Evil*, 85–86.

65. Milton, *Paradise Lost*, 65 (book 3, l.496).

66. Edgar Allan Poe, "The Fall of the House of Usher," in *Tales of Mystery and Imagination* (Hertfordshire, U.K.: Wordsworth, 2000), 156.

67. Bataille, *Literature and Evil*, 83.

68. Milton, *Paradise Lost*, 216 (book 9, ll.1187–89).

69. Emma Goldman, "The Psychology of Political Violence," in *Anarchism and Other Essays* (New York: Dover, 1969), 80.

70. Walter Benjamin, "The Paris of the Second Empire in Baudelaire," in *Selected Writings*, vol. 4, trans. Harry Zohn (Cambridge, Mass.: Harvard University Press, 2003), 8.

71. See Gianfranco Sanguinetti, *On Terrorism and the State*, trans. Lucy Forsyth and Michel Prigent (London: Chronos, 1982).

72. Marla Hanson, Christ Zois, and Abel Ferrara, *The Blackout*, revised script, 9 July 1996, 37 (privately accessed).

73. Zoë Lund, *Bad Lieutenant*, final revised script, 3 October 1991, 59 (avaliable at the *Internet Movie Script Database*, www.imsdb.com/scripts/Bad-Lieutenant.html).

74. St. Augustine of Hippo, *Confessions*, trans. R. S. Pine-Coffin (London: Penguin, 1961), 62.

75. Lund, *Bad Lieutenant*, 26.

76. Sébastien Clerget, "Hérédité du crime" (Heredity of crime), *Simulacres* 7 (November 2002): 64.

77. Christ L. Zois and Margaret Scarpa, *Short-Term Therapy Techniques* (New York: Jason Aronson, 1997), 34.

78. Hegel, *Phenomenology of Spirit*, 239.

79. For a literary remake of this sequence, see Bret Easton Ellis, *American Psycho* (New York: Vintage, 1991), 126–32.

80. St. Augustine of Hippo, *The Trinity*, book 13, sec. 26 (Washington, D.C.: Catholic University of America Press, 1963), 408.

81. Kracauer, *Le roman policier*, 53.

82. Nicholas St. John, *The Addiction*, draft, July 1991, 16 (privately accessed).

83. Primo Levi, *If This Is a Man and the Truce*, trans. Stuart Woolf (London: Abacus, 1995), 188–89.

84. Friedrich Nietzsche, *Untimely Meditations*, ed. Daniel Breazeale, trans. R. J. Hollingdale (Cambridge: Cambridge University Press, 2001), 72.

85. Clinical definitions from *Thérapeutique et Informations*, "Glossary of Mental Disorders," http://thera.info/icd9–cm/icd9–cm-glossary-mental-diseases.pdf.

86. See Adrian Martin, "The Misleading Man: Dennis Hopper," in *Stars in Our Eyes: The Star Phenomenon in the Contemporary Era*, ed. Angela Ndalianis and Charlotte Henry (Westport, Conn.: Praeger, 2002), 2–19.

87. See Daniel Lagache, "Passions et psychoses passionnelles" (Passions and passionate psychoses), in *Les hallucinations verbales et travaux cliniques* (Verbal hallucinations and clinical works), vol. 1: 1932–46 (Paris: PUF, 1977), 136–54.

88. Julien-Daniel Guelfi, *DSM-III: Manuel diagnostique et statistique des troubles mentaux* (manual diagnostic and statistics of the mental disorders) (Paris: Masson, 1986), 186.

89. See André Green, "Le travail du négatif et l'hallucinatoire (l'hallucination negative)" (Work of the negative and the hallucinatory [negative hallucination]), in *Le travail du négatif* (Manual diagnostic and statistics of the mental disorders) (Paris: Minuit, 1993), 217–87.

90. Sylvie Le Poulichet, "Toxicomanies" (Drug-related manias), in *L'Apport freudien* (Paris: Bordas, 1993), 448.

91. S. Nacht and P. C. Racamier, "La théorie psychanalytique du délire" (The psychoanalytic theory of delirium), *Revue française de Psychanalyse* 22.4–5 (1958): 439.

92. Ibid., 439.

93. Ibid., 497.

94. Maurice Merleau-Ponty, *Husserl at the Limits of Phenomenology* (Evanston, Ill.: Northwestern University Press, 2002), 132–54.

95. Ludwig Binswanger, *Délire: Contribution à son étude phénoménologique et daseinalytique* (Delirium: A contribution to its phenomenological and deseinalytic study) (Paris: Jérôme Million, 1993).

96. Binswanger's definition was first elaborated in his *Mélancholie et manie: Études phénoménologiques* (Melancholia and mania: Phenomenological studies). It is quoted in *Délire*, 48.

97. Ibid., 91.

98. Nietzsche, *Ecce Homo*, trans. R. J. Hollingdale (London: Penguin, 1992), 29.

99. See Dennis Hopper and Henry T. Hopkins, "The Seductive Sixties," in *Dennis Hopper: A System of Moments*, ed. Peter Noever (Ostfildern-Ruit: Hatje Cantz, 2001), 35.

100. Binswanger, *Délire*, 29.

101. Emile Durkheim, *On Morality and Society*, 56.

102. François Albera, "Avant-Propos," in Sophocles, Friedrich Hölderlin, Bertolt Brecht, Jean-Marie Straub, Danièle Huillet, and Bernd Alois Zimmermann, *Autour d'Antigone* (Lausanne: Université de Lausanne, 1993), 7.

103. Brenez, "Come into My Sleep."

104. André Bazin, "The Ontology of the Photographic Image," in *What Is Cinema?* vol. 1 (Berkeley: University of California Press, 1967), 9–16; Maurice Blanchot, "Two Versions of the Imaginary," in *The Station Hill Blanchot Reader: Fiction and Literary Essays*, ed. George Quasha (New York: Station Hill, 1999), 417–28.

105. See Gherardo Ortalli, *La Pittura Infamante nei Secoli XIII-XVI* (Infamante painting in the thirteenth to sixteenth centuries) (Roma: Jouvence, 1979).

106. See Paul Schimmel, ed., *Out of Actions: Between Performance and the Object, 1949–1979* (London: Thames and Hudson, 1998).

107. Clerget, "Hérédite du crime," 67.

108. William Gibson, "New Rose Hotel," in *Burning Chrome and Other Stories* (London: HarperCollins, 2000), 137.

109. Dora Panofsky and Erwin Panofsky, *Pandora's Box: The Changing Aspects of a Mythological Symbol* (Princeton, N.J.: Princeton University Press, 1978).

110. Mikhail Bulgakov, *The Master and Margarita,* trans. Michael Glenny (London: Collins Harvill, 1988).

# An Interview with Abel Ferrara |

The following is the transcription of a question-and-answer session following a screening of 'R Xmas at the Cinémathèque Française in Paris on 9 April 2003. Ferrara appeared with his producer and frequent collaborator, Frank DeCurtis. Jean-François Rauger is the director of the Programation Department.

ABEL FERRARA: All right, so, I hope everyone enjoyed the film. So, speak, talk, somebody . . .

JEAN-FRANÇOIS RAUGER: May I start? I think that the film is very close to *Bad Lieutenant,* because it's about good and evil, and the fact that you may do wrong things, but you cannot know that you are wrong. Am I right?

AF: Right! [Gestures to the lights in his face.] Kill it, man, please! [Lights go off.] All right, yeah, what does everybody think? Does anybody have a reaction to that? Don't be shy! Somebody, somebody break the ice!

SPECTATOR 1: I would disagree with Jean-François's comment . . .

AF: Stand up so we can hear you! What's your name? Talk to everybody. Don't be shy. Speak in French, somebody can translate.

S1: What struck me in this film is that you're coming much closer to the reality of social life.

AF: And how does that make it cinema? I mean, if we're filming . . .

S1: No, no. What you are doing here, what strikes me rewatching it, are the continuous dissolves and fades, which bring the film closer to *The Addiction,* with its theme of vampirism. But I'm not a critic.

AF: It's okay, we're all critics. Well, the point is, this is the other side of *King of New York.* Here, one gunshot goes off and he shoots the basketball, as opposed to God knows how many gunshots were fired in *King of New York.* We make these films, all these people getting killed, and maybe we're not feeling what we should be feeling. It's not a film about gunshots but about the reality. If a gun went off, in the reality of this situation, everybody would be hiding under their cars and not coming out of their houses for weeks. Friends of mine couldn't stand the film because the hero of the film, Lillo Brancato, was afraid. He was scared. He gave up the information right off the bat. Which is somebody I could relate to a lot more than I can to Larry Fishburne or Frank White in *King of New York.* That makes sense, but is it cinema? So, what do you guys feel about the film? Would you rather see *King of New York,* or this, or something different?

S1: May I go on?

AF: Keep going, baby! Please, please. We're here for four or five hours. I've got a two-hour speech.

S1: I would like to compare the film to *Body Snatchers* in their approach to consumerism and society. But also, you're focusing on the emotions between the principal characters.

AF: Right! Very good!

FRANK DECURTIS: Very well put!

AF: [Picks up the microphone.] Yo! HOW'S EVERYBODY DOING? ONCE UPON A TIME IN THE GHETTO! [Laughs, puts microphone back.] So, somebody in the back, 'cause I know people in the back always have the most wonderful things to say.

SPECTATOR 2: Are your films about redemption?

AF: Well . . . redemption is a twenty-four-hour, seven-days-a-week process, I mean, who wants to be redeemed? I think these people . . . we put "to be continued," or "to be cunt" [laughs], "cont. . . ." [He points at DeCurtis.] That was his choice of words. In the end, I think these people needed to be educated before they could be redeemed.

JFR: But there is no difference between good and evil in your films. God is not watching, he's blind.

AF: God is blind! God wears sunglasses! [Laughs.] God's not blind! He's all-seeing and He's all-knowing. And He made the trees. . . . For Ice-T there is a God, that's what he feels, he's telling her [Drea de Matteo] she's feeding drugs to children. I think he is speaking for a very . . . you know . . . moral high ground. He's saying that what you're doing is a hundred percent wrong. She's confronted with the fact that she's doing wrong. She's trying to deny what she even does. Nobody even takes drugs in this movie, you don't see anybody doing drugs. She's blind, and all she wants to know about is the money. And in her mind, well, she's helping people go to school, she's helping this, she's doing that, she's like the Godfather, she's like Brando. That's why she's so protected. The same way that they could never get close to . . . Escobar, someone like that. But still, she's denying what she's doing. And now, what is she gonna do when she confronts it? That's why it's "to be continued," because we've only led them to the point of, okay, this is what's going on, this is what's happening. They're pushed to the wall on all phases of their life. Now what's going to happen? I mean, we couldn't end the film like that. It's "to be continued." [To the audience:] Hello!

SPECTATOR 3: I'd like to ask . . .

AF: Stand up!

S3: Is there a subtext about the social politics developed by Giuliani?

AF: Yeah, of course . . . [He mumbles with DeCurtis.]

FDC: The rules have changed.

AF: He's talking about the difference between Giuliani and . . . and . . .

FDC: . . . anybody!

AF: Well . . . when he came in . . . at that point, believe me, the cavalry came into town. There was no more dealing on the street, there was none of this even considered anymore. Not that there were any more or less drug dealers or drugs in New York, but . . . not like that! And the main point is, the police here realized there was no way they were gonna get any help from the justice system if they arrested these guys, so they had to take it into their own hands. After this, today, believe me, these guys would have been arrested, they would have been run right through the system, and they would have been in jail. . . . The Rockefeller laws are still intact. From 1970, '73. I mean, there are mandatory sentences for drug dealing. Which puts a lot of pressure on the drug dealers, and puts a lot of pressure on the police, and . . . who are they gonna arrest? Because in terms of sentences, it's a very heavy deal. I'll tell ya, I have these horrible fucking nightmares of the way we watched the military going into Iraq. What if they let these guys loose back at home in New York and said, "We've just got rid of the Iraqis, let's get rid of the drug dealers!" How would you get any drugs with all those guys walking around in their outfits? For Giuliani, that would be the ultimate world—zero freedom. Anyway . . .

SPECTATOR 4: To date, 'R Xmas is one of the most beautiful films I've seen about a woman loving a man.

AF: Oh! That's so sweet! [Laughs.] I can't believe it. That's fantastic! About her, that's the bottom line. Because in that situation, that machismo of the Latin culture, she had to support Lillo. Even though she was the strength, she was the power. It was her. You see, the story that continues is that Lillo was tapping the bags, and he did have a habit. That's why he's reluctant to go to the Bronx with the black group. Those were his friends. The street people, the Puerto Ricans in that street, the daytime street dealers, they were her relatives of some sort, and they were doing the right deal, they were taking care of business and making the money, and she was with them. These guys in the Bronx were tapping the bags then trying to . . . you know . . . create some smokescreen to deny it. He . . . when he's giving all these raps of [imitating Lillo's accent], "I wouldn't know, I do the bags, I do 'em all the same, I'm at the table myself"—he was robbing the stuff and doing it himself. So we find out when we start chapter 2 here that he has a habit, and he's supporting this habit, and that's what is leading to his downfall. And now he has seventy-five thousand dollars he owes the Colombians, or wherever the priest gets that cigar box, and those people want the money. So it becomes an interesting story for the continuation. Very interesting. I mean, I hope everybody followed that. Anybody else?

SPECTATOR 5: Abel, when you go to the video store and there are no more Godard films left, what do you look at?

AF: People are making films, films that are out there. . . . I don't know, y'know? I'm into more or less taking chances. I wouldn't go to a video store, but . . . I mean, there's like thirty, fifty television stations. My kids have got cable, so whenever you turn it on you see all kinds of interesting films.

S2: Who are the filmmakers that move you today?

AF: Well . . . while we're here, I'd say it is not just Godard or Jean Vigo, but the ones they loved. You know, Joseph Losey, Nicholas Ray, Robert Aldrich was on the plane. . . . What is the name of the film? The cowboy movie with Burt Lancaster and Gary Cooper?

FDC: *Vera Cruz* [1954].

AF: Yeah, there are so many . . . Hitchcock, John Ford, Pasolini, Fellini, Rossellini [laughs], Bertolucci. . . . You can't name them, we keep watching movies.

FDC: If you make a film, we'll watch it. That's what we do!

AF: I see so many great films, bits and pieces. Stan Brakhage, Michael Snow, you know, all kinda screwy stuff, documentaries, Wiseman, the Maysles brothers, I mean, Orson Welles. . . . That's a funny question, there are so many great films, great documentaries, everything . . . and free baseball.

S1: I'd like to free you from that list and move back to the film.

AF: THANK YOU!

S1: Could you tell us about your collaboration with cinematographer Bojan Bazelli? What is he doing now?

AF: He shoots commercials.

FDC: He's making big bucks!

AF: [Laughs.] He's making the big money. He went for the swimming pool! I mean, Bojan is a fantastic DP. We've never worked together, me, Frank, and Bojan, but we work with Ken Kelsch, and he's like an ex-Vietnam Green Beret. He can just pick that camera up. Ken is a big, big dude. And it's all the marbles, it's all at stake. He never not brings his best game to the table. And he has his group, and he has his truck, and he has his . . . y'know what I mean? If worse came to worst, we could, like, go to war with his equipment.

FDC: I don't know if Bojan could have shot 'R Xmas.

AF: The thing is, I don't know, he'd have to change. I mean, with Bojan, it was about the shot. And then there's about giving the actor the freedom to work. Y'know, you go for the shots, you go for . . . to make it beautiful in a certain way. But you've got to allow the actor to be free. It's a fine line. And in this film you get the feeling that you're a fly on the wall. But it's not a fly on the wall, 'cause first of all this was shot in June, so this Christmas bit was in summertime. And you can't imagine how many trees . . . I cursed every tree in New York. [Laughs.] Because everything is designed, everything, even if we leave it alone, it's designed in the fact that we left it alone. It was all brought . . . which is what you want to do. I mean, you have to bring every element to the thing, and every frame has to be there, y'know? And then the actors have to . . . We started doing this film with Annabella Sciorra and John Leguizamo, and both of them . . . we had a very not-good relationship. We rehearse a lot to get to the point where we feel that we can feel like . . . you have to really feel comfortable and feel like you have it all in front of you—the lines, where to go, everything—then you can, you know, improvise it, to get to where they can be free within the frame. But Leguizamo and Annabella could not liberate themselves, whereas Lillo could. I mean, Lillo's a dear friend, but we're having a lot of problems with him lately. He's been rebellious!

FDC: A maniac! [Laughs.]

AF: Yeah, maniac, he doesn't take to unemployment well. . . . Anyway, I thought he was very brilliant in this. And Drea . . . it's a woman's film, man! It's like *Ms .45* or *The Addiction*. I mean, without her you had no film. And Annabella is brilliant and great at all times, but she wasn't then, she wasn't there for us. And this girl . . . she's like Kim Novak in *Vertigo,* nobody looks like that, smoking cigarettes like that. But what does everybody think about her? [Long pause.] Is everybody stunned into silence by this movie? I mean, come on! Somebody say something!

SPECTATOR 6: It reminds me of Scorsese who, like you, still makes gangster movies. What do you think of his films?

AF: Scorsese? Well, he's a fucking genius, I mean, he's the man! But what do you think of him? How many people have seen *Gangs of New York* [2002]? . . . Keep your hands up. Now, how many liked it? . . . Oh, no! Well . . . we all have our bad days! He had a bad two hundred! [Laughs.] Like I said before, *'R Xmas* is the opposite of *King of New York*, which is a make-believe version of how to deal drugs in Manhattan, where you take over the Colombians in three days and you're carrying around fifty-gallon drums and you're having car chases with the cops. It's a game, it's cinema as metaphor. Whereas we're attempting here to do another thing, you know?

s6: I think this movie is more intimate, and *King of New York* is more . . .

AF: . . . entertaining! The point is to be intimate and entertaining. I mean, how important is entertainment to everybody here? I'm just curious.

s6: I would disagree with you, I think *King of New York* is perfect . . .

AF: . . . as entertainment. But it's not intimate, is it?

JFR: There is some intimacy in the film, in the relationship between Christopher Walken and his buddies.

AF: Yeah . . . his boys! [Laughs.] I mean, the intimacy is between Chris Walken and the audience, that's the intimacy in *King of New York*. There was a gangster, Notorious B.I.G., who checked into hotel rooms as Frank White. He saw the movie a thousand times. That's the intimacy in the film. You live and die with Christopher. Here, at least somebody feels we captured the relationship between a man and a woman. The great thing about making movies is that you can make one like this, you can make one like that. One of the great things is that now we can do something different than either one of them. I mean, hopefully. Although I would really like to go back and do the sequel to this. And we're doing a prequel to *King of New York.* Back to the beginning. Which is not necessarily about Frank White. But the guy's name is Frank.

FDC: We're doing a prequel, then we're doing a sequel! [Laughs.]

AF: Yeah, it's a prequel, and then we'll do the sequel. [Gets up and addresses the crew.] Alright, so where is everybody going? Let's go party! What movie's playing tomorrow? *Ms .45*? Oh my god, we have a dedication to Zoë [Lund], our girl, who came to France . . . and you guys killed her! I'm only kidding. [Applause.] Just a final word. It's a very historical place here, and you have to support cinema, man! 'Cause film is twenty-four frames a second, and when you sit in a room, between every fucking frame is a little bit of black. So, at the end of the fucking hour-and-a-half movie, everybody here sat in the dark for maybe thirty minutes. When you watch tapes, it's a constant obliteration of your mind. In these thirty minutes of darkness, there is a symbiosis between the audience and the film. That's when you make your own film. And you also watch a film with everybody all around you, everybody here at the same time and that's not like watching video, man, even if videos saved our lives. Anyway, support the Cinémathèque.

*Recorded and transcribed by Charles-Antoine Bosson; revised and corrected by Brad Stevens.*

**From around 1967 to 1970, Ferrara made many amateur shorts.**

*Nicky's Film* (1971; short)
Director: Abel Ferrara
Screenplay: Nicodemo Oliverio and Abel Ferrara
Cast: Nadia Von Loewenstein, Nicodemo Oliverio, Abel Ferrara
Black and white
16 mm
6 min.
Silent
A sketch-film made with friends, using crime-genre iconography and told as a
  woman's dream.

*The Hold Up* (1972; short)
Producer: John Howard
Director: Abel Ferrara
Screenplay: Nicodemo Oliverio and Abel Ferrara
Photography: Habi Vogel
Cast: Ken Fowler (Johnny, dubbed by Abel Ferrara), Mary Kane (wife),
  Robert Denson (Bob), Joe Guida (Joe)
Black and white
16 mm
14 min.
Ken, Bob, and Joe work in a factory. Ken has married the boss's wife. Bob and
  Joe are university graduates. Short of money, they hold up a gas station,
  helped by Ken. All three are arrested, but thanks to the intervention of
  Ken's father-in-law, only Bob and Joe remain in prison.

*Could This Be Love* (1973; short)
Producer: Claude Ramirez
Director: Abel Ferrara
Screenplay: Abel Ferrara

Photography: Jon Rosen
Editor: Joseph Burton
Sound: John Paul McIntyre
Music: The Rolling Stones and Dennis Gray
Cast: Nadia Von Loewenstein (Jacky), Dee Dee Rescher (Renee), Casandra
    Cortez (Cathy), Carl Low (Mr. Gatto), David Pirell (Michael), Lanny
    Taylor (Stephen), Dennis Gray (Dennis)
Color
16 mm
26 min.
Ferrara describes the film as "the story of a rich, married bourgeois couple
    who get tired of living in Greenwich, Connecticut. One day they go to New
    York, pick up a prostitute, take her home, make love, pay her, then take
    her to an upmarket restaurant where they pass her off as a sister. . . . It's
    extremely erotic." Jacky is a painter, and Cathy the prostitute is presented
    as an archeology student.

*9 Lives of a Wet Pussy* (1976; short feature)
Producer: Navaron Films
Director: Abel Ferrara (pseudonym: Jimmy Boy L.)
Screenplay: Nicholas St. John (pseudonym: Nicholas George)
Photography: Francis Delia (pseudonym: Francis X. Wolfe)
Editor: K. James Lovttit
Sound: Larry Alexander
Music: Joseph Delia
Cast: Pauline LaMonde (Pauline), Dominique Santos (Gypsy), Joy Silver
    (Nacala), David Pirell (wife), Shaker Lewis (stable boy), Nicholas St. John
    (chauffeur), Abel Ferrara (Old Man)
Color
16 mm
63 min.
Epistolary porno film. Gypsy, the narrator, describes her passion for Pauline,
    a free-living young woman incapable of resisting her desires, who shares
    her sexual experiences by mail. At the end, Gypsy burns the letters, and
    Pauline delivers this lesson worthy of Marx or Adorno: "False unity is
    no unity. There is no reality except human reality." A flashback depicts
    the rape of Pauline's ancestor (played by Ferrara) by his two daughters,
    explicitly modeled on the biblical tale of Lot's children.

*Not Guilty: For Keith Richards* (1977; short)
Directors: Abel Ferrara and Babeth [Mondini-Vanloo]
Music: The Rolling Stones
Cast: Abel Ferrara, Susan Andrews

16 mm
5 min.
Lost film.

*The Driller Killer* (1979; feature)
Producer: Navaron Films
Director: Abel Ferrara
Screenplay: Nicholas St. John
Photography: Ken Kelsch
Editors: Orlando Gallini, Bonnie Constant, Michael Constant, Abel Ferrara
  (pseudonym: Jimmy Laine)
Music: Joseph Delia
Cast: Abel Ferrara [Jimmy Laine] (Reno Miller), Carolyn Marz (Carol),
  Baybi Day (Pamela), Rhodney Montreal (Tony Coca-Cola), Harry Schultz
  (Dalton Briggs), Alan Wynroth (landlord)
Color
16 mm
96 min.
Reno, a bohemian painter in New York, lives in a threesome with Carol and
  her lover, Pamela. Obsessed with completing a painting and irritated by
  the endless rehearsals of a rock band, The Roosters, Reno becomes a serial
  killer. At first, his victims are homeless people. Carol, worn down by Reno's
  egotistical behavior and artistic failures, leaves him to reunite with her
  former boyfriend, Steven. Reno bumps off an art dealer who is incapable
  of grasping the beauty of his masterpiece, then attacks Steven and finally
  Carol. In some prints, the film is dedicated "to the people of NYC—City of
  Hope."

*Ms .45* (a.k.a. *Angel of Vengeance;* 1981; feature)
Producer: Navaron Films
Director: Abel Ferrara
Screenplay: Nicholas St. John
Photography: James Lemmo (pseudonym: James Momèl)
Art Director: Ruben Masters
Editor: Christopher Andrews
Sound: John McIntyre
Music: Joe Delia
Cast: Zoë Tamerlis (Thana), Bogey (Phil the dog), Albert Sinkys (Albert),
  Darlene Stuto (Laurie), Helen McGara (Carol), Nike Zachmanogiou
  (Pamela), Abel Ferrara [pseudonym: Jimmy Laine] (first rapist and party
  dancer), Peter Yellen (second rapist)
Color
35 mm

81 min.

Raped first in the street and then at home, Thana, a young worker at a garment workshop, kills her second attacker in a state of legitimate defense. In the morning she cuts up his corpse and spreads the pieces throughout Manhattan. Thana metamorphoses into an avenger whose target becomes ever broader: first she kills sexual predators, but eventually any man at all. During a Halloween party, Thana, dressed as a nun, kills everyone present, starting with her boss. The film is dedicated to Alfred J. Ferrara, the director's father.

*The Beds* (1982; short)
Producer: Mary Kane
Director: Abel Ferrara
A pre-MTV "long-form rock-and-roll video" showcasing several songs by The Beds (lead singer, Merle Miller) and a group of dancers.

*Fear City* (1984; feature)
Producer: Rebecca Productions, for Zupnik-Curtis Enterprises
Director: Abel Ferrara
Screenplay: Nicholas St. John
Photography: James Lemmo
Costume Designer: Linda M. Bass
Editors: Jack Holmes and Anthony Redman
Sound: Jim Tanenbaum and Anthony R. Milch
Music: Dick Halligan
Cast: Tom Berenger (Matt Rossi), Billy Dee Williams (Wheeler), Jack Scalia (Nicky), Melanie Griffith (Loretta), Rossano Brazzi (Carmine), Rae Dawn Chong (Leila), Joe Santos (Frank), Michael V. Gazzo (Mike), Jan Murray (Goldstein), Janet Julian (Ruby), John Foster (Pazzo)
Color
35 mm
96 min.

Matt, an ex-boxer haunted by guilt over having killed one of his opponents in the ring, is now (with his friend Nicky) involved in running a strip-tease agency. His co-workers include Ruby, Nicky's fiancée, and Matt's ex-girlfriend Loretta, with whom he reunites, despite her intimate relationship with Leila, another dancer. The strippers are stalked by Pazzo, a serial killer and sword virtuoso, who eliminates Leila, among others. All the film's protagonists hunt for Pazzo: Matt, Nicky, the police, and the Mafia. Matt confronts Pazzo in a final duel, pitting western boxing against martial arts.

*Miami Vice* (1985; television series)
Producer: Michael Mann
Photography: James A. Contner
Costume Designer: Jodie Tillen
Production Designer: Jeffrey Howard
Sound: Michael R. Tromer
Music: Jan Hammer

"The Home Invaders" (episode 20)
Director: Abel Ferrara
Screenplay: Chuck Adamson
Editor: Joel Goodman
Cast: Don Johnson (Sonny Crockett), Saundra Santiago (Gina
    Calbrese), Michael Talbott (Switek), Edward James Olmos
    (Castillo), John Diehl (Zito), Olivia Brown (Trudy Joplin), Paul
    Calderon, Esai Morales, David Patrick Kelly (burglars), Sylvia Miles
    (Mrs. Goldman)
Color
35 mm
49 min.
Sonny Crockett eradicates a gang of young, immigrant crooks from a
    rich, white sector of Miami.

"The Dutch Oven" (episode 27)
Director: Abel Ferrara
Screenplay: Maurice Hurley
Editor: Robert A. Daniels
Cast: Don Johnson (Sonny Crockett), Philip Michael Thomas
    (Ricardo Tubbs), Saundra Santiago (Gina Calbrese), Michael
    Talbott (Switek), Edward James Olmos (Castillo), John Diehl (Zito),
    Olivia Brown (Trudy Joplin), Cleavant Derricks (David), Giancarlo
    Esposito (Adonis)
Color
35 mm
49 min.
Trudy Joplin, an associate of Crockett and Tubbs, inadvertently kills a
    criminal during a sting. Tormented by remorse, she takes up with
    an ex-lover, David. He is a friend of Adonis, a drug dealer. Trudy
    exposes Adonis to Crockett, who traps and arrests him.

*The Gladiator* (1986; telefeature)
Producer: Walker Brothers/New World Television
Director: Abel Ferrara

Screenplay: William Bleich
Photography: James Lemmo
Costume Designer: Heidi Kaczenski
Production Designers: Richard E. LaMotte and George Sack
Editor: Herbert H. Dow
Sound: Don Summer
Music: David Frank
Cast: Ken Wahl (Rick Benton), Nancy Allen (Susan Neville), Robert Culp
    (Frank Mason), Stan Shaw (Joe Barker), Rosemary Forsyth (Loretta
    Simpson), Bart Braverman (Dan), Brian Robbins (Jeff Benton), Jim Wilkey
    (Death Car Driver)
Color
35 mm
98 min.
Rick and his brother Jeff are attacked by a serial killer who drives a black
    car. Jeff dies. Crazy with grief, Rick transforms himself into a modern-
    day gladiator and his car into a vehicle capable of stopping dangerous
    automobiles. Every night, Rick cruises in search of evil drivers; Susan,
    one of his clients and also his lover, talks ceaselessly about the Gladiator's
    exploits, unaware of his true identity. Realizing that he is becoming a
    dangerous role model, Rick abandons his hunt, but not before crossing
    paths with and vanquishing the Death Car in a final duel.

*Crime Story* (1986; TV pilot)
Producer: Michael Mann
Director: Abel Ferrara
Screenplay: Chuck Adamson, David J. Burke, Gustave Reininger
Photography: James A. Contner
Costume Designer: Michael Kaplan
Production Designer: Linda Sutton
Editor: Jack Hofstra
Sound: Allen Bernard
Music: Todd Rundgren
Cast: Dennis Farina (Michael Torello), Anthony Denison (Ray Luca), William
    Smitrovich (Danny Krychek), Steve Ryan (Nate Grossman), Eric Bogosian
    (DeWitt Morton), David Caruso (Johnny O'Donnell)
Color
35 mm
96 min.
Chicago, 1963. A cop, Mike Torello, tracks a gang of burglars, an eminent
    member of which is the son of Johnny, a childhood friend. During a
    burglary, Wes, Mike's associate, is killed by Luca, the gang leader. Luca
    also kills his accomplice, Johnny, for becoming too greedy. During a final

burglary, Mike kills all the criminals except for Luca who escapes, and with whom he engages in final arm-to-arm combat. This is the pilot for a television series that ran for forty-three episodes between 1986 and 1988.

*China Girl* (1987; feature)
Producer: Vestron Pictures
Director: Abel Ferrara
Screenplay: Nicholas St. John
Photography: Bojan Bazelli
Costume Designer: Richard Hornung
Production Designer: Dan Leigh
Editor: Anthony Redman
Sound: Petur Hliddal and Greg Sheldon
Music: Joe Delia
Cast: James Russo (Alby Monte), Richard Panebianco (Tony Monte), Sari Chang (Tye), David Caruso (Mercury), Russell Wong (Yung Gan), Joey Chin (Tsu Shin), Judith Malina (Mrs. Monte), James Hong (Gung Tu)
Color
35 mm
90 min.
Italian businesses in Little Italy, New York, are being slowly replaced by businesses from Chinatown. In this climate of economic and cultural competition, Tony, a young Italian, falls in love with Tye, a young Chinese girl. Alby, Tony's brother, responds to the economic invasion with violence. Gan, Tye's brother, upholds Chinese autonomy against American integration. After the bombing of a Chinese restaurant, the ethnic war is resolved from above by an agreement between the Mafia and the Triad, but their subordinates keep pursuing reprisal. After Alby's death, Tony and Tye flee and hide, but one of their Chinese friends finds and kills them.

*The Loner* (1988; short telefeature)
Producer: Aaron Spelling
Director: Abel Ferrara
Screenplay: Larry Gross
Photography: Tony Richmond
Costume Designer: Anid Harris
Production Designer: Larry Warwick
Editor: Anthony Redman
Sound: Vince Garcia
Music: Joe Delia
Cast: John Terry (Michael Shane), Vanessa Bell (Jane), Constance Towers (Kate Shane), Larry Hankin (Abner Gibson), Clare Kirkconnell (Jessica), Michael Medeiros (Kyle)

Color
35 mm
49 min.
Michael, an independently wealthy, celibate dandy and music buff, works for the Los Angeles police. He and his partner Carver successfully hunt down a gang of burglars and killers led by Kyle. This inquiry into the underworld allows him to meet Jessica, a young, rich, and beautiful gallery owner, and to momentarily forget his fixation on an overbearing mother.

*Cat Chaser* (1988; feature)
Producer: Vestron Pictures/Whiskers Productions
Director: Abel Ferrara
Screenplay: James Borrelli and Elmore Leonard, from Leonard's novel
Photography: Anthony B. Richmond
Costume Designer: Michael Kaplan
Production Designer: Dan Leigh
Editor: Anthony Redman
Sound: Henry Lopez
Music: Chick Corea
Cast: Peter Weller (George Moran), Kelly McGillis (Mary De Boya), Charles Durning (Jiggs Scully), Frederic Forrest (Nolen Tyler), Tomas Milian (Andres De Boya), Juan Fernández (Rafi), Kelly Jo Minter (Loret), Tony Bolano (Corky), Phil Leeds (Jerry)
Color
35 mm
90 min.
Dominican Republic, 1965. George, a marine, is part of the American invasion of Santo Domingo. He is almost killed, but Luci, a Dominican resistance fighter, spares him. Twenty years later, George, who now runs a hotel in Miami, decides to return to Santo Domingo to find Luci. Instead, he finds Mary, a lover from his youth, now the wife of the despot Andres De Boya. Despite the fraudulent maneuvers of Jiggs, a grasping American detective, and the cruel power machinations of De Boya, George manages to wrest Mary from her husband's control while preserving her marital fortune.

*King of New York* (1989; feature)
Producer: Reteitalia SPA/Scena International SRL
Director: Abel Ferrara
Screenplay: Nicholas St. John
Photography: Bojan Bazelli
Costume Designer: Carol Ramsey

Production Designer: Alex Tavoularis
Editor: Anthony Redman
Sound Editors: Greg Sheldon and Drew Kunin
Music: Joe Delia
Cast: Christopher Walken (Frank White), David Caruso (Dennis Gilley),
    Larry Fishburne (Jimmy Jump), Victor Argo (Bishop), Wesley Snipes
    (Thomas Flanigan), Janet Julian (Jennifer), Joey Chin (Larry Wong),
    Giancarlo Esposito (Lance), Paul Calderon (Joey Dalesio), Steve Buscemi
    (Test Tube)
Color
35 mm
103 min.
"Reformed" Frank White leaves prison. His mission is to save the city
    from corruption and build a children's hospital in the South Bronx. To
    accomplish this, Frank—with his gang and legal representatives—sets
    about eliminating rival gangs and reclaiming his drug empire. He cuts
    down Colombian, Italian, and Chinese gangs. An official ceremony to
    unveil the hospital plan honors the new "King of New York." Confronted
    with this triumph, Bishop, a law-abiding cop, and Dennis, his driven
    partner, look for any way to end Frank's reign. After killing Bishop on a
    train, Frank bleeds to death in a traffic-jammed Manhattan.

"King of New York" (1990; music video)
Director: Abel Ferrara
Photography: Ken Kelsch
Music: Schoolly D
Cast: Schoolly D, Larry Fishburne, Theresa Randle
Color and black and white
35 mm
3 min.

*FBI: The Untold Stories* (1991; TV pilot)
"The Judge Wood Case" (episode 1)
Producer: The Arthur Company
Director: Charles Braverman (and Abel Ferrara, uncredited)
Screenplay: Donna Kanter (and Zoë Lund, uncredited)
Photography: Donald McCuaig (and Ken Kelsch, uncredited)
Editor: M. Edward Salier
Music: Bill Fulton and Richard Bowers
Cast: Gregory Sierra (Jimmy), Barry Cullison (Charles), Vic Trevino (Joe)
Color and black and white
25 min.

*Bad Lieutenant* (1992; feature)
Producer: Pressman Films
Director: Abel Ferrara
Screenplay: Zoë Lund and Abel Ferrara
Photography: Ken Kelsch
Costume Designer: David Sawaryn
Production Designer: Charles Lagola
Editor: Anthony Redman
Music: Joe Delia
Cast: Harvey Keitel (L. T.), Zoë Lund (Zoë), Victor Argo (Bet Cop), Paul
    Calderone (Cop 1), Leonard Thomas (Cop 2), Anthony Ruggiero (Lite),
    Robin Burrows (Ariane), Victoria Bastell (Bowtay), Frankie Thorn (Nun),
    Fernando Velez (Julio), Joseph Micheal Cruz (Paulo), Paul Hipp (Jesus)
Color
35 mm
96 min.
Against the backdrop of a baseball championship series, L. T., a cop who
    is the father of a young family and a multiple addict (crack, alcohol, sex,
    and gambling), pursues an investigation into the rape of a nun in the hope
    of getting the reward. His investigation becomes a quest: he finally frees
    the guilty parties, who turn out to be two teenagers. L. T. is killed in the
    middle of Manhattan, in front of the Trump Plaza, by Large, the head
    bookie. Bo Dietl, the model for L. T. (he investigated a nun's rape), appears
    in a cameo as a cop.

*Body Snatchers* (1993; feature)
Producer: Warner Brothers
Director: Abel Ferrara
Screenplay: Stuart Gordon, Dennis Paoli, and Nicholas St. John, based on
    Jack Finney's novel *The Body Snatchers*
Photography: Bojan Bazelli
Costume Designer: Margaret Mohr
Production Designer: Peter Jamison
Editor: Anthony Redman
Sound: Mike Le-Mare
Music: Joe Delia
Cast: Gabrielle Anwar (Marti Malone), Terry Kinney (Steve Malone), Meg
    Tilly (Carol Malone), Reilly Murphy (Andy Malone), Billy Wirth (Tim
    Young), Forest Whitaker (Dr. Collins), Christine Elise (Jenn Platt), R. Lee
    Ermey (General Platt), Kathleen Doyle (Mrs. Platt), G. Elvis Phillips (Pete)
Color
35 mm widescreen
87 min.

Steve, a scientist sent by the Environmental Protection Agency, sets up house with his family at a military base in Alabama. Steve learns that the atmosphere is saturated with toxic chemicals, and his daughter Marti discovers that people have been replaced by an army of extraterrestrial invaders who reduce humans to ashes while they sleep and take on their appearance. The replacement of the Malone family begins with the stepmother, Carol. Marti resists and flees, eventually obliged to kill the "snatched" Steve and Andy. In the company of a solider, Tim, Marti flees the military base in a helicopter. They bomb the camp.

*Dangerous Game* (a.k.a. *Snake Eyes;* 1993; feature)
Producer: Cecchi Gori Group/Maverick
Director: Abel Ferrara
Screenplay: Nicholas St. John
Photography: Ken Kelsch
Costume Designer: Marlene Stewart
Production Designer: Alex Tavoularis
Editor: Anthony Redman
Sound: Greg Sheldon
Music: Joe Delia
Cast: Harvey Keitel (Eddie Israel), Madonna (Sarah Jennings), James Russo (Frank Burns), Nancy Ferrara (Madlyn), Reilly Murphy (Tommy), Victor Argo (Director of Photography), Heather Bracken (stewardess), Anthony Redman (swinger), Randy Sabusawa (producer)
Color
35 mm
109 min.
Eddie, a film director, takes leave of his wife Madlyn and son Tommy in New York to shoot *Mother of Mirrors* in Los Angeles. His leading actors, Sarah and Frank, are at loggerheads. As the shoot proceeds, the relations between its participants become exacerbated: Frank identifies with Eddie, Eddie embarks on an affair with Sarah, and his real family is reduced to the status of raw material to fuel his inspiration. The relations of reciprocal identification and vampirization reach their apogee in a scene from *Mother of Mirrors* where Frank shoots Sarah, a gesture that is undecidably actual or virtual.

"I Know You Want to Kill Me" (1994; unreleased music video)
Producer: Sony
Director: Abel Ferrara
Music: Schoolly D
Cast: Schoolly D
Color
35 mm
4 min.

*The Addiction* (1995; feature)
Producers: Denis Hann and Fernando Sulichin
Director: Abel Ferrara
Screenplay: Nicholas St. John
Photography: Ken Kelsch
Costume Designer: Melinda Eshelman
Production Designer: Charles Lagola
Editor: Mayin Lo
Sound: Ray Karpicki
Music: Joe Delia
Cast: Lili Taylor (Kathleen Conklin), Christopher Walken (Peina), Edie Falco
    (Jean), Annabella Sciorra (Casanova), Father Robert Castle (narrator/
    priest), Paul Caldaron (Professor), Heather Bracken (nurse), Jay Julien
    (Dean), Leroy Johnson, Fred Williams (homeless victims), Kathryn Erbe
    (anthropology student)
Black and white
35 mm
82 min.
Kathleen, a philosophy student in New York, attends an illustrated lecture on
    the Vietnam War. She discusses with her pal Jean the historic responsibility
    that comes from witnessing such acts. Casanova, an elegant vampire,
    snatches Kathy off the street and bites her. Contaminated, Kathy in turn
    attacks friends, students, her teacher, homeless people, and passersby,
    all the while reflecting on the question of evil. She meets Peina, the
    vampire king, who declares his superiority and attacks her. Kathy obtains
    her doctorate and transforms the celebratory party into a bloodbath. She
    appears to die in the hospital but resurrects fleetingly as her own double.

"Nigger Entertainment" (1995; music video)
Producer: Randy Sabusawa
Director: Abel Ferrara
Photography: Ken Kelsch
Music: Schoolly D
Cast: Schoolly D, Randy Sabusawa
Color
Video
5 min.

*The Funeral* (1996; feature)
Producers: October Films/MDP Worldwide/C and P
Director: Abel Ferrara
Screenplay: Nicholas St. John
Photography: Ken Kelsch

Production Designer: Charles M. Lagola
Costume Designer: Melinda Eshelman
Editors: Bill Pankow and Mayin Lo
Sound: Greg Sheldon
Music: Joe Delia
Cast: Christopher Walken (Ray), Chris Penn (Chez), Vincent Gallo (Johnny), Annabella Sciorra (Jean), Isabella Rossellini (Clara), Benicio Del Toro (Gaspare), Gretchen Mol (Helen), Paul Hipp (Ghouly), John Ventimiglia (Sali), Victor Argo (Julius)
Color
35 mm
99 min.
New York, circa 1935. Johnny, the youngest member of a Mafia family, is gunned down as he leaves a movie theater. During his wake, events and recollections interweave. Ray and Chez, Johnny's two older brothers, hunt the murderer. They suspect Gaspare, whose wife was Johnny's lover. Despite the pleas of his wife Jean, Ray abducts Gaspare, who claims innocence. Even when this is proven, Ray does not hesitate in ordering Gaspare to be killed in front of his family. Then he kills the real murderer, a humble mechanic. At dawn, Chez buries the body, then arrives at Ray's where he shoots the henchmen, Johnny's corpse, Ray, and finally himself.

"California" (1996; music video)
Producer: Toutankhamon S.A.
Director: Abel Ferrara
Photography: Ken Kelsch
Music: Mylène Farmer
Cast: Mylène Farmer, Giancarlo Esposito
Color
35 mm
5 min.
An affluent couple is mirrored by a prostitute and a pimp. The society woman finally becomes the whore, whose death she avenges.

*Love on the A Train*, in *Subway Stories: Tales from the Underground* (1997; telefeature)
Producers: HBO NYC/Clinica Estetico/Ten in a Car Productions
Director: Abel Ferrara
Screenplay: Marla Hanson
Photography: Ken Kelsch
Editor: Elisabeth Kling
Music: Meca Bodega
Cast: Rosie Perez (the girl), Mike McGlone (John T.), Gretchen Mol (wife)

Color
35 mm
8 min.

Every morning, John T. takes the A train. One day, he meets a mysterious woman who, through her gestures, invites him to fondle her. They meet like this daily, and a ritual forms. But when he tries to change this adventure into a relationship, she abandons him. One day, he crosses her path while in the company of his pregnant wife, who demands to learn the other woman's identity. Three times he denies knowing her. (Other episodes are directed by Bob Balaban, Patricia Benoit, Julie Dash, Jonathan Demme, Ted Demme, Alison Maclean, Craig McKay, Lucas Platt, and Seth Zvi Rosenfeld.)

*The Blackout* (1997; feature)
Producers: Les Films Number One/CIPA/MDP Worldwide
Director: Abel Ferrara
Screenplay: Marla Hanson, Christ Zois, Abel Ferrara
Photography: Ken Kelsch
Costume Designer: Melinda Eshelman
Production Designer: Richard Hoover
Editor: Anthony Redman
Music: Joe Delia and Schoolly D
Cast: Matthew Modine (Matty), Dennis Hopper (Mickey), Béatrice Dalle (Annie 1), Claudia Schiffer (Susan), Sarah Lassez (Annie 2), Christ Zois (psychiatrist)
Color
35 mm
98 min.

Matty, a Hollywood star, asks his fiancée Annie to marry him. She has had an abortion at his request, as a tape recording attests. Annie takes the leading role in *Nana Miami,* a video artwork directed by Mickey in Miami. Annie disappears. Drunk from pain, alcohol, drugs, and guilt, Matty meets a young waitress also named Annie and, goaded by Mickey, strangles her. Mickey thereby captures the murder scene he needs for his video. In New York, eighteen months later, a cured Matty lives with Susan and sees a psychoanalyst who uses video. Matty returns to Miami in an attempt to relive and understand his "blackout."

*New Rose Hotel* (1998; feature)
Producer: Edward R. Pressman Film Corporation
Director: Abel Ferrara
Screenplay: Abel Ferrara and Christ Zois, based on the short story by William Gibson

Photography: Ken Kelsch
Costume Designer: David C. Robinson
Production Designer: Frank DeCurtis
Editors: Jim Mol and Anthony Redman
Sound: Mathew Price
Music: Schoolly D
Cast: Christopher Walken (Fox), Willem Dafoe (X), Asia Argento (Sandii),
  Yoshitaka Amano (Hiroshi), Gretchen Mol (Hiroshi's wife), Annabella
  Sciorra (Madame Rosa), John Lurie (distinguished man), Ryuichi
  Sakamoto (Hosaka executive)
Color
35 mm
92 min.
Fox and X decide to snag Hiroshi, top scientist in the field of genetic
  manipulation, from Maas corporation and deliver him to the rival Hosaka
  corporation. They recruit the prostitute Sandii, with whom X falls in
  love. Sandii succeeds, and Hiroshi abandons his wife and employer. But
  suddenly X and Fox learn that their bank account is empty and that Sandii
  has spread a virus that has wiped out major genetics experts. They realize
  that Sandii must have been a Maas agent. Fox hurls himself to death, and X
  holes up in the New Rose Hotel, where he thinks back over his affair with
  Sandii.

"Iowa" (1998; music video)
Director: Abel Ferrara
Music: The Phoids
Cast: The Phoids
Color
Video
3 min.

"Don't Change Your Plans" (1999; music video)
Director: Abel Ferrara
Music: Ben Folds Five
Cast: Gretchen Mol, Ben Folds, Robert Sledge
Color
Video
4 min.

'R Xmas (2001; feature)
Producers: Studio Canal and Pierre Kalfon
Director: Abel Ferrara
Screenplay: Scott Pardo and Abel Ferrara, based on a story by Cassandra de
  Jesus

Photography: Ken Kelsch
Costume Designer: Debra Tennenbaum
Production Designer: Frank DeCurtis
Editors: Bill Pankow, Suzanne Pillsbury, Patricia Bowers
Sound: Jeff Pullman
Music: Schoolly D
Cast: Drea de Matteo (wife), Lillo Brancato Jr. (husband), Ice-T (kidnapper), Victor Argo (Louie), Naomi Morales (niece), Lisa Valens (daughter), Clarence Dorsey (dealer), Roman Rivera (Felipe), Anthony "Dust" Ortiz (dealer), Gloria Irizarry (aunt)
Color
35 mm
85 min.
Christmas Eve, New York, 1993: A man looks in vain for a doll that his little daughter wants. He and his Puerto Rican wife are affluent professional drug dealers, a faithful, loving couple, caring and devoted parents, and dispensers of charitable community works. While the wife looks for the doll, the husband is kidnapped by an African American gang. She must find the ever-escalating ransom money. Even the husband's mother refuses to help; only the street sellers assist. On Christmas morning, he miraculously, mysteriously appears. The final title reads: "Less than a month later, Rudolf Giuliani becomes the 107th Mayor of New York."

"Flowerland" (2002; unreleased music video)
Director: Abel Ferrara
Music: Flowerland
Cast: Flowerland
Concert filmed January 2002.
Video

"Rain" (2003; music video)
Producer: Nkunim
Director: Abel Ferrara
Music: Abenaa
Cast: Abenaa
Color
Video
3 min.

"You Don't Look So Good" (2003; music video)
Producer: Frank DeCurtis
Director: Abel Ferrara
Photography: Jim Mol

Editors: Jim Mol (Ferrara's cut), Ruth Maria Mamaril (band's cut)
Music: Dead Combo
Cast: Dead Combo
Color
Video
3 min. 18 sec. (Ferrara's cut), 3 min. 46 sec. (band's cut)

"Move with Me" (2004; music video)
Directors: Abel Ferrara and Toni D'Angelo
Photography: Fabio Cianchetti
Music: Krysten
Cast: Krysten
Color
Video

*Mary* (2005; feature)
Producer: Central Films
Director: Abel Ferrara
Screenplay: Abel Ferrara, Simone Lageoles, and Mario Isabella
Photography: Stefano Falivene
Production Designer: Frank DeCurtis
Editors: Fabio Nynziata and Langdon F. Page
Music: Francis Kuipers
Cast: Juliette Binoche (Marie Palesi/Mary Magdalene), Matthew Modine
    (Tony Childress/Jesus), Heather Graham (Elizabeth Younger), Forest
    Whitaker, (Ted Younger)
Three characters are linked by the biblical figure of Mary Magdalene. Tony
    Childress, an infamous, egotistical, and obsessive actor/director is playing
    the lead role of Jesus in his controversial new film *This Is My Blood*. When
    the shoot wraps, Marie Palesi, his lead actress, is left alone in Jerusalem,
    drained and wandering. Into her empty spirit is poured the spirit of Mary
    Magdalene, and Marie embarks on a journey towards enlightenment.
    Meanwhile, in New York City, a television journalist, Ted Younger, begins
    his own quest for spiritual truth through making a documentary about
    the life of Christ. When the premiere of Tony's film becomes the target of
    bomb threats by the vengeful religious Right, the lives and paths of these
    three characters intersect.

**Films about Ferrara**

*Dans les coulisses du clip California* (In the wings of the clip "California";
    1996; documentary short)
Producer: Toutankhamon S.A.

Director: François Hanss
Photography: François Hanss
Editor: Corinne Cahour
Music: Mylène Farmer
Color
Video
27 min.
A portrait of Ferrara directing the music video "California."

*Abel Loves Asia* (1998; documentary short)
Producer: Nihil
Directors: Asia Argento and Marco Giusti
Editor: Dario Cece
Cast: Abel Ferrara, Asia Argento, Anthony Redman
Video
33 min.
Argento's intimate video diary of the *New Rose Hotel* shoot.

*High* (2001; experimental short)
Producer, Director, Photography, and Editor: Othello Vilgard
16 mm/video
7 min.
A visual poem based on *The Addiction,* offering an in-depth analysis of Lili
    Taylor's performance.

*Not Guilty: Abel Ferrara* (2003; feature)
Producer: AMIP/ARTE/INA
Director: Rafi Pitts
Photography: Olivier Guéneau
Editor: Danielle Anezin
Sound: Jean Minondo
16 mm
80 min.
A portrait of Ferrara in his hometown of New York City, made for
    the celebrated television series *Cinéastes, de notre temps.* Ferrara's
    collaborators Abenaa, Victor Argo, Lillo Brancato, and Frank DeCurtis
    appear.

*Odyssey in Rome* (2005)
Director: Alex Grazioli
A documentary on the preparation and shooting of Ferrara's *Mary,* featuring
    interviews with cast and crew members.

**Discography**

*The Funeral,* soundtrack (Critique, 1996).
Compilation of songs featured in the film; does not contain Joe Delia's score.

*The Blackout,* soundtrack (Mother, 1997).
Includes songs used in the film and Delia's score. "The Player (Theme from
*The Blackout*)" by Schoolly D and Delia was also released as a CD single.

*Closed on Account of Rabies: Poems and Tales of Edgar Allan Poe* (Mouth
Almighty Records, 1998).
Ferrara, in a church before a crowd, reads Poe's "The Raven." The other
performers are Christopher Walken, Marianne Faithfull, Ken Nordine,
Deborah Harry and the Jazz Passengers, Gavin Friday, Diamanda Galás,
Dr. John, Jeff Buckley, Gabriel Byrne, Ed Sanders, and Iggy Pop.

Filmography by Nicole Brenez and Adrian Martin. Summaries of the films by
Nicole Brenez.

## I. By Abel Ferrara

ESSAYS

Ferrara, Abel. "Le champion." In *Feux croisés: Le cinéma américain vu par ses auteurs (1946–1997)* (Crossfire: The American cinema as seen by its auteurs, 1946–1997). Ed. Bill Krohn. Lyon: Institut Lumière/Actes Sud, 1997. 261–62.

———. "Five Questions." *Projections* 7 (1997): 106–7.

———. Foreword to *Captured: A Lower East Side Film and Video History.* Ed. Clayton Patterson. New York: Seven Stories Press, 2005. xii–xiv.

INTERVIEWS

Colon, Gilbert. "The Mark of Abel on a Classic: An Interview with Abel Ferrara." In *They're Here . . . Invasion of the Body Snatchers: A Tribute.* Ed. Kevin McCarthy and Ed Gorman. New York: Berkley Boulevard Books, 1999. 149–62.

Desanglois, Lucie. "Tous les films ne sont pas faits pour tout le monde" (Not all films are made for everyone). *Le Mensuel du cinéma* 11 (November 1993): 67–70.

French, Olivier, and John Strausbaugh. "*Bad Lieutenant*'s Director Still Struggles to Find Screens." *New York Press* 15.27 (July 2002): 28–29.

Garel, Alain, and François Guérif. "American Boy." *La Revue du Cinéma* 436 (March 1988): 47–52.

Jarecki, Nicholas. "Abel Ferrara: The Driller Killer." In *Breaking In: How Twenty Film Directors Got Their Start.* New York: Broadway Books, 2001. 114–23.

Schnabel, Julian. "Harvey Keitel, Zoë Lund, and Abel Ferrara—The Unholy Trinity That Makes *Bad Lieutenant* a Religious Experience." *Interview* (December 1992): 139–40.

Smith, Gavin. "Dealing with the Now." *Sight and Sound* 7.4 (April 1997): 7–9.

———. "The Gambler." *Sight and Sound* 3.2 (February 1993): 20–23.

————. "Moon in the Gutter." *Film Comment* 26.4 (July–August 1990): 40–46.

Strauss, Frédéric, and Camille Nevers. "La passe de trois" (The master key of three). *Cahiers du Cinéma* 473 (November 1993): 18–23.

Voinchet, Marc. "Des ombres argentées" (Silvery shadows). *Entrelacs* 2 (October 1994): 101–5.


## II. Ferrara's Collaborators

Argento, Asia. *Je t'aime Kirk.* Trans. Marie Blaison. Paris: Florent Massot, 2001.

Hopper, Dennis. "Invitation to the Void: A System of Moments." In *Dennis Hopper: A System of Moments.* Ed. Peter Noever. Ostfildern-Ruit: Hatje Cantz, 2001. 15–21.

Jones, Kent. "'Hör mal-warum sind wir überhaupt auf der Weit?' Ein Gespräch mit dem Orebuchator Nick St. John" ("Listen—Why are we on the face of the earth?": An interview with screenwriter Nicholas St. John). *Meteor* 4 (1996): 15–21.

Jousse, Thierry, and Frédéric Strauss. "Entretien avec Béatrice Dalle." *Cahiers du Cinéma* 513 (May 1997): 61–67.

Lund, Zoë. *Bad Lieutenant.* Final revised script, 3 October 1991. *Internet Movie Script Database,* www.imsdb.com/scripts/Bad-Lieutenant.html.

————. "'I Had To Do It in My Life as Well as in the Film': An Interview with Zoë Lund." *Rouge* 10 (2006), www.rouge.com.au/stars/04.html.

————. "Interview with Zoe Lund (Part 1)." *Zoë (Tamerlis) Lund,* http://www.lundissimo.info/Zoe/docs/CF-interviews/interview1-0796.html.

————. "The Nun's Confession." *Zoë (Tamerlis) Lund,* http://www.lundissimo.info/Zoe/docs/NunConfession.html.

————. "The Ship with Eight Sails (and Fifty Black Cannons)." *Rouge* 10 (2006), www.rouge.com.au/stars/02.html.

————. "The Vampire Speech." *Zoë (Tamerlis) Lund,* http://www.lundissimo.info/Zoe/docs/VampireSpeech.html.

Martin, Adrian. "The Misleading Man: Dennis Hopper." In *Stars in Our Eyes: The Star Phenomenon in the Contemporary Era.* Ed. Angela Ndalianis and Charlotte Henry. Westport, Conn.: Praeger, 2002. 2–19.

Smith, Gavin. "Interview with Christopher Walken." *Film Comment* 28.4 (July–August 1992): 56–65.

Zois, Christ L., and Margaret Scarpa. *Short-Term Therapy Techniques.* New York: Jason Aronson, 1997.

Zois, Christ L., with Patricia Fogarty. *Think Like a Shrink: Solve Your Problems Yourself with Short-Term Therapy Techniques.* New York: Warner Books, 1992.

## III. On Abel Ferrara

BOOKS

Baj, Pietro, ed. *Abel Ferrara*. Rome: Dino Audino Editore, 1997.
Danese, Silvio. *Abel Ferrara: L'anarchico e il cattolico* (Abel Ferrara: The anarchist and the Catholic). Genova: Le Mani, 1998.
Herrgott, Elizabeth. *Abel Ferrara*. Paris: Kfilms Editions, 1999.
Johnstone, Nick. *Abel Ferrara: The King of New York*. London: Omnibus Press, 1999.
Kiefer, Bernd, and Marcus Stiglegger, eds. *Die bizarre Schönheit der Verdammten—die Filme von Abel Ferrara* (The bizarre beauty of the damned: The films of Abel Ferrara). Marburg: Schüren Presseverlag, 2000.
Legendre, Claire. *Making Of.* Paris: Éditions Hors Commerce, 1998.
Nazzaro, Giona A., ed. *Abel Ferrara: La tragedia oltre il noir* (Abel Ferrara: Tragedy beyond noir). Rome: Stefano Sorbini Editore, 1997.
Pezzotta, Alberto. *Ferrara*. Milan: Il Castoro, 1998.
Stevens, Brad. *Abel Ferrara: The Moral Vision*. London: FAB Press, 2004.

CHAPTERS

Brenez, Nicole. "Frankly White: Actualités de l'abstraction dans la construction figurative" (Frankly white: The current state of abstraction in figurative construction). In *De la figure en général et du corps en particulier: L'invention figurative au cinéma* (On the figure in general and the body in particular: Figurative invention in cinema). Brussels: De Boeck Université, 1998. 225–38.
Hawkins, Joan. "No Worse Than You Were Before: Theory, Economy, and Power in Abel Ferrara's *The Addiction.*" In *Underground USA: Filmmaking beyond the Hollywood Canon.* Ed. Xavier Mendik and Steven Jay Schneider. London: Wallflower Press, 2002. 13–25.
Lyons, Donald. "Abel Ferrara." In *Independent Visions: A Critical Introduction to Recent Independent American Films.* New York: Ballantine Books, 1994. 23–31.

DOSSIERS

*Admiranda* 11/12 (December 1996). Texts (in French) by Thomas Boisdelet, Nicole Brenez, Sébastien Clerget, Stéphane du Mesnildot, Virginie Naader, Antoine Raison, Emmanuelle Sarrouy, and Zoë Lund.
*Balthazar* 3 (Autumn 1998). Texts (in French) by Cyril Béghin, Sophie Charlin, Stéphane Delorme, Florent Guézengar, and Emeric de Lastens.
*Balthazar* 5 (Spring 2002). Texts (in French) by Nicole Brenez, Sophie Charlin, Agathe Dreyfus, Sébastien Clerget, Richard Hell, and Zoë Lund.
*Simulacres* 7 (November 2002). Texts (in French) by Nicole Brenez, Sébastien Clerget, and Fabienne Duszynski.

GENERAL ESSAYS

Blumenfeld, Samuel. "Recherche Carlos désespérément" (Desperately seeking Carlos). *Les Inrockuptibles* 52 (10–16 April 1996): 15–19.

Brenez, Nicole. "Abel Ferrara versus XX° siècle: Une Passion critique" (Abel Ferrara versus the twentieth century: A critical passion). *Trafic* 43 (Autumn 2002): 47–59.

———. "Fonction critique du grand criminel: Notes sur la figure du Serial Killer en tant qu'elle structure l'œuvre de Ferrara" (Critical function of the great criminal: Notes on the serial-killer figure as it structures Ferrara's work). *Simulacres* 1 (1999): 68–75.

Daverat, Xavier. "Abel Ferrara et le mal" (Abel Ferrara and evil). In *Why Not? Sur le cinéma américain.* Ed. Jean-Baptiste Thoret and Jean-Pierre Moussaron. Pertuis: Rouge Profond, 2002. 150–61.

Gallagher, Tag. "Geometry of Force: Abel Ferrara and Simone Weil." *Screening the Past* 10 (June 2000), www.latrobe.edu.au/screeningthepast/firstrelease/fro600/tgfr10d.htm.

Jones, Kent. "Abel Ferrara—The Man: Who Cares?" *Lingo* 4 (1995): 30–40.

———. "Désordre et contemplation dans les films d'Abel Ferrara" (Disorder and contemplation in the films of Abel Ferrara). *Trafic* 19 (Summer 1996): 32–45.

Lehman, Peter. "The Male Body within the Excesses of Exploitation and Art: Abel Ferrara's *Ms .45, Cat Chaser,* and *Bad Lieutenant.*" *Velvet Light Trap* 32 (Autumn 1993): 23–29.

Martin, Adrian. "Neurosis Hotel: An Introduction to Abel Ferrara." Program, *Twelfth Brisbane International Film Festival* (July 2003): 84–89.

Rauger, Jean-François. "Abel Ferrara: La passe de trois." *Cahiers du cinéma* 473 (November 1993): 16.

ESSAYS ON INDIVIDUAL FILMS

Benoliel, Bernard. "*Snake Eyes:* Borderline." *Le Mensuel du Cinéma* 11 (November 1993): 40–41.

Brenez, Nicole. "The Actor in (the) Place of the Edit." *Rouge* 9 (2006), www.rouge.com.au/stars/01.html.

———. "Come into My Sleep." *Rouge* 6 (2005), www.rouge.com.au/rougerouge/sleep.html.

Charlin, Sophie. "*Ms .45:* Angel, Femme Fatale, Seamstress." *Rouge* 10 (2006), www.rouge.com.au/stars/03.html.

Hoberman, Jim. "Paranoia and the Pods." *Sight and Sound* 4.5 (May 1994): 28–31.

Jones, Kent. "*Bad Lieutenant.*" In *The Hidden God: Film and Faith.* Ed. Mary Lea Bandy and Antonio Monda. New York: The Museum of Modern Art, 2003. 198–201.

Martin, Adrian. "Black Holes." *RealTime* 27 (1998): 17.

Matarasso, David, and Stéphane du Mesnildot. "Fatale beauté." *L'Ecran fantastique* 184 (April 1999): 59.

Rauger, Jean-François. "L'enfer du même" (The Hell of the same). *Cahiers du cinéma* 469 (June 1993): 78–80.

Scorsese, Martin. "*Bad Lieutenant.*" *Projections* 7 (1997): 93–94.

Viletard, Simon. "La maison de tous les pêchés." *L'Ecran fantastique* 184 (April 1999): 58.

Page numbers for illustrations are in boldface.

abandonment, 28, 91
*Abel Ferrara: The Moral Vision* (Stevens), 5
Abenaa, 87
Abuba, Ernesto: as King Tito, 64, 71
acknowledgment, 113–14, 141, 144
actionism. *See* Viennese Actionists
actor's role, 93, 98–101
actor trilogy, 90. See also *The Blackout; Dangerous Game;* and *New Rose Hotel*
*Addiction, The* (1995), 2, 3, 6, 12, **19,** 23, 26, 32, **48,** 50, 60, 112, 117, 123, 142, 156; Abel Ferrara on, 170; acknowledgment in, 113; death in, 78, 80, 81, 118; devouring in, 69, 74–75, 83, 116; ending of, 14; fury in, 46; and history, 8–10, 18, 20, 114, 135, 136, 137; knowledge in, 108, 109, 110; morality and revolution in, 57; and philosophy, 18; protagonist's trajectory in, 34, 35, 38, 46, 51, 70, 80, 114, 135, 152; and the question of evil, 31, 47, 111, 115
adjuration, 156
Adorno, Theodor W., 1, 27, 61, 64
*After Hours* (Scorsese), 30
agitprop, 109
AIDS, 9, 45, 46
alcoholism, 103, 140–42
Aldrich, Robert, 169
*Alice's Adventures in Wonderland* (Carroll), 21, 142
alienation, 10

allegory, 12–13, 18, 28, 46, 74, 79, 114, 116, 129
Alvarez, Santiago, 54, 137
American cinema, 5, 22
"American Condition, The" ("La Condition américaine"), 53, 59, 67
American economy, 45
American ideology, 27
American imaginary, 150
American imperialism, 9, 61, 126
American "No Wave," 38
American Way of Life, 150
Amino, Yoshitaka: as Hiroshi, 24, 153, 154, 156
amorality, 6, 15, 66
anamnesis, 22, 50, 106, 146
anamorphosis, 13–14, 29. *See also* Ferrara's films: anamorphic structure of
*Andy Warhol's Exploding Plastic Inevitable* (Nameth), 32
anger, 41, 45, 49
anguish, 18, 34, 110, 113
*Ann Uyen,* 57
*Antigone* (Straub/Huillet), 150
Anwar, Gabrielle, as Marti, 7, 13, 20, 69, 83, 85, 106, 151
archetype, 3, 4, 12, 29, 50, 81, 84, 101, 156
Argento, Asia: as Sandii, 24, 26, 38, 50, 51, 69, 87, 90–92, 119, 153–56
Argento, Dario, 51
Argo, Victor: as Cop Bishop, 45
art dealers, 120
artistic torment, 37. *See* torment
artist trilogy, 118–23

atonement, 115
Augustine, 67, 114, 116, 132
Auschwitz, 11. *See also* Nazism: Nazi or
    death camps
avant-garde, 4, 109, 137

B., Scott and Beth, 38
*Bad Lieutenant* (1992), 3, 12, 14, 31, 39,
    56, 62, 77, 108, 112, 123, 128, 165;
    death in, 75, 78, 118; dreams and
    visions in, 86, 131; forgiveness, 2, 110;
    formal invention in, 32, 56, 87; the
    protagonist's trajectory, 15, 26, 32–35,
    44, 68–69, 70, 80, 111, 113–16, 132–34,
    142; rage in, 44; about redemption in,
    14, 38; structure of the film, 15, 16, 17
Baldwin, James, 54
barbarity, 74–75
Bataille, Georges, 1, 26, 35, 36, 37, 39,
    70, 74, 100
Baudelaire, Charles, 12, 116
Bazelli, Bojan, 169, 170
Bazin, André, 151
Becker, Jacques, 53
Ben Folds Five, 87
Benjamin, Walter, 28, 64, 67, 109
Berenger, Tom: as Matt, 42, 80, 85, 86,
    108, 111, 112, 124, 126
Bergman, Ingrid, 9, 52
Bertolucci, Bernardo, 169
Bickford, Charles: as Oliver Niles, 103
Binoche, Juliette: as Marie Palesi/Mary
    Magdalene, 58, 111, 157
Binswanger, Ludwig, 145, 149
*Black Liberation,* (*Black America; Silent
    Revolution*) (Laurot, Edouard de),
    54, 57
*Blackout, The* (1997), 3, 12, 24–25, 27,
    118, 122, 128, 138, **139**, 152, 153; alle-
    gory in, 79; creating images, 119; critics
    on, 3, 140; death in, 28, 70; drinking in,
    87, 112–13 (*see also* alcoholism); epi-
    logue of, 121, 155–56; facing the crime,
    78; facing violence, 111; figurative
    elements in, 28, 29; figure of the serial
    killer in, 49, 52; forms of disruptive
    perception, 132, 141–51; Matty and
    Mickey, 24, 116, **117**, 120; the protago-

nist of, 26, 28, 32, 38, 69, 78, 80, 108,
    110, 114–15; purpose of delirium, 142;
    reception of, 5; representing psychic
    images, 132, 141; structure of, 15, 129,
    140
Black Panthers, 54
Blake, William, 35
Blanchot, Maurice, 151
Blank, Les, 93
Blasetti, Alessandro, 53
bloody balls, 73–75, 90
body exploitation. *See* sexual abuse
*Body Snatchers* (1993), 6, **9**, 10, 12, 29,
    67, 69, 98, 105, 119, 166; alienation and
    the double in, 82–83, 85, 146, 151; alle-
    gory in, 13, 22, 47; and evil, 7–**8**; family
    questions in, 84, 92; and history, 7, 73,
    150; the individual in, 26; influences on,
    32; metamorphosis in, 20, 80, 106, 123;
    as a remake, 103; serial killer figure in,
    45–46; status of the feminine, 155
*Body Snatchers, The* (Jack Finney), 6
Boetticher, Budd, 32
Bogdanovich, Peter, 5
Boltanski, Christian, 113
Brakhage, Stan, 2, 169
Brancato, Lillo: as The Man, 166, 168,
    170
Brando, Marlon, 167
*Bringing Out the Dead* (Scorsese), 14,
    15, 30
Bronx, the, 2, 58, 157, 168. *See also* New
    York
Brooks, Louise, 154
Brus, Günther, 151
Bulteau, Michel, 152
Bulgakov, Mikhaïl, 156
*Burden of Dreams* (Blank), 93
Burroughs, William S., 116
Burrows, Robin: as Ariane, 133, 134

Cabral, Amílcar, 57
Cage, Nicolas, 14, 15
"California" (1996), 3, 82, 85, 86, 87–89,
    108
capitalism, 6, 8, 30, 47, 65–67; as catastro-
    phe, 9; figures of, 10
*Carlito's Way* (De Palma), 22

Carpenter, John, 22, 61
Carroll, Lewis, 21
Carruthers, Ben, 54
Caruso, David: as Mercury, 23, 44
*Casino* (Scorsese), 22, 67
Cassavetes, John, 11, 12, 22, 54, 90, 91
*Cat Chaser* (1989), 21, 112, 123, 126, 127, 128
*Cat People* (Tourneur), 136
Cavalcanti, Alberto, 109
Chang, Sari: as Tye, 42, 43
Chaplin, Charles, 5
characters: ethical existence of, 33, 36, 98, 17; projects of, 23, 28, 41, 42, 43, 45, 81
Chin, Joey: as Larry Wong, 43; as Tsu, 43
*China Girl* (1987), 2, 21, 23, 42, 43, 44, 67, 112
Christian imagery, 56, 56–57, 114–16, 134, 138
Christianity, 58
CIA, 54
*Cineaste,* 53, 54
cinema: and contemporary evil, 5, 9, 13 (*see also* evil); as delirious apparatus, 149; and history, 6–9, 18–20, 27 (*see also* history); as psychic apparatus, 150
Cinema Engagé (Engaged Cinema) group, 53, 56, 59
Cinémathèque Française, 5, **61,** 165, 171
Cinéthique group, 54
Clerget, Sébastien, 153
*Closed on Account of Rabies: Poems and Tales of Edgar Allan Poe,* 111
Clouzot, Henri-Georges, 53
compassion, 14, 157
conjuration, 156
conscience trilogy, 113–18, 123
consciousness, 20, 22, 34, 40, 74–75, 110, 117–18, 123, 147, 153
consumerism, 101, 166
conversion, 17, 18, 76, 101, 114, 132
Cooper, Gary, 169
corruption, 9, 15, 18, 33, 42, 45, 47, 52, 66
*Coup d'Etat,* 61
creation, 92–97, 100–102, 118–19, 121, 129

crime, criminal logics, order, 2, 5–7, 9, 12, 14, 16, 24, 30, 35–38, 42, 43, 45, 49, 52, 65–67, 70–72, 105, 111, 127, 144, 152
*Crime Story* (1986), 3, 123
criminal figures, 40. *See also* serial killer
cruel, cruelty, 3, 38, 96, 109
Cruz, Joseph Micheal: as Paulo, 132
Cukor, George, 102, 103, 104, 105, 106, 107
cultural consumption. *See* culture industry
culture industry, 1, 2, 4, 5, 11, 38, 91

Dafoe, Willem: as X, 24, 51, 91, 153, 154, 156
Dalle, Béatrice, 4, 107, **139;** as Annie 1, 25, 28, 49, 69, 78, 90, 91, 92, 103, 107, 116, 119, 122, 140, 141, 143, 145, 146, 147, 149
*Dangerous Game (Snake Eyes,* 1993), 3, 108, 119, 120; artist trilogy, 112, 118; avidity in, 67; death in, 68; delirium in, 128, 129, 137–38; destruction in, 56, 121–22, 152; devouring, 99–102; double in, 90; film within the film, 92; identity, 20, 26, 83; status of the actor, 84, 92, 96–99; script, 59, 156
*Darty Report, The* (Godard), 96
Davies, Ossie, 54
Day, Baybi: as Pamela, 119
Dead Combo, 87, 93
*Dead Man* (Jarmusch), 22
death, 12, 23, 28, 38, 39, 45, 49, 57, 84, 96, 104, 108, 110, 113, 116, 118, 121, 123, 146, 149–53; and creation (*see* creation); and its archaic resonances, 68–82. *See also* murder; suicide
DeCegli, Nicholas: as a dealer, 32
DeCurtis, Frank, 165
*Deer Hunter, The* (Cimino), 17
Dee Williams, Billy: as Detective Wheeler, 124
Delia, Joe, 11
delirium, 97, 101, 114, 123; clinical forms, 144–45; films, 128–38, 140–44, 146, 149, 151; local, 123–28; opposed to normal perception, 145; total, 128–38

Del Sarto, Andrea, 151
dementia, 144–45
democratic capitalism: American, 27
denial, 30, 31, 33, 60, 108, 113, 155, 156
De Niro, Robert, 41, 42
De Palma, Brian, 22, 36
devastation, 117–18, 122
devouring, 69, 95, 99, 100, 113, 116
Dick, Vivienne, 38
disillusion, 142
dissolution, 117–18, 123
documentary image. *See* image
*Don Quixote* (Welles), 53
Dostoyevsky, Fyodor, 39
double, 21, 23, 82–90, 151
*Driller Killer, The* (1979), 2, 10, 13, 47,
    48, 132; artistic torment in, 37, 118–20,
    152; delirium in, 128–29; formal struc-
    tures of, 15, 46, 108, 122; fury in, 23,
    41, 44, 81; murder in, 75, 86, 91, 112;
    music in, 87; parties in, 68, 74; tramps
    of, 109
drugs, addictions, booze, junkies: 2, 9, 10,
    15, 26, 31, 33, 40, 46, 52, 111, 131, 132,
    138, 146, 147, 167–68. *See also* alcohol-
    ism; delirium
Duras, Marguerite, 14
Durkheim, Emile, 28
"Dutch Oven, The" (episode 27). See
    *Miami Vice*
Dylan, Bob, 102
Dziga Vertov group, 54

economic alienation, 10. *See* capitalism
ecstasy, 3, 37, 38, 112, 144
editing, 82, 88, 116, 148. *See also* mon-
    tage
*8 and a Half* (Fellini), 120
engulfment, 95–96, 143
Ermey, R. Lee: as General Platt, 7
*Escape from L.A.* (Carpenter), 61
Esposito, 2. *See also* Ferrara, Abel
Esposito, Giancarlo, 86
ethical stakes in Ferrara's œuvre, 1, 52,
    63, 110; depiction of death, 71–73;
    figurative deontology or ethic of forms,
    24, 38, 82; from one film to another,
    23–24

*Europa 51* (Rossellini), 9, 14
Eustache, Jean, 150
evil, 3, 5, 22, 101, 165, 167; attributes
    of, 15, 30, 101; collective, 7, 8, 115,
    152; facing evil, 111; history of, 6, 14;
    modern evil, 9; origin of all, 47, 49, 64,
    67–75, 156; the question of evil, 13, 30,
    40n, 136; reflection and evil, 35–36,
    113, 142; as spatial and mental inva-
    sion, 7, 8, 95, 117, 136; transformation
    of, 38, 115, 157
exaltation, 3
existentialism, 4, 54, 55
expiation, 115
exploitation, 16, 127, 128

fable, 4, 7, 14, 22, 58, 67, 80, 91, 153
Factory, Warholian, 119. *See also* Warhol
Falco, Edie: as Jean, 46, 116, 135
"Fall of the House of Usher, The" (Poe),
    99
family issues, 2, 6, 7, 20, 22, 27, 30, 40,
    49, 52, 69, 84–85, 97, 99, 100, 101,
    133–34
Fanon, Frantz, 56, 57
*Far from Vietnam. See* Ray, Michèle
*Far from Vietnam* (Marker), 57
Farina, Denis: as Michael Torello, 123
Farmer, Frances, 4
Farmer, Mylène, 82, 86, 89. *See also*
    "California"
Fassbinder, Rainer Werner, 11, 12, 13,
    38, 52
*Fear City* (1984), 2, 74, 88; delirium in,
    123–26, 128; figure of the double in,
    82, 83, 85–86, 108; fury and serial kill-
    ing in, 41–43, 80; violence in, 111, 112
Fellini, Federico, 53, 120, 169
femme fatale, 24, 38
Ferrara, Abel: birth and early years of, 2;
    early films of, 9; on film and video, 172;
    as the first rapist, 130–31; on God, 167;
    his conception of history, 6 (*see also*
    history); on his films, 165–77; his proj-
    ects, 3, 171; his relation to music and
    cinema, 86–87; and other filmmakers,
    1, 2, 4, 5, 11, 12; on other filmmakers,
    169; on politics, 23 (*see also* politics);

public image, 4; as Reno, 23, 37, 41, 44, 68, 74, 79, 80, 81, 91, 108, 112, 118, 119, 120, 121, 129, 130, 152, 15; self-portrait as a corpse, 152; team of collaborators, 11; as tragedian, 14, 27; videos, 3 (*see also* "California")
Ferrara, Nancy, 144; as Madlyn, 92, 97, 99, 100, 138
Ferrara's cinema: aesthetic limitations, 4; and American audiences, 5; American studios, 5; anthropological horizons of, 20; within cultural industry, 3, 5; dynamics of, 16; ethical stakes in (*see* ethical stakes); figurative work in, 6; and genre cinema, 2, 3; importance of the image, 4 (*see also* image); between industry and avant-garde, 4; international recognition of, 3, 5, 31; polemical enterprise of, 9, 11–12; prototypes in, 110–13 (*see also specific film titles*); remakes, 103; social issues in, 3
Ferrara's films: anamorphic structure of, 14–20, 22, 49, 88, 108; the "artist" and "consciousness" trilogies, 112–22; beauty in, 12; delirium, 128 (*see also* delirium); dynamics among, 13; narrative structures in, 15, 91, 108–9; retrospective of, 5. *See also* specific film titles
film and music, 2
*Film Culture,* 53
film within the film, 69, 92. *See also* mise en abyme
Finney, Jack, 6
Fishburne, Larry: as Jimmy Jump, 44, **72,** 112, 166
*Fitzcarraldo* (Herzog), 93
Fleming, Victor, 21
Ford, John, 169
forgiveness, 2
Foster, John: as Pazzo, 41, 42, 43, 45, 49, 85, 108, 123, 124
"490," 63. *See also* Lund
*Fox and His Friends* (Fassbinder), 11
Frankfurt School, 26
fraternity, 70
Free University of New York, 54
French underground, 53

Freud, Sigmund, 78
Fukasaku, Kinji, 1
*Funeral, The* (1996), 3, 5, 27, 49, 59, 110, 112, 127, 129, 153; characters in, 23, 27, 38; death and sacrifice in, 75, 77, 80, 81, 108; ending of, 14; a family fable, 26, 27, 30, 69, 70; fury in, 78; the narrator in, 156, 56; politics in, 66–67
fury, 23, 40, 42–46, 78

Gallo, Vincent: as Johnny, 23, 49, 59, 66, 69, 70, 76, 108, 153
*Gangs of New York* (Scorsese), 171
Garel, Alain, 5
Garland, Judy, 107; as Vicky Lester, 103, 104, 105, 107
Gazzara, Ben, 22
genocide, 18
genre cinema, 1–3, 4, 85
Gentry, Minnie: as the old woman, 132
*Germany Year Zero* (Rossellini), 13
Getino, Octavio, 54
Giuliani, Rudolph, 168
*Gladiator, The* (1986), 3, 123, 125, 126, 127, 128
Godard, Jean-Luc, 13, 23, 38, 52, 58, 96, 146, 169
Goldman, Emma, 109
*Gospel According to Matthew, The* (Pasolini), 11, 56
grace, 115
Gramsci, Antonio, 64
*Grandeur and Decadence of a Small-Time Filmmaker* (Godard), 13, 96
Grand International Revolutionary Style, 54
Griffith, D. W., 5, 57
Griffith, Melanie: as Loretta, 85
Guérif, François, 5
Guevara, Ernesto "Che," 56, 57
guilt, 13, 18, 22, 25, 67–68, 78, 83, 85, 86, 97, 101, 110, 116, 124, 128; collective historical, 18
Gulf War, 7. *See also* war
Gutaï Independent Group. *See* Japanese performers

*Hail Mary* (Godard), 58
hallucination, 31–32, 77, 103, 110, 114–
    15, 126, 128, 129, 131–32, 141–43, 154
Hamill, Pete: as a journalist, 65, 66
Hanson, Marla, 59
Hark, Tsui, 1
HBO. See *Love on the A Train*
Hegel, Georg W. F., 20, 33, 35, 36, 37, 38,
    39, 40, 63, 74
Hellman, Monte, 5
Henry, Patrick, vii, 63
Heraclitus, 10
Hershey, Barbara, 58
Herzog, Werner, 93
Hesiod, 81
Hipp, Paul: as Ghouly, 66
Hiroshima, 6, 10, 13, 27, 46
historical abomination, 7. See also AIDS,
    evil, Nazism, war
historical guilt, 13, 18. See also guilt
historic evil, 6, 18. See also evil
history: reflections on, 8, 18–20, 29–30,
    46, 47, 49, 59
Hitchcock, Alfred, 21, 36, 169
Hobbes, Thomas, 35, 64
Ho Chi Minh, 56
*Hold Up, The* (1972), 9
Hollywood, 61, 80, 91, 102, 137, 150;
    within, 3
Holocaust, 46, 135, 136, 152
*Holocaust* (Chomsky), 137
"Home Invaders, The" (episode 20). See
    *Miami Vice*
Hopper, Dennis, 141; as filmmaker, 93; as
    Mickey, 23, 24, 49, 50, 78, 80, 81, 91,
    93, 103, 104, 105, 106, 107, 110, 116,
    **117,** 119, 120, 138, 140, 143, 144, 145,
    146, 147, 148, 149, 154
Horkheimer, Max, 1
*Hot Ticket* (Lund), 62–64. See also Lund
Howard, Freddy: as Emilio Zapa, 64
*How Can We Bear It?* (Boltanski), 113
hubris, 80–81. See also fury, rage
Huillet, Danièle, 150
human, 21, 25–27, 29, 35, 39, 45, 47, 64,
    80, 150; future of, 10; psyche, 13
Husserl, Edmund, 144–45

hypermorality, 22, 26, 30–37, 39, 86
hyperrealism, 115, 131

Ice-T: as the cop, 15, 167
iconography of crime, 66. *See also* spe-
    cific film titles
identity, 3
idol, 91
illusion, 144, 145
image: depicting the world, 21, 22, 52;
    documentary image, 18, 47, 114 (see
    also *The Addiction*); importance of,
    4; making images, 107, 116 (*see also*
    creation); mental or psychic, 23, 24,
    25, 38, 41, 47, 50, 105, 114, 118, 123,
    126, 149, 152 (*see also* delirium; per-
    ception; psychic event; *and specific
    titles of films*); the missing image, 140,
    153–55 (see also *The Blackout; New
    Rose Hotel*); of the mother (*see* mother
    imagery); power of the, 18, 50, 96;
    relation between metal and concrete
    image, 23, 41, 47, 114, 118, 153; status
    of the, 47, 50, 96, 118, 135; as trauma,
    18, 34, 110
individual, 2–3, 6–7, 25–31, 39, 58, 59,
    82, 92, 110, 111, 125, 152
industrialization, 10, 25, 27, 30, 47
industrial pollution, 6
inebriation, 3, 34, 50, 77, 110, 113, 138
infinitude, 22, 39–40, 78
infinity, 122
intoxication, 112
introjection, 113
*Invasion of the Body Snatchers*
    (Kaufman), 103
*Invasion of the Body Snatchers* (Siegel),
    103
Iraq War, 150, 168

Jack the Ripper, 42
Jankowski, Celene, 57
Japanese fascism, 151
Japanese performers, 151
Jarmusch, Jim, 1, 22
Jesus, 4, 58. *See also* Christian imagery
Johnson, Don: as Sonny Crockett, 24

Jones, Kent, 5
Julian, Janet: as Jennifer, 60, 64, 65, 66
Julien, Jay: as Abraham, 65
*Juliet of the Spirits* (Fellini), 53

Kane, Mary, 11
Kant, Emmanuel, 33
Karina, Anna, 52
Kaufman, Philip, 103
Keitel, Harvey, 75, 138; as Eddie, 68, 69,
    70, 80, 81, 85, 92, 93, 95, 97, 98, 99,
    100, 101, 102, 108, 112, 119, 120, 138;
    as L. T., 12, 15, 17, 26, 31, 32, 33, 34,
    35, 36, 38, 44, 47, 68, 69, 70, 75, 76,
    77, 80, 108, 110, 111, 112, 113, 114,
    115, 116, 118, 123, 131, 132, 133, 134,
    138, 142
Kelsch, Ken, 11, 169
Kennedy, John F.: presidential campaign,
    54
Keres, goddesses of punishment, 51
*Killing of a Chinese Bookie, The* (Cas-
    savetes), 22
Kim Phuc, 136. See also *The Addiction*
King, Martin Luther, Jr., 57
*King of New York* (1990), 2, 3, 9, 31, 56,
    60, 87, 112, 142; Abel Ferrara on, 166,
    171; crime in, 43, 72; death in, 68, 70,
    71, 73, 75, 78, 118; drug economy, 10,
    47; ending of, 76; Frank's project, 44,
    45, 73, 80, 81, 123; the individual in,
    26, 68; mafia in, 67, 86; passion in, 108,
    110; revolt, 52; violence in, 111
Kinney, Terry: as Steve, 7, 8, 9, 151
Kitano, Takeshi, 15
knowledge, 18, 20, 35, 36, 51, 110–13,
    115–17, 138, 141–42, 144

lack, 24, 28–29, 31, 34, 79, 80, 106, 107–
    8, 118, 140, 144–45, 153, 155
Lacombe, Georges, 109
Lancaster, Burt, 169
Lang, Fritz, 25
*La Revue du cinéma,* 5
Lassez, Sarah: as Annie, 2, 24, 49, 70, 78,
    90, 92, 104, 106, 107, 116, 119, 121,
    122, 143, 145, 146, 148, 149

*Last Movie, The* (Hopper), 93
*Last Temptation of Christ, The* (Scors-
    ese), 57, 58
Laurot, Edouard de, 52–61, 63
law, 24, 40, 76, 80, 85, 112, 124, 125
Léaud, Jean-Pierre, 13
Lee, Bruce, 85
Leguizamo, John, 170
Lenin, Vladimir Ilych, 56
*Letter to Freddy Buache* (Godard), 96
Levi, Primo, 136
*Lili Marleen* (Fassbinder), 12
*Listen America* (de Laurot), 54
Locarno Film Festival, 4
*Loner, The* (1988), 69
Lorenzetti, 151
Losey, Joseph, 169
loss, 113, 143, 147, 149
*Lost Highway* (Lynch), 22, 147
*Love Meetings* (Pasolini), 11
*Love on the A Train* (1997), 59–60, 156
*Lucky to be a Woman* (Blasetti), 53
Lucretius, 10
Lund, Zoë, 52, 53, 54, 57, 61, 62, 64,
    171–72; as co-scriptwriter, 16, 56, 114;
    as director (see *Hot Ticket*); as Thana,
    3, 11, 16, 23, 41, 42, 45, 68, 70, 74, 80,
    86, 89, 90, 91, 108, 111, 119, 130; as
    writer, 56, 62; as Zoë, 39, 115, 133
Lynch, David, 22

madness, 124–25
Madonna, 4, 91, 99, 100; as Sarah/Claire,
    26, 67, 86, 90, 91, 92, 94, 95, 98, 99,
    100, 101, 102, 112, 119, 122, 137
mafia, 6, 43, 73, 78, 86, 112, 126; and
    capitalism, 67; Chinese Triad, 42, 43,
    112; Italian Mafia, 42; mafia logic,
    72–73, 76
*Main Line* (Bulteau), 152
Malcolm X, 54, 57
Mao Tse Tung, 56
Manhattan, 76, 80, 118. *See also* New
    York
Marker, Chris, 54
Martin, Adrian, 3
Marx, Karl, 56

Marxist-Leninism, 55, 61
*Mary* (2005), 5, 56, 58–59, 111, 156–57; script, 4, 156
Mary Magdalene, 58, 157
Marz, Carolyn: as Carol, 79, 119, 129
Mason, James, 107; as Norman Maine, 103, 104, 105, 106, 107
massacres, 18, 73, 76–78, 81, 87; My Lai, 18, 57; Serbian massacre, 47, 114. See also *The Addiction*
Massina, Giulietta, 10
*Master and Margarita, The* (Bulgakov), 156
maternal: depiction of the, 8. *See also* mother imagery
Matteo, Drea de: as the wife, 15, 38, 70–71, 111, 167, 168, 170
McGillis, Kelly: as Mary, 127, 128
McGlone, Mike: as John T., 59
McIntyre, John Paul, 2
*Mean Streets* (Scorsese), 14, 30
*Medea* (Pasolini), 11, 27
Medusa: myth of, 84
Meins, Holger, 109
Mekas, Adolfas, 54
Mekas, Jonas, 2, 53, 54
memories, 124
*Menschen am Sonntag* (Siodmak), 109
mental image. *See* image
metamorphosis, 13, 15–20, 34, 41, 71, 74, 89, 103, 106–7, 111, 142
*Miami Vice,* (1985), 3, 24; "The Dutch Oven" (episode 27), 24; "The Home Invaders" (episode 20), 24
Milian, Tomas: as Andres De Boya, 126, 127
Milton, John, 93, 95
*Minima Moralia* (Adorno), 27
*Mirage, The* (Weiss), 53
mise en abyme, 4, 96. *See also* film within the film
mise en scène, 4, 16, 99
Modine, Matthew, 107; as Matty, 13, 24, 26, 28, 29, 38, 49, 50, 69, 70, 78, 79, 80, 81, 90, 91, 92, 102, 103, 104, 105, 106, 107, 108, 110, 111, 112, 113, 114, 115, 116, 117, 118, 119, 120, 121, 122, 132, 138, 140, 141, 142, 143, 144, 145,

146, 147, 148, 149, 154; as Tony Childress, 58
Mol, Gretchen: as the pregnant wife, 60; as singer, 79
monochromes, 79, 121, 129
Monroe, Marilyn, 4
montage, 37, 86, 87–89, 104, 107, 116, 122, 149
Montreal, Rhodney (Douglas Metrov): as Tony Coca-Cola, 119
morality, 2, 6, 15, 24, 41, 73 (*see also* ethical stakes); unbearable as hypermorality, 26, 30, 35 (*see also* hypermorality; negativity)
Morrison, Mrs. Norman, 57. See also *Far from Vietnam*
Moss, Lambert: as Veronica, 133
mother imagery, 7, 10, 20, 25, 70, 83–85, 91–92, 105–6, 156
*Mother of Mirrors,* 67, 92, 93, 94, 96, 97, 99, 100, 119, 120, 121, 122, 137. See also *Dangerous Game*
*Ms .45 (Angel of Vengeance,* 1981), 13, 62, 85, 86, 108, 170, 171; delirium, 128–31; evil in, 111; fury, 42; revenge, 23, 45; serial killer in, 41, 119; 112; sexual abuse, 2, 60, 89; solitude of the protagonist, 70, 74; structure of the film, 15, 16, 17, 134
Munk, Andrzej, 54
murder, 1, 6, 24, 33, 37, 45–46, 49, 66, 70–72, 76, 85–86, 91, 95, 96, 100, 103, 112, 113, 116, 126, 143, 144, 149; by snatching, 46
Murnau, F. W., 43
Murphy, Reilly: as Andy, 7, 10, 20, 83; as Tommy, 69, 95
music video, 3, 38, 82, 85, 86, 87, 120, 145

Nagasaki, 6, 27
Nameth, Ronald, 32
Nazism, 7, 9, 30, 46, 151; moral catastrophe provoked by, 13; Nazi or death camps, 10, 18, 47, 114, 135, 152
negation, 1, 14, 41, 74, 157; and evil, 3
negative, 11, 38, 39, 44, 60, 68, 79, 95, 105–6, 107, 157

negativity, 31–32, 34, 102, 122; as moral source, 26–29, 30, 52; as a speculative asset, 35–37, 41, 74, 106, 108, 157
*New Rose Hotel* (1998), 3, 5, 9, 25, 29, 49, 81, 84, 87, 128; confusion in, 69; evil in, 111; forms of lack in, 31, 153, 154, 155; the human in, 10, 30; image of the capitalist system in, 10, 67; plot of, 24; simulation, 90, 91; status of the feminine, 26, 38, 92, 119, 156; structure of, 129, 156; the universal killer in, 50–52
Newsreel group in America, 54
New York, 15, 36, 95, 157, 109, 148, 168
Nietzsche, Friedrich, 26, 116, 137
nightmare, 133–34
*9 Lives of a Wet Pussy* (1976), 2, 13, 87, 112, 123
Nitsch, Hermann, 151
*Nosferatu* (Murnau), 43
Novak, Kim, 170

œuvre, 121. *See also* Ferrara's cinema; works of art
Oliverio, Nicodemo. *See* St. John
*Oskar Langenfeld* (Meins), 109

*Paisà* (Rossellini), 13
Palestine, 58, 157
palinopsia, 143
Pandora: the myth of, 24, 25, 29, 50, 81, 154, 155
Panebianco, Richard: as Tony, 42, 43
*Paradise Lost* (Milton), 93
Paramount, 5
party, parties, 90. *See also* bloody balls
Pasolini, Pier Paolo, 11, 12, 13, 38, 54, 56, 57, 75, 169
passion, 16, 34, 40, 62–63, 95, 141
Penn, Chris, 5; as Chez, 26, 28, 37, 49, 68, 69, 75, 76, 77, 78, 108, 153
perception: deregulation of the fundamental principles of, 145, 146–48
Perez, Rosie: as "the girl," 60
permanence, 106
persistence, 106
Philonenko, Alexis, 33
Phoids, The, 87
*Photos d'Alix* (Eustache), 150

Poe, Edgar Allan, 99
Polanski, Roman, 37
polemical enterprise. *See* Ferrara's cinema
Polish underground, 53
political critique: forms of, 6–7, 9, 11, 45, 66. *See also* capitalism; revolution
political questioning, 18, 22, 24, 167–68. *See also* ethical stakes
political radicalism, 52–59, 62–63, 89. *See also* Laurot; revolt; revolution
politics: in Ferrara's films, 18, 23, 45, 52, 89
popular culture, 1, 38, 87, 100
possession, 143
*Prison Notebooks* (Gramsci), 64
"Prolepsis" (Laurot), 55
"Promethea" (Laurot), 56
propagation, 118, 135
Proust, Marcel, 36
Psyche, 123, 152
psychic event, 110; image, state, process or complex, 17, 78, 102–4, 112, 118, 123, 138, 142, 152, 155 (*see also* image); investigation, 111
punk films, 38

rage, 40, 42, 70, 84
rape. *See* sexual abuse
Rauger, Jean-François, 5, 165
Ray, Michèle, 137
Ray, Nicholas, 4, 169
realism, 149
reality, 113, 114, 144, 146. *See also* perception
redemption, 12, 14, 24, 38, 104, 118, 124, 167
Redman, Anthony, 11
reflection, 38, 80, 96
reflexivity, 115
Reinhardt, Ad, 105
remanence, 81, 105, 144
reminiscence, 124. *See also* memories
*Rendez-vous de Juillet* (Becker), 53
reparation, 23, 70, 101, 150, 157
repentance, 13, 23, 25, 115
*Repulsion* (Polanski), 37
*Reservoir Dogs* (Tarantino), 138

Resnais, Alain, 54
revelation, 18, 20, 30, 34, 75, 98, 103, 104, 107, 108, 118, 132
revenge, 42, 44, 77, 130. *See also* vengeance
revolt, 6, 12, 41, 52, 81, 109
revolution, 44, 55–57, 59, 63–64, 109, 127
revolutionaries, 6
*Rien que les heures* (Cavalcanti), 109
*Rise and Fall of Legs Diamond, The* (Boetticher), 32
*Rome Open City* (Rossellini), 13, 73
Rosenbaum, Jonathan, 5
Rossellini, Roberto, 6, 9, 13, 14, 22, 38, 52, 73, 169
Rotterdam Film Festival, 62
Ruggiero, Anthony: as Lite, 31, 32
Ruperto, Maria: as Luci, 126, 127
Russo, James: as Frank Burns/Russell, 67, 90, 92, 95, 99, 100, 101, 102, 119
'*R Xmas* (2001), 3, 5, 14, 21, 26, 30, 38, 52, 67, 69, 87, 111, 112, 115, 165, 166–69, 170, 171

sacrifice, 2, 24, 35, 45, 57, 76, 77, 78, 96, 101, 104, 106, 115, 138
Santiago, Saundra: as Gina, 24
Santo Domingo. See *Cat Chaser*
Sartre, Jean-Paul, 54, 55
*Scénario du film Passion* (Godard), 146
*Scenes from Rotterdam* (ass. De Jong). See *Hot Ticket*
Schelling, Friedrich, 36
Schiffer, Claudia, 91; as Susan, 12, 69, 78, 79, 92, 105, 119, 120, 131, 148
*Schindler's List* (Spielberg), 137
Schneemann, Carolee, 137
Schoolly D, 71, 87
Schultz, Harry: as Briggs, 75, 120
Schygulla, Hannah, 12
Sciorra, Annabella, 170; as Casanova, 18, 74, 75, 80, 115, 136; as Jean, 49, 110; as Madame Rosa, 154
Scorsese, Martin, 14, 22, 30, 57, 58, 67, 75, 170, 171
*SCUM Manifesto* (Solanas, V.), 88
Second Front, 61
self: annihilation, 12, 20, 30, 35, 39,

47, 75, 105; consciousness, 117–18; destruction, 80, 113; liquidation, 83; revelation, 20, 75
Selznick, David O., 53
serial killer, 14, 41–52, 85, 90, 124, 125
*79 Springs* (Alvarez), 137
sexual abuse, sexual harassment, body exploitation, violence, rape, 16, 42, 60, 86, 89, 95, 99, 102, 110–12, 130–31
*Shadows* (Cassavetes), 54
Siegel, Don, 103, 107
Siodmak, Robert, 109
Smith, Gavin, 5
Snatchers, 7, 20, 85, 105
snatching, 6, 46, 150
Snow, Michael, 169
Solanas, Fernando, 54
Solanas, Valerie, 88
solitude, 68–70
somatization, 18, 22, 34, 35, 41, 46, 49, 78, 104, 113, 135, 138, 152
soundtrack, 135
Spelling, Aaron, 69
standard imagery, 4. *See also* culture industry
Stanislavski/Strasberg Method of Acting, 98
*Star Is Born, A* (Cukor), 102, 103, 104, 105, 106, 107
*Starship Troopers,* (Verhoeven), 3
*Les Statues meurent aussi* (Marker/Resnais), 54
status of the image, 154
Stembera, Peter, 152
*Stendhal Syndrome, The* (Argento, D.), 51
Sternberg, Josef von, 4
Stevens, Brad, 5, 69, 171
St. John, Nicholas, 2, 9, 11, 57, 59, 66, 96, 135
"strange cinema," 146–47
Straub, Jean-Marie, 150
Strawberry, Darryl, 34, 118
stroboscope: use of, 31–32
Stroheim, Erich von, 4
*Stromboli* (Rossellini), 13
Strummer, Joe, 1
Stuto, Darlene: as Laurie, 89, 90, 108

substitution, 86
*Subway Stories: Tales from the Under-
ground* (1997), 111. See also *Love on
the A Train*
suicide, 105–7, 115, 116, 121, 138, 144,
149, 150
*Sylvie and Bruno* (Carroll), 21

Tarantino, Quentin, 138
*Taxi Driver* (Scorsese), 30, 41, 42
Taylor, Lili, 4; as Kathy, 12, 18, 19, 20, 23,
30, 34, 35, 36, 38, 46, 47, 48, 51, 57, 69,
70, 74, 75, 80, 81, 83, 108, 109, 110,
111, 113, 114, 115, 116, 118, 119, 134,
135, 136, 142, 152, 154
Terry, John: as Michael Shane, 69
*Theorem* (Pasolini), 11
*Theory of Religion* (Bataille), 74
*They Live* (John Carpenter), 61
*Thing Called Love, The* (Bogdanovich), 5
Thorn, Frankie: as the raped nun, 12, 34,
71, 86, 133
*Through the Looking Glass* (Carroll), 21
Tilly, Meg: as Carol, 10, 83, 84
Titans: the myth of the, 81
Titian, 13
torment, 6, 18, 34, 42, 47, 78, 79, 110,
113, 152; artistic or creative torment,
37, 41, 80; tormented characters, 17,
85
Tourneur, Jacques, 136
tract: film-tract, 3; visual, 87
trance, 110, 123, 129, 138, 143
transgression, 38, 39, 43, 68, 70, 102, 105
translation: visual, formal, 13, 22, 23,
88–89, 122, 123, 129–30, 133–34, 157
trauma, 17, 22, 47, 110, 113, 115, 125,
128, 142, 146, 157
Triad, The. *See* mafia
*Truck, The* (Duras), 14
Trump, Donald, 76
truth, 33, 34, 36, 51, 67, 72, 75, 78, 82,
86, 93, 98, 103, 104, 108–13, 142, 146

*Un altro Festival* (de Laurot, Munk), 54
unbearable, 24, 38, 85, 98, 106, 110–11,
135, 141, 146
unconsciousness, 34, 77

United States, 5. *See also* American cinema industry, Ferrara
universality, 70, 123
unlimited: forms of the, 51, 78

vampire, vampirism, 2, 8, 18, 26, 34–36,
38–39, 47, 69, 74–75, 80, 84, 116,
135–36, 142, 166
vampirization, 98, 119
Velez, Fernando: as Julio, 132
vengeance, 51, 70, 86
Venice Film Festival, 5
*Vera Cruz* (Aldrich), 169
Verhoeven, Paul, 3
*Vertigo* (Hitchcock), 21, 147, 170
Vertov, Dziga, 54
Viennese Actionists, 151
*Viet-Flakes* (Schneemann), 137
Vietnam War, 2, 9, 18, 30, 46, 54, 63, 74,
109, 126, 137; images of, 34, 47, 114,
135
video, 87, 97, 120, 145. See also *The
Blackout;* "California"; music video
Vidor, King, 4
Vigo, Jean, 169
*Village of the Damned* (Carpenter), 22
violence, 17. *See also* massacres; murder;
sexual abuse
*Violent Cop* (Kitano), 15, 21
visionary, 6, 110
visions, 77, 110, 123. *See also* hallucina-
tion

*Wager, The,* 54, 57
*Wages of Fear* (Clouzot), 53
Wahl, Ken: as Rick Benton, 125, 126
Walken, Christopher, 171; as Fox, 24, 69,
111, 153, 154; as Frank White, 23, 26,
36, 43, 44, 45, 49, 60, 64, 65, 66, 68, 71,
73, 75, 76, 80, 81, 108, 110, 111, 118,
142, 166; as Peina, 19, 29, 36, 50, 74,
81, 116, 117, 142, 154; as Ray, 28, 49,
67, 69, 70, 72, 73, 76, 77
war, 7. *See also* Gulf War, Iraq War, Vietnam War
Warhol, Andy, 53, 88
Warner Brothers, 5
Weiss, Peter, 53

Weller, Peter: as George Moran, 126, 127
Welles, Orson, 4, 5, 25, 53, 169
West, Mae, 4
Western civilization, 18, 35, 109
Western conception, 25
Western economic world, 109
Western imaginary, 16
Western philosophy, 18–20
Western subjectivity, 115
Whitaker, Forest: as Major Collins, 7, 8, 26, 27; as Ted Younger, 58
Wiseman, Frederick, 169

*Wizard of Oz, The* (Fleming), 21
*Woman under the Influence, A* (Cassavetes), 90
Wong, Russell: as Yung, 43
works of art, 121–22
Wynroth, Alan: as the landlord, 37

Yomini Independent Group, 151

Zois, Christ, 140, 153; as the psychoanalyst, 50, 110, 120
*Zone, La* (Lacombe), 109

NICOLE BRENEZ teaches cinema studies at the University of Paris-1 Panthéon-Sorbonne. Her books include *Shadows de John Cassavetes* and *De la figure en général et du corps en particulier*. She is the editor of several books, including *Poétique de la couleur—Une Anthologie, Cinéma Politique—série 1, La Vie nouvelle—Nouvelle Vision*, and *Jean-Luc Godard: Documents*. She has organized many film events and retrospectives, notably "Jeune, dure et pure, une histoire du cinéma d'avant-garde en France" for the French Cinémathèque in 2000. She has been the curator of the Cinémathèque française's avant-garde film sessions since 1995 and received the Film Preservation Award of the Anthology Film Archives in 2000.

ADRIAN MARTIN is Senior Research Fellow at Monash University and co-editor of the online film magazine *Rouge* (www.rouge.com.au). He is the author of *The Mad Max Movies* and *Once upon a Time in America*. He won the Pascall Prize for Critical Writing in 1997 and the Australian Film Institute Byron Kennedy Award in 1993.